*f*P

HALFWAY
to HEAVEN

My White-knuckled—and Knuckleheaded—
Quest for the Rocky Mountain High

Mark Obmascik

Free Press
NEW YORK • LONDON • TORONTO • SYDNEY

FREE PRESS

A Division of Simon & Schuster, Inc.
1230 Avenue of the Americas
New York, NY 10020

First Free Press hardcover edition May 2009

FREE PRESS and colophon are trademarks of Simon & Schuster, Inc.

For information about special discounts for bulk purchases, please contact
Simon & Schuster Special Sales at 1-866-506-1949 or
business@simonandschuster.com

The Simon & Schuster Speakers Bureau can bring authors to your live event. For
more information or to book an event, contact the Simon & Schuster Speakers
Bureau at 1-866-248-3049 or visit our website at www.simonspeakers.com

Designed by Paul Dippolito

Map by Paul J. Pugliese

Manufactured in the United States of America

1   3   5   7   9   10   8   6   4   2

Library of Congress Cataloging-in-Publication Data
Obmascik, Mark.
Halfway to heaven: my white-knuckled—and knuckleheaded—quest for the
Rocky Mountain high/Mark Obmascik.
p.   cm.
Includes bibliographical references.
1. Mountaineering—Colorado—Anecdotes. 2. Hiking—Colorado—
Anecdotes. 3. Middle-aged men—Colorado—Anecdotes. I. Title.
GV199.42.C6026 2009
796.52209788—dc22   2008049192

ISBN-13: 978-1-4165-6699-1
ISBN-10:   1-4165-6699-6

To Merrill

Contents

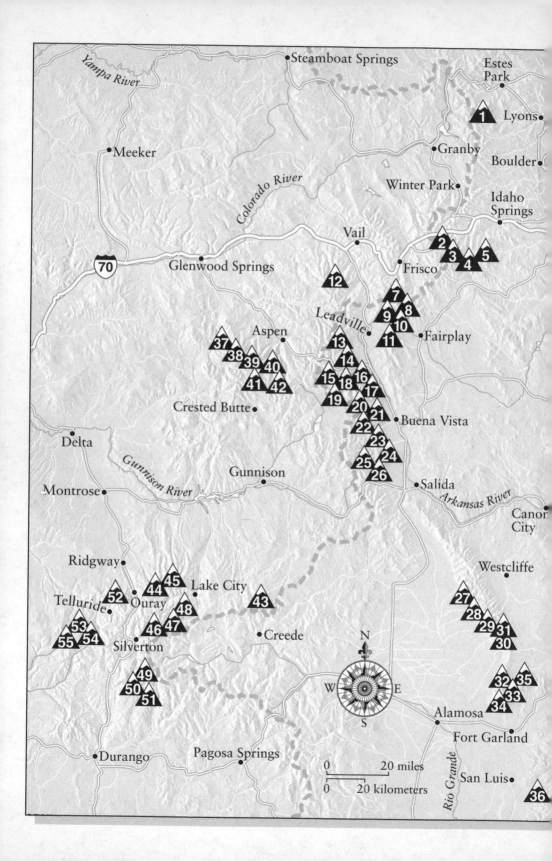

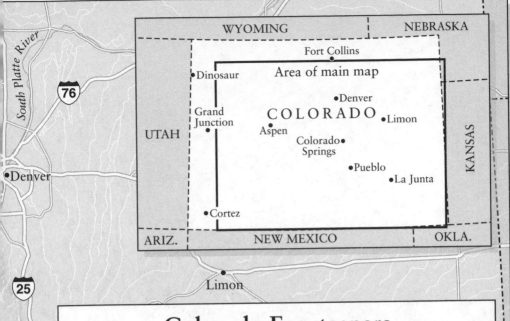

Colorado Fourteeners

Mount Antero 14,276 Feet	24.	Mount Lindsey 14,042 Feet	35.
Mount Belford 14,203 Feet	16.	Little Bear Peak 14,037 Feet	34.
Mount Bierstadt 14,060 Feet	4.	Longs Peak 14,259 Feet	1.
Blanca Peak 14,345 Feet	33.	Maroon Peak 14,163 Feet	40.
Mount Bross 14,172 Feet	10.	Mount Massive 14,421 Feet	13.
Capitol Peak 14,130 Feet	37.	Missouri Mountain 14,074 Feet	18.
Castle Peak 14,279 Feet	42.	North Maroon Peak 14,019 Feet	39.
Challenger Point 14,081 Feet	27.	Mount Oxford 14,160 Feet	17.
Mount Columbia 14,077 Feet	21.	Pikes Peak 14,115 Feet	6.
Crestone Peak 14,294 Feet	29.	Mount Princeton 14,204 Feet	23.
Crestone Needle 14,197 Feet	30.	Pyramid Peak 14,025 Feet	41.
Culebra Peak 14,047 Feet	36.	Quandary Peak 14,271 Feet	7.
Mount Democrat 14,155 Feet	9.	Redcloud Peak 14,034 Feet	47.
El Diente Peak 14,159 Feet	55.	San Luis Peak 14,014 Feet	43.
Mount Elbert 14,440 Feet	14.	Mount Shavano 14,231 Feet	26.
Ellingwood Point 14,042 Feet	32.	Mount Sherman 14,036 Feet	11.
Mount Eolus 14,083 Feet	50.	Mount Sneffels 14,150 Feet	52.
Mount Evans 14,265 Feet	5.	Snowmass Mountain 14,099 Feet	38.
Grays Peak 14,278 Feet	3.	Sunlight Peak 14,059 Feet	49.
Handies Peak 14,058 Feet	46.	Sunshine Peak 14,001 Feet	48.
Mount Harvard 14,421 Feet	20.	Tabeguache Peak 14,162 Feet	25.
Mount of the Holy Cross 14,009 Feet	12.	Torreys Peak 14,275 Feet	2.
		Uncompahgre Peak 14,321 Feet	45.
Humboldt Peak 14,064 Feet	31.	Wetterhorn Peak 14,015 Feet	44.
Huron Peak 14,010 Feet	19.	Mount Wilson 14,246 Feet	54.
Kit Carson Peak 14,165 Feet	28.	Wilson Peak 14,017 Feet	53.
La Plata Peak 14,336 Feet	15.	Windom Peak 14,082 Feet	51.
Mount Lincoln 14,293 Feet	8.	Mount Yale 14,200 Feet	22.

HALFWAY
to HEAVEN

Introduction

I was fat, forty-four, and in the market for a vasectomy. My mortgage was half gone, but so was my hair. Crabgrass bugged me.

After sixteen years of marriage, my wife and I completed each other's sentences. Most were about our boys. We had three, though they sounded louder. Because Merrill traveled for her job, and I stayed home for mine, my three sons saw a lot of me. I changed their diapers, cooked their meals, coached their soccer, and harped about their homework. I was around so much that when our three-year-old woke in the middle of the night, he usually screamed for me. Our pubescent twelve-year-old, however, usually screamed at me. The eight-year-old could go either way.

It was a chaotic life, but a fun life, and I knew how to live it—until an emergency phone call rocked my world.

"Dad," our twelve-year-old said from his Colorado summer camp, "they're taking me to the hospital."

Turns out Cass and a bunch of camp buddies were climbing Pikes Peak, elevation 14,115 feet, when he tripped and slashed open his shin to the bone. Now I was the one screaming.

"Dad," he said, "calm down. I summited. It was amazing. I saw the sunrise from the top of the mountain. I slipped on the way down, but I made it to the top—two-and-a-half miles above sea level."

"How bad does it hurt?"

"I summited, Dad. I summited."

With ten surgical staples in his leg, Cass actually let me hug him in front of his friends. He even hugged me back. Then we did something more surprising: We talked.

He told me that mountains over 14,000 feet were called Fourteeners, and that Colorado had a bunch of them. He asked if I knew anything about them.

I did.

Our home state has fifty-four peaks higher than 14,000 feet—more than any other state or province in North America. Every year more than 500,000 people try to climb a Fourteener, but fewer than 1,300 people have ever reported standing atop them all. Colorado's Fourteeners have been summited by skiers and snowboarders, racers and amputees, dogs, cats, cockatiels, monkeys, and horses, people as young as one and as old as eighty-one. One Texan spent three weeks pushing a peanut to the summit of one peak with his nose. There have been gunfights and cannibalism, avalanches and helicopter crashes. Hundreds have died and thousands have been maimed.

One blond boy even survived America's most famous Fourteener with a Frankenstein scar on his leg.

Nice one, Dad, he said, but how do you know all this?

Once upon a time, before I was a husband or a father—back in the days when my inseam had more inches than my waistline—I somehow managed to climb a few Fourteeners.

My son was shocked. For a fleeting millisecond, he even looked at me as if I were almost not embarrassing. Teetering on the edge of a truly touching father-and-son moment, I was ready for another hug, but he was overcome by another surge of testosterone.

Dad, how about if we climb a Fourteener together?

Well, when I was climbing mountains—that was a lifetime ago, back when I liked to exercise. These days I like to eat. I've packed so much on my hips it would be like climbing with a pony keg of beer in my fanny pack. Imagine lugging all that extra weight up the 1,860 steps of the Empire State Building, four times, and doing it in high-altitude air with about a third less oxygen than Manhattan. All that work would be just one Fourteener.

He looked at me. I looked at him.

My mind was racing: Could I do it? Was it even possible for me to try? Back when I was in shape, those five Fourteener summits were still about the hardest sport I'd ever taken on—harder than two-a-day football practices as a high school punk, harder than weeklong bike tours that sent me, an alleged adult, four hundred miles over and around the mountain ranges of Colorado. Still, the beauty of the Fourteeners was something to remember. Standing on the roof of the Rockies, high above the trees and the clouds and the everyday worries, always made me feel like I was halfway to heaven. Now I'm forty-four, and my life is halfway there too.

Cass kept looking at me. I wondered what he saw. Someone to argue with? Someone to avoid? Someone who once did something cool, but way before he was even born? My face must have betrayed my fear: The older I get, the better I was.

Then he said the magic words: Dad—please.

I couldn't resist.

Chapter 1

Failure

GRAYS PEAK 14,278'
TORREYS PEAK 14,275'

There's one thing harder than climbing a Fourteener: waking up a preteener to climb a Fourteener. Because nothing scares me more than lightning, I insist on an alpine start—on the trailhead before dawn to get off the top of the peak by noon to beat Colorado's regular afternoon thunderstorms. Which all means I must somehow wrestle our twelve-year-old out of bed by 4 a.m.

After nudging, shaking, rocking, bouncing, and rolling, he's still not moving. I threaten the nuclear option—Kelly Clarkson, shrieking "Since U Been Gone," through his iPod headphones—but he knows it's an empty threat. No man can stomach an American Idol two hours before sunrise. So I try another tack and ask him simply, please. Magically, it works. Plus I promise food.

When I stop at 7-Eleven for our breakfast of champions (chocolate doughnuts, Mentos, and Kit Kat bars) I check the backseat and see that he has sprawled back into hibernation. For the one-and-a-half-hour drive to the trailhead, I hear only my own thoughts. They are not pleasant visitors.

What made me think I could do this? For the past year or so, my toughest daily exercise was to clean-and-jerk our three-year-old into his car seat. One night a week, after the kids were asleep, I met a bunch of dads in a Catholic school gym to play what we called basketball, but actually was closer to nonprofessional wrestling. My jumping ability was so pathetic that once, after I snared a rebound, a wisecracking opponent stopped our game to marvel that he may have seen a shadow beneath my feet. Though we vowed to run longer in the gym than we drank afterward in a bar, this rule was strictly enforced only during Lent. After we went around the bar table detailing our kitchen sink of health woes—ACL that burned like a waffle iron; lower vertebrae with more shavings than a coffee grinder; prostate the size of a grapefruit—we hardly had time left for the main subject of interest, namely, how good we used to be. The sad truth: The only part of my body with any serious cardio training was my flapping jaw.

At the trailhead, my son snaps awake to a scene of glorious beauty: dawn over the Rockies. Five cars are in the parking lot—one from Washington, one from Wyoming, one from Texas, two from Kansas—but we're on the trail before them. In just a few steps, Cass goes from groggy to confident. I shine my headlamp in his face and see a big, fat grin. You OK, Dad? I try to answer, but can't. The trail begins at 11,280 feet, and somebody has filled my lungs with sand. You OK, Dad?

I'm not OK, but I'm not quitting either. My twelve-year-old is smoking me up the trail. Dad, you OK? I open my mouth to talk, but what comes out is a sound described by my son as a goose that swallowed a bugle. He laughs. I do too. Enough father-son communication for now. I waddle another fifty steps and taste something alien in my throat. It's two chocolate doughnuts and a Kit Kat bar. They tasted better the first time. The bugle has turned into a tuba.

My symphony wins my son's sympathy. He offers to stop right there and turn around and head all the way back to Denver, but I feel strangely calm. Maybe my problem was jittery nerves. Onward and upward, I proclaim, but my son seeks assurance that I'm talking about my feet, not my breakfast.

At 12,000 feet, the first yellow rays of dawn spill over the trail, and the view reminds me why I'm trying this. It's spectacular: a massive wall on our left, a talus peak on our right, and a breathtaking rock amphitheater dead ahead. Above it all stand our intended targets—the summits of Grays Peak and Torreys Peak, which stretch about three-quarters of a mile apart, linked by a high saddle that dips 550 feet in the middle. We're planning to stand atop both before most people back home in Denver are cemented to their work desks for the day. I had summited these two peaks years before I was married. With a well-maintained four-mile trail that requires 3,500 feet of climbing, Grays and Torreys are among the most popular mountain climbs in Colorado. They are often described in guidebooks as two of the state's easiest Fourteeners. Whatever that means.

Now the trail really goes up. We take twenty steps, rest, and push twenty more. There's a jackhammer pounding my eardrums, which alarms me at first, until I'm able to cite it as evidence to my son that I truly do have a heart. Just a few years ago he saw me as the hero who was stronger, faster, smarter, and funnier than all the other dads. Lately, though, I'm the guy who says no—no to too much television, video gaming, Web surfing, mess making, junk-food eating, music blaring, yelling, swearing, disrespecting—all the stuff that generally makes a teenager a teenager. Of course, I had inflicted all the same woes (minus the technological "advances") upon my parents aeons ago, but I had never quite confessed my duplicity to him. Now seems as good a time as any. I stare at my feet and struggle for the right words to start explaining that as a teenager, I had also felt many of the same feelings that he is feeling today, even if, years later, I am totally clueless and possibly the world's stupidest father.

Unfortunately, when I glance up, I realize he's in no shape for surprises. On the trail ahead his feet are wobbling like he's in his fifteenth round with Muhammad Ali. I remember that malady, which comes when you're dizzy from altitude or worn out from climbing. Either way, it's not a good sign.

We rest and I try to revive him with the smelling salts of history. Grays and Torreys, I tell him, were named after the two greatest

American botanists of the nineteenth century. Asa Gray was the student of John Torrey, but together they wrote the first comprehensive plant catalog of the New World, *Flora of North America*. Though Gray eventually won the hearts of scientific plant lovers by shepherding construction of one of the world's great herbariums, at Harvard University, he was best known to Americans for promoting and defending Charles Darwin's concept of natural selection. Grays Peak is the tallest point on the Continental Divide in North America.

Tallest point? That pegs the testosterone meter for Cass. We trudge higher.

At 13,500 feet, we had scaled the equivalent of one-and-a-half Sears Towers, and the burden shows. He takes five steps, rests, and then wobbles five more. While we sit, four extremely loud hikers pass, and they're chattering with accents from an easily identifiable state renowned in Colorado for sending us so many vacationing cowboys who are all hat and no cattle. Cass easily guesses the state. I wait for the hikers to move beyond earshot, then prime the boy for a story about Dick Lamm, our former governor, who, like all proud Coloradans, loved few things more than the mountains and a good joke about Texans.

A few years back, I tell him, Lamm opened his speech to a Texas education conference by claiming there had been an awful accident on the slopes earlier that day at Vail. It seemed the biggest oilman in Texas was skiing fast down the slopes when he crashed smack-dab into a pine tree. He was killed instantly. The ski patrol quickly discovered the true size of the oilman: The body was so large that the ski patrol needed three sleds to carry him down the mountain to the resort medical clinic. That's where things really turned dicey. In all of Colorado, no one could find a coffin big enough to contain the body of the biggest oilman in Texas. So they gave him an enema and sent him home in a shoe box.

If laughter could power legs up a mountain, we'd have summited in minutes.

We progress a few hundred more feet before his boots go goofy

again. We sit and he asks for another joke. Problem is, I can't think
of one. Reality is, I can't think of much of anything. We're only about
400 feet short of the summit of Torreys Peak, and the altitude has
vacuumed every repeatable thought from my head. About one of five
flatlanders venturing above 8,000 feet typically suffers some kind of
health woe, Colorado health officials say. The higher you go, the
colder and drier it gets. There's less oxygen and more ultraviolet ra-
diation. Lungs and the heart must work harder, even when the body
is at rest. If a body is not at rest—and is in fact trying to haul its sorry
ass up a mountain—then it's more likely to succumb to headaches,
nausea, dizziness, or, in more serious cases, acute mountain sickness.
That requires an immediate retreat to lower elevations.

Luckily, I'm more tired than sick. I'd still like to try something to
motivate my son. Then it hits: another Dick Lamm story. When he
wasn't insulting Texans, this governor also liked to climb Fourteeners. On one of his last peaks, he started complaining about the load
in his backpack. Don't worry, his hiking partners told him, just keep
moving. The higher Lamm hiked, the heavier the pack felt. He moaned
and groaned and wondered aloud whether he had the strength to
continue. Maybe he was coming down with a bug. Maybe it just
wasn't his day. No matter, his buddies kept encouraging him to press
forward. Finally, after a draining scramble to the summit, Lamm
wearily plopped off his backpack, which led one of his buddies to
announce: Man, I sure have a taste for watermelon. Two thousand
feet above timberline, Lamm could hardly see any live plants, much
less any edible fruit. He opened his backpack and found a giant, ripe
watermelon, which he nearly cracked over the heads of his friends.
Lamm made them pack down all the rinds.*

My son looks at me with an idea: Dad, how about if you carry my
backpack? No big deal, I tell him, and stuff his daypack into my
larger sack. He stands to take another step and nearly somersaults
backward. No more happy feet—just wacky feet.

---

* I learned later that Lamm may have been in on the joke.

How close are we? he asks. Doesn't matter, I tell him. The mountain will always be here. We can try again another day.

I hold his arm and we turn tail in retreat. Cass gains strength with every step down, and we're soon low enough for him to walk by himself. I tell him how proud I am of him. It takes a lot more maturity to turn around on a peak than to press ahead and put yourself in danger.

Yada, yada, yada, he says, and then yaks it up for the next hour hiking back down. He's blabbering on about school, friends, summer camp, girls, cell phones—the full cornucopia of preteen stuff—without any encouragement from me. I chalk it up to altitude drunkenness, but I'm not complaining. It's fun to be buddies again. This time I don't even need nausea to bring us together.

He falls asleep as soon as his head hits the car backseat, and once again I'm left with my own thoughts. I was so focused on getting him up the mountain that I forgot about my own struggles. Strangely, they weren't so bad. After a shaky start, I climbed slowly and steadily, like an ox but without the horns. We stopped 400 feet shy of the summit, but I could have made it. At least I think I could have made it. Could I? Would I?

Chapter 2

Religious Experience

MOUNT OF THE HOLY CROSS 14,009'

There's a bear outside my tent.

It's 2 a.m., I'm camped alone just below Half Moon Pass, elevation 11,600 feet, and I'm wondering how in the hell I'm going to de-
fend myself. Quick survival check: no gun, no knife, no guts.
Entombed in my down mummy sleeping bag, I wear only boxer
shorts. Piled somewhere in the tent are my clothes and boots, but on
this no-moon night I see nothing.

I can, however, hear something. It's big, rooting around, and moving closer. Another twig snaps, and I realize that he smells bad too.
Maybe it's the scent of his earlier kill. Or maybe it's just me. City-boy
deodorant is no match for raw mountain fear.

At this point I figure I have two options: curl up in a ball and die,
or fight back and die. Not much choice for any man who grew up
watching John Wayne at a matinee. So I slowly, quietly, unzip my
sleeping bag, grope in the dark for my mountaineer's headlamp, and
suck in a deep breath.

Like a bat out of hell—or maybe just more like Meat Loaf—I blast
out of my tent. Arms waving, feet stomping, eyes bulging, I'm screaming, "Bear! Go away, bear! Out of here, bear!"

Only it's not a bear.

It's an elk, antlerless and female, but still clearly an elk. Given the time of year, she must be approaching the rut and searching for a mate.

She looks at me and I at her, and the look in her eyes makes me really uncomfortable. Hey, I'm a married man. She turns, blows out the world's biggest load of crap in my direction, and hightails it into the night.

And there I am, left shivering outside in the dark, in my underwear, flush with testosterone from screaming at a girl.

I retreat to my mummy bag and manage after a few minutes to finally stop shivering. I toss and turn and turn and toss—no easy feat in a feathered sarcophagus—but fail to fall back asleep. I count sheep, then elk, and finally bear. My mind, however, keeps wandering back to one overwhelming question: Why in the hell am I here?

The simple answer, I suppose, is because I was driving everyone nuts at home. Though I was justifiably proud of our son for toughing it up to 13,900 feet on Torreys Peak, I couldn't shake my focus on the final, but unclimbed, 375 feet. I had surprised myself that day by climbing so high with a body so over the hill. Maybe my once-a-week dads' basketball game really was enough to prepare me for some of the continent's highest mountains. Or maybe I, too, was just steps from suffering my son's same high-altitude crazy feet. This had all been the topic of considerable thought during my subsequent walks to school, shuttles to summer day camps, and drives to the orthodontist, plus conversations during breakfast, lunch, dinner, and sofa-lazing time.

One week of my hand-wringing convinced my wife that I should chase my dream. Or, more accurately, what Merrill said was, "If you go out and do it, will you stop bugging everyone about it?"

My bluff was called. That meant I had to pick a peak.

I wanted something dramatic. Torreys, shmoreys—that was a Denver day hike. Plus I had already summited it years ago. To really test myself, I needed something farther, harder, and more famous. If any peak could fit that bill, then the Mount of the Holy Cross was it.

Two hours from our house by highway, and then another hour by dirt road, the trailhead to Holy Cross was far enough from the parking space of a carpool dad to feel like a real expedition. And the climb itself was no walk in the park—more than a mile of vertical gain (5,625 feet) and twelve miles of hiking over trail and talus, that jumble of oven-size blocks that makes up the higher reaches of so many peaks. In other words, a lot more territory than I had ever covered in dads' basketball, even when they had started enforcing the three-second rule.

Plus this mountain offered the fame factor. For decades, Holy Cross was one of the best-known mountains in America, thanks to that lovesick nineteenth-century hardman William Henry Jackson.

A Civil War veteran, Jackson returned home to Vermont from the Battle of Gettysburg to find his heart torn by two passions. The first was for a young beauty named Caddie Eastman, whom Jackson called the "Belle of the Town." Caddie's stepfather was among the richest men in their small town; Will and Caddie were soon engaged to be married.

Jackson's second passion was for a fledgling invention called photography. Working as a retouch man for a local portraitist, he picked up some great experience, but got the bug to call more of his own shots. Serendipitously, a better photographer sixty miles away in Burlington offered up a job.

Jackson's dilemma: stick with the new fiancée in small-town Rutland, or ditch her for a $25-a-week gig in the big city. For several months, he tried to do both, but ran himself ragged. On one Sunday in April, the young lovers started arguing over who had started an argument. "She had spirit, I was bullheaded, and the quarrel grew," explained Jackson.

She dumped him.

He was distraught. He was humiliated. He was depressed.

So he moved to Omaha, Nebraska.

In the nineteenth century, Omaha actually seemed like a good idea. Urged on by Horace Greeley's advice to "go West, young man, and grow up with the country," tens of thousands did. Jackson signed on as a bullwhacker for a wagon train on the Oregon Trail, and checked every fort along the way for a letter of forgiveness from his sweetie. Alas, the Belle of the Town wasn't ringing. Gradually, though, the magnificent western landscape worked to heal his broken heart.

In the railroad-and-farm boomtown of Omaha, Jackson found a place large enough to start his own portrait photography business. It thrived. Better yet, Omaha was also large enough for Jackson to find a new love, Mollie Greer. They married in May 1869, and honeymooned on a steamboat ride to St. Louis. Jackson couldn't believe his luck: He had found a woman who understood his wanderlust. She even put up with his occasional hankering to hop a Union Pacific train to take pictures of the interior West.

Jackson's railroad photographs were fine enough to attract the attention of Dr. Ferdinand V. Hayden, a Civil War surgeon and adventurer trying to put together an expedition. His destination: some faraway western place that, rumor held, was rife with fire and brimstone and waterfalls that spouted not down from a stream but upward to the heavens. When asked to join Hayden's western survey, Jackson could not resist.

There was one complication: Mollie was pregnant. She agreed to stay home in Omaha to run the photo studio while William went wild exploring the West. By summer's end, he was to return home to fatherhood and domestication.

He made the most of his time afield. Hauling more than three hundred pounds of gear—three giant cameras, a tent darkroom, gallons of chemicals, and more than four hundred photographic glass plates—Jackson ended up publishing the world's first pictures of the spectacular geysers, hot springs, and canyons of the region that came to be known as Yellowstone.

Mollie was thrilled with her husband's success. But after a summer of being pregnant, alone, and running a business in Nebraska, she was ready for her man to be home. Then his boss, Dr. Hayden, placed an emergency demand.

Jackson's photos of Yellowstone were so breathtaking that naturalists wanted more prints, pronto, to bring to Washington, D.C. There was a new bill calling for Yellowstone to become the world's first national park, and the hope was that Jackson's glorious images just might inspire politicians to protect a place that few had ever seen. Jackson left his pregnant wife with his parents in New York, then hustled to Washington to make more prints and lobby Congress. A folio of his photos was placed on the desk of every senator and representative. Few could resist Yellowstone's charms.

Congress overwhelmingly approved the bill, and on March 1, 1872, President Ulysses S. Grant signed the legislation to make Yellowstone into a national park.

For Jackson, though, political success carried a horrible price. While he was in Washington, Mollie fell into premature labor. She died during childbirth. Their baby daughter died shortly after.

Horror, guilt, grief—name the awful emotion, and Jackson battled it. For a time he tried to work through the tragedy in Washington, but felt an irresistible force pulling him from the city and to the unsettled, to the mountains, to the West. Within four months of Mollie's death, he had returned to the frontier to heal, or at least strengthen, his broken heart.

With his white mule, Molly, and his bulky 11x14 camera, Jackson set off on years of expeditions that turned him into the premier photographer of the West, capturing iconic images of the Tetons of Wyoming, the gold camps of Denver, the Garden of the Gods along Pikes Peak, the Anasazi cliff dwellings of Mesa Verde—and a mountain that he helped make into one of the world's most famous. Jackson wrote:

> In the Middle Ages there was the legend of the Holy Grail. In Colorado there was the legend of a snowy cross upon a mountain.
>
> No man we talked with had ever seen the Mountain of the Holy Cross. But everyone knew that somewhere in the far reaches of the Western highlands such a wonder might exist.

Hadn't a certain hunter once caught a glimpse of it—only to have it vanish as he approached? Didn't a wrinkled Indian here and there narrow his eyes and slowly nod his head when questioned? Wasn't this man's grandfather, and that man's uncle, and old so-and-so's brother the first white man ever to lay eyes on the Holy Cross many, many, many years ago?

The cross was no myth. In August 1873, Jackson and two other survey members stumbled three days along Ute trails, plowed through dark timber, waded hip-deep snowmelt streams, and battled mightily to protect cameras from a soaking thunderstorm. After Jackson scrambled up slopes too jagged and steep for mules, the Rocky Mountain storm clouds finally lifted, and the men saw it: a 1,200-foot cross of snow, carved into the side of the mountain.

To a nation convinced that God had blessed westward expansion as Manifest Destiny, Jackson's photograph of the 14,009-foot Mount of the Holy Cross became an instant sensation. Men who couldn't afford portraits of their own families managed to scrape together enough coin for a print of that glorious Colorado mountain. The Mount of the Holy Cross was framed in Christian homes, rectories, and churches everywhere. When the western landscape painter Thomas Moran crafted his own magnificent five-by-six-foot version, embellished with a canyon and waterfall in the foreground, the faithful swooned. Jackson decided to beef up his own print sales by borrowing the painter's romanticized vision. In the darkroom Jackson retouched his photo to strengthen one arm of the cross and add a creek and waterfall in the valley below.

The great fireside poet Henry Wadsworth Longfellow was so moved by Jackson's photograph that he wrote "The Cross of Snow," which likened the summer ice on the mountain in the Rockies to his continuing love for his deceased wife:

> *There is a mountain in the distant West*
> *That, sun-defying, in its deep ravines*

Displays a cross of snow upon its side.
Such is the cross I wear upon my breast
These eighteen years, through all the changing scenes
And seasons, changeless since the day she died.

Some believers still had to see the great peak for themselves. By the turn of the century, priests were offering Holy Communion atop adjacent Notch Mountain. By the Great Depression, thousands of pilgrims descended upon the peak to pray. Some bathed in the cool waters of Cross Creek. Others dipped a handkerchief in the Bowl of Tears, the mountainside tarn. A few even talked of miracles.

By 1929, pilgrimages had become so popular that President Herbert Hoover turned the Mount of the Holy Cross into a protected national monument. At about that time, however, the cross couloir started to become less and less prominent. Most blamed the deterioration of the cross's right arm on erosion and rockfall, though there were persistent rumors that some local tourism promoter, eager to extend the pilgrimage season, had made matters worse by attempting to deepen the arm with miner's dynamite. Either way, the number of visits to the peak had plummeted enough by 1950 to persuade President Harry Truman to rescind the national monument status.

One other explanation for the drop-off in Holy Cross visits: This was a damned difficult hike, even if you weren't worrying about bear or elk.

At 2:30 a.m., with eyes wide open in a pitch-black tent, I concede that all hope for sleep is lost. It's time to put that elk-related adrenaline to use. I put on my socks by feel.

I know it's important to eat breakfast on the day of a big hike, but at this hour the only sustenance my body is trained to accept is cold pizza and beer. Neither would get me up the mountain. I hike on an empty stomach.

Walking alone in the dark on a narrow mountain trail eight miles from the nearest paved road isn't the greatest way to relax. I'm wearing a headlamp, which helpfully illuminates the boulders I keep tripping on, but also leaves me feeling slightly dizzy. I see nothing beyond the meager power of my four raindrop-size LEDs. The only other time I experienced this kind of tunnel vision was watching Jacques Cousteau scuba diving into a cave on PBS.

And then there are the nighttime noises. Scruffs, grunts, scratches, and rubs—what almost certainly is a refreshing breeze in the daytime becomes the pant of a bloodthirsty mountain lion at night. After a half-mile or so on the trail, though, I'm breathing heavily enough to block out most other ear distractions.

I look up and stifle a gasp: Stars! Billions and billions of them. The Milky Way beams from mountain to mountain while Mars lords above it all as a pale red disk. Even my lousy eyes can pick out nine gleaming stars of the Pleiades. From the eastern horizon rises the great hunter Orion. I do a double take. Orion is a winter constellation, master of the Christmas sky. Can I really be seeing it the first week of August? I search to the west for Scorpius, the scorpion that killed Orion with a sting to the heel. After their fight to the death, Scorpius and Orion were banished by the Greek gods to opposite ends of the heavens, so that one would never appear in the sky with the other. Sure enough, I now see that Scorpius, the summer constellation, is gone. Working a trail at three in the morning miles from the light pollution of a city gives me a sneak peak at the next season's sky.

At the base of the Half Moon Trail I hear the babbles and swirls of East Cross Creek. In the trees my headlamp beam bounces off the reflective tape of three dome backpacking tents. Those campers are still; I am moving. Sweaty and nervous, but feeling pretty exhilarated, actually. Do I really have a shot at the summit?

A few minutes past the creek crossing and I'm slapped back to reality. Ugh, the taste of lungs for breakfast. The whole first part of my hike this morning had been a 1,000-foot descent from the top of Half Moon Pass. Now I'm dropped all the way down to 10,700 feet, and I must make up all the elevation I lost. My legs doth protest. Suddenly the night sky doesn't feel so wondrous. It feels lonely.

One wrong turn. Then another. And another. Surely this trail can't be so hard to find in the daytime. I double back and find a small man-made tower of stacked rocks—a cairn. I'm back on track into a world where one dark step hurts even more than the other. I sit down and take a slug of water, hoping the liquid will push back my heart from my throat. Instead, I find I'm breathing so hard that the water squirts out my nostrils, accompanied by a jellyfish of snot. Call Sigourney Weaver—there's an alien to battle in my sinus. I'm too tired to care. My jacket now sports a slimy racing stripe. In the throes of exhaustion, the first thing that goes is personal hygiene.

Finally I clear the trees, and my spirits lift. Measurable progress! I don't know whether to be thrilled that I've come this high without suffering a massive coronary, or humbled to realize that I have another 2,000 vertical feet to go. The Milky Way seems to point toward the summit. I take it as a sign, and climb on.

Or, more accurately, I plod on. Five steps, gasp, another five steps, pant. I can't take it anymore. I sit, but my folded-over gut pinches off my air supply. I hunch and wheeze. My throat churns with bile. What the hell am I doing here? My bet is it would take a lot less time to hike back to my tent than to try a suicide drive to the summit. I know I'm not supposed to do it, but for the first time I look back down the mountain. And I am horrified.

In the distance I see two lights bobbing up the trail. Two hikers, coming my way. They must have started from the trailhead this morning. (To cut down on the day's climb, I had backpacked one-and-a-half miles and 1,300 vertical feet the day before to camp at the top of Half Moon Pass.) My head start means nothing to these guys. They're closing on me.

Of course, that's only if I let them. Nothing kicks in the testosterone like competition. I may scream at randy elk in my boxer shorts, but I've got enough personal pride to keep these hikers from passing me on the trail. I think. I hope.

I push myself enough to double my pace—ten steps instead of five before I stop to blow out my lungs with deep breaths. Still, they gain on me. Worse, in this thin mountain air I can hear them. And they're laughing. What kind of superhuman can spare the oxygen at timberline for a belly laugh? They must be laughing at me and my feeble headlamp.

No more am I a plodder. There's a Niagara Falls of sweat erupting from my beanie, and a bass drum of heartbeats throbbing in my wrists, but I'm definitely not plodding. I'm climbing.

I stop for another lung blow, and turn downhill to measure the progress of the headlamps. Only the headlamps are gone. In my determination to push up the mountain I've ignored the fact that the sun has risen behind my back. Below me is a moonscape of gray-and-blue talus. The trail switchbacks through the sea of stone, but the landscape is so massive there's no way to pick out two approaching climbers. Plus, the gray skies of dawn have been accompanied by a gentle breeze. No way to hear any talking now, especially with so much sweat pooled in my ears. Still, they must be gaining on me.

The breeze turns into a wind, and I shiver every time I stop to pant. My fingers have swelled to the size of Vienna sausages. At first I assume this is an inevitable hallucination from my ill-advised decision to skip breakfast, but then I realize it's probably my hands' retribution for my feet's decision to venture above 13,000 feet. Is my wedding ring slashing the blood circulation to my fingertip? I'm too damn cold to take off my mitten to check. The wind whistles. My head spins. My feet go . . .

Not so crazy. I haven't eaten a thing but mucus this morning, so I stop and tear open an energy bar wrapper with my teeth. In these temperatures, the bar is as solid as chalk, and tastes like it too. I huddle from the wind behind a rock, and fill my mouth with water to turn the energy bar into a slurry that slides down my gullet. Not exactly the breakfast of champions, but I feel a little stronger.

I'll need all the energy I can get. I top out the north ridge at 13,400 feet, and the hulking mass of Holy Cross stretches above me. There's no trail to the top, just 600 vertical feet of boulder-hopping. For the first time all day, the sun warms my face. It's go time.

Right foot, left foot, a hop, a skip, a right hand for balance—I'm a kid on a playground jungle gym. One rock at a time, I move higher and higher. Should I bounce to this chunk or that? It's problem solving on a massive scale, and for the first time all day I don't feel tired or cold or slow. I'm just having fun.

And then, just as soon as I settle into my most joyful rhythm, it happens: There's no more up. I find a small rock shelter around a palm-size brass medallion from the U.S. Geological Survey that proclaims MT HOLY CROSS. 250 DOLLARS FINE FOR DISTURBING THIS MARK. Next to it some lovebird has left behind a rock carved with this inscription: "To Abby. My vow to you in stone. This day 7 3 06." Abby may have found her true love here—or maybe she didn't; is that why the engraving was left on the summit?—but right now there is no doubt I'm the happiest one on the mountain.

I want to jump. I want to dance. I want to shout.

Unfortunately, when I stand up quickly, I get dizzy, so I sink to my duff to celebrate.

From the summit I can see from here until tomorrow, even though tomorrow is seventeen hours away. There are jagged peaks and rolling forests and cascading creeks and blue skies and no sign whatsoever of the hikers who trailed me in the dark. In fact, the only sign of man's handiwork is the trail up Holy Cross's north ridge. The view is breathtaking—literally. And I want to share it.

Though I packed it to use only in an emergency, I pull out my cell phone and find a signal, which grows even stronger when I rise to my feet. (One bar at 14,009 feet, but three bars at 14,015 feet.) Our home phone rings three times. Our three-year-old answers, and cuts to the chase.

"Dad, did you fall down the mountain?" Wesley asks.

"No, son, I did not. Right now, I'm standing on top of it."

Chapter 3

The Mission Takes Shape

HURON PEAK 14,010'

QUANDARY PEAK 14,271'

LA PLATA PEAK 14,336'

MOUNT SHERMAN 14,036'

MOUNT YALE 14,200'

MOUNT PRINCETON 14,204'

At home that afternoon I circle the kitchen in a glorious victory lap, and babble to my wife and kids like a brook tumbling from the Continental Divide.

You guys should have seen that mountain! It was so beautiful! I was the first one to climb it this morning! I had the whole summit to myself! I didn't think I could do it, but then I did!

That's great, Dad, says our eight-year-old, Max. Now can we get something from the ice cream truck?

Of course we can! Let's all celebrate!

With the calliope music of the ice cream truck bouncing off the walls of our house, I reach for my wallet and feel something strange. Somebody has inserted a sledgehammer between my shoulder blades. My spine feels like cement; my thighs are Jell-O. My wife hands me a bottle of Advil for dessert, and I Frankenstein my way into bed.

You seem really happy, Merrill tells me.

I am, I say. My eyes shut, and stay that way until morning.

It takes one day for me to lose the sledgehammer, two for the Jell-O. The spine remains incommunicado.

The biggest body change, however, is in my eyes. They see things differently. Walking to the park with the kids, I notice for the first time that some homes along the block have bricks that can be climbed like a rock wall. At the playground, instead of chasing my kids up the stairs of the jungle gym, I scramble up the slide. Some kid loses a Frisbee up a Ponderosa pine, and I climb up after it. What's a ten-foot branch when I've stared down an eight-hundred-foot couloir? When our three-year-old cries in his bedroom, I take the stairs two at a time.

Merrill is quick to notice the difference. Sad fact is, I'm not the man she married sixteen years ago. When I gained my first ten pounds, I blamed it on my heavy work schedule. The next ten, after I became the father of two. The ten after that had arrived by the time of our third son, when I was working even more, and the fourth ten were added in the blur that followed. Excavating clothes from the back of the closet was a depressing stumble down memory lane—first the college pants, then the loose-fit jeans, then the baggy shirts.

The last few years I had stopped sucking in my gut at the beach; nobody was looking, anyway, at a guy who grew hair faster on his ears than his scalp. Fortunately for me, the new fashion trend of untucked shirts arrived at about the same time as Chipotle's big burrito restaurants. Coincidence or conspiracy? I wasn't arguing.

My wife, however, could still tuck in her shirt. Despite a travel job and three pregnancies, she had gained no weight whatsoever since college. Merrill was a runner. Weekdays she woke up at 5 a.m. to do it. Last year she had even won a Top 10 medal for her age class in a 10K race with fifty thousand runners. She was thin, fast, and brimming with the unfathomable willpower that allowed her to walk past a plate of fries without diving in. If I stood in front of her on a sunny day, she would pale under my solar eclipse.

So whenever my wife saw me moving, by choice, and not toward the refrigerator, she was full of encouragement.

Climbing that mountain seemed like something you enjoyed, she told me, and I think you should try another one.

Really?

Really.

The idea was to pick hiking days when she was not traveling for her job. She could hang out with our three kids. No big deal at all.

And so for one day a week the rest of the summer, I became the dad on the block with the weird ritual—putting the kids to bed at night, driving two hours through the dark to sleep in my car at a trailhead, rising before dawn, struggling but ultimately succeeding in summiting a mountain, and returning home by dinnertime.

Every hike, I felt cold and lonely and a little scared. Every hike, I felt like quitting. Every hike, I thought: This is my last one.

Every hike, though, something happened that rejuvenated me enough to keep me keeping on.

On Huron Peak, I missed a turnoff in the dark and hiked a full mile before realizing that my trail was much too gentle and enjoyable to be the correct route up a Fourteener. I retraced my steps after sunrise, found the sign to the right turnoff, smacked my forehead in frustration, and suffered up an endlessly rising and twisting trail that had me keeling over at every switchback. Ah, but the view of the spectacularly jagged Three Apostles was better than any postcard. On my way down, however, I saw something just as breathtaking: a lone hiker, moving swiftly up the same switchbacks and never stopping. Who was this übermensch? As we drew nearer, I noticed something a little odd about him—his gait and his posture seemed a little off. When I finally met him on a switchback, I told him that he was cruising up the same switchbacks that required a pit stop from me. He told me it was his third attempt at this mountain. The first time, he got lost; the second time, he ran from a thunderstorm. Finally I couldn't resist, and asked him his age. "I'm sixty-eight," said John Sanborn, a retired schoolteacher from Chapman, Kansas. "I climbed Longs Peak, my first Fourteener, in 1958." That was three years before I was born. I shook his hand and staggered away. Suddenly I wasn't tired. I was inadequate.

On Quandary Peak, I popped a heel blister about five hundred feet from the summit. I sat and felt sorry for myself until a yellow Labrador retriever ahead on the talus looked down on me and seemed to urge me on. When I had met this dog for the first time at the trailhead this morning, I had assumed he belonged to another hiker on the mountain. But after we summited together, I learned that this wasn't just any yellow Lab. This was Horton the Quandary Dog, who lived with his family in a house near the trailhead. His owner, a former *National Geographic* photographer, told a local radio station that his eight-year-old pooch had summited Quandary nine hundred times, including some days when he climbed the mountain four separate times with different groups of hikers. At night, Horton slept like a dog. After he guided me to the top, I could understand why.

On La Plata Peak, I took the less-visited southwest slopes route to enjoy some solitude. I got my wish, and I soon regretted it. I became lost in the dark again, but this time in a swamp with shin-deep mud and ice water. After that came a steep scree slope that had me taking two steps forward before sliding one step back. Then I was confronted by a talus field so steep that I had to use my hands to help pull myself up. Was this really the route? I concluded that this mountain was dissing me, and I was not going to let it win. When I finally summited, I saw a nasty black cloud barreling my way from the west. To escape the coming lightning storm, I ran down a mountain that I barely had energy to walk. I slipped and tore an eight-inch gash on the rear of my pants, which flapped in the wind as I tried, unsuccessfully, to outrun a hellacious downpour. I returned home with a racing stripe of mud up my boxers.

On Mount Sherman, I was lulled by reports calling this the easiest Fourteener. I slept in, and didn't arrive at the trailhead until 7 a.m. My reward was a fog-and-wind whiteout, complete with horizontal snow—in August!—along a ridge that, according to maps, had a six-hundred-foot drop. (The pea soup was too thick for me to see the bottom.) The summit of Sherman was long and flat enough to have hosted a successful emergency landing by a four-passenger charter plane four decades ago. With a numb nose, wind-seared eyes, and chattering teeth, I wished that charter were still around for me to hire for the trip back down.

On Mount Yale, I ran off the summit from another approaching thunderstorm. On my race to the car I met Gary Huckabay, fifty-eight, a man of many callings—former air force combat pilot with a doctorate in archaeology who now did classified work for the military in Colorado Springs. One of his other fields of expertise is lightning. On a backcountry survival course, he was a hundred yards away from three buddies when a bolt hit the tree they were hiding under. One friend was killed, two were paralyzed. Not long after that, another friend was hit in the head by another lightning bolt. He survived, but with life-changing problems. And just a few months ago, Huckabay himself had retreated on La Plata when an incoming storm carried enough of an electrical charge to make hikers' hair stand on edge. So why was I running down the mountain while he was hiking up? He thought it still looked safe. By the time I reached the parking lot, all hell was breaking loose up on the summit, or at least where I thought the summit should be. The sky was black. Lightning bolted. I breathed easier when I saw no stories in the next day's newspapers about hikers being electrocuted on Mount Yale, but I was still curious. I called Huckabay at home, who told me the lightning remained "pretty far away." How far away was that? "About three miles," he said, though to me that meant the lightning was as little as a minute away. I would have wet my pants in fear, but Huckabay said something that made me wonder if he'd been negotiating all those lightning bolts with some inside information. Turned out the man of many callings had one extra one—he was a retired minister.

After each of these peaks, I returned home with a little more pride and skill and stamina, plus the humility to realize that nothing I could do on a mountain would ever be as hard or rewarding as staying home for the past three years with our three kids. Still, I was grateful for the time away. It hurt to admit, but I think the kids were grateful for the break. They seemed to be having a blast without me. My wife too.

Though I felt guilty saying it, I was having fun on my own. On a mountain, nobody told me what to do. I had the freedom to eat, sleep, sweat, piss, moan, swear, belch, fart, sing, laugh, yodel, and nap whenever and wherever I wanted. The views were magnificent. The people on the trail were friendly. The fears were life-affirming. I could not think of any other pursuit that so perfectly tested my physical and emotional limits. At home those years with the kids I had learned to revel in the little victories—the covered sneeze, the unprompted thank-you, the testosterone-fueled argument between brothers that was resolved without a sock in the nose—but I still ended some days wondering if I had lost more ground than I had gained. The mountain, however, offered little ambivalence. I either summited or I didn't. It was hard work that could be measured. It was straightforward. It was satisfying. I longed to do more.

There was, of course, one hitch: My solo hiking was driving Merrill nuts. Or, more precisely, giving her nightmares, and, on some nights, preventing any sleep whatsoever. At first I responded by telling her about the joys of solitude—the soul-cleansing quiet, the pleasure of proceeding at my own pace, the time to think about something in particular or nothing at all.

She asked: What if something happened—something bad?

Well, these are just hiking routes. No climbing. No real danger.

What about the lightning?

I had no good answer for that one.

What if you twisted an ankle? What if you slipped when you were alone on some mountain—could you die of a sprained ankle?

No good answer for that one either.

Though Merrill was almost always right, I didn't like to admit it. So I fell back on my argument of last resort:

I can't hike with anyone, because I don't have anyone to hike with.

We both knew this claim was true, even if it hurt me to say so. The reality was, I was firmly ensconced in a middle-aged rut. I'd had the same set of friends for years. There were some guys who would drink with me, and some who would fish, or play cards, or watch a ball game with me. A few guys also played golf, but certainly not with me, especially after I'd sliced two houses in a particularly notorious walk around eighteen holes a few years back.

Did I know anyone who would rise before dawn to stagger up a cold mountain on a day off work? Who in their right mind would do that by choice? Friend—or nutcase?

Well, said my wife, what about Gottlieb?

Ah, Gottlieb.

To my wife, Gottlieb—his actual name was Alan Gottlieb, but few of my friends had first names that got much use—was the perfect dinner party guest. He was a Peace Corps veteran and bighearted father, raised as an agnostic Jew, but married to the world's most elegant and charming Episcopal priest. He was a newspaperman who switched over to a small nonprofit that worked to save inner-city public schools. He wrote thriller novels in his spare time. Like my wife, he ran twenty miles a week.

There was another side to Gottlieb too. The last time I summited a mountain with him was fifty pounds ago, on a backpacking trip two weeks before my wedding day, when we hiked one of the easier Fourteeners (Humboldt Peak), returned to camp to knock off a bottle of gin with a few other buddies, passed out, woke up at 3 a.m., failed to fall back asleep, said what the hell, and scrambled up one of the nastier Fourteeners, Crestone Needle, with a pounding hangover—while a mountain goat kicked down boulders on us. We celebrated in base camp with macho grunts and ibuprofen.

At the time we felt like studs. In hindsight we both figured out that we had been fools.

We went on to embarrass ourselves in other outdoor endeavors. Our employer at the time, the *Denver Post*, sponsored an annual weeklong bike tour across Colorado called Ride the Rockies. We volunteered to pedal it for the paper mainly because it got us out of covering the rapists, robbers, murderers, and politicians that made up the bulk of our newspaper reporting work.

On the bike tour, Gottlieb and I soon found ourselves on the wrong side of a cultural divide. The vast majority of the tour's two thousand other bikers—no, excuse me, they preferred to be called *cyclists*—rode dainty road bikes and dressed like psychedelic praying mantises. We rode mountain bikes with fat knobby tires and wore freebie shirts with permanent half-moons below the underarms. The cyclists shaved grams from their components and hair from their legs; we held a burping contest up Wolf Creek Pass. They nibbled PowerBars; we bogarted burritos. We smelled bad. We spit. We finished last.

On one defining night in the venerable old mining town of Leadville, when all the other cyclists had retired by 10 p.m. to their tents in a community campground, Gottlieb and I started up in a miners' bar and drank beer and played pool and told lies and drank even more.

Stumbling back to camp without a flashlight, I discovered that my tent, an REI gray dome, was the most popular type in Colorado that year. That night I unzipped and tried to enter three of the wrong tents by accident; the next morning Gottlieb mercifully let me ride behind him with my head hung low, hoping that everyone else on the bike tour had lost interest in trying to kill that stumbling midnight tent intruder who stank like a pool hall.

Of course I should call Gottlieb, I told my wife, who was under the impression that this would be a safe and responsible thing. I wasn't about to dissuade her.

Though Gottlieb agreed to try Mount Princeton with me, he had an obligation at his wife's church that prevented him from meeting in the mountains until the dawn of our hike. This left me with a Friday night to kill in the Arkansas River Valley, home to the highest peaks of the Rockies. They won't stay that way forever. The Fourteeners have had some vast geologic ups and downs.

About 1.7 billion years ago, Colorado was an island floating around the world when it smashed into Wyoming. The collision crinkled the earth up toward the sky, and the result was Colorado's first mountain range. With no vegetation to protect the rock, however, the relentless forces of erosion won the upper hand. The peaks were ground down enough to make them dip back below the surface of the sea.

My home state stayed flat and wet for millions more years. About 315 million years ago, though, the vast tectonic plates went at it again, butting heads hard enough to push two new ranges up out of the sea. The big mountain islands, near the present-day Front and San Juan ranges, were called the Ancestral Rocky Mountains. They dominated the landscape for 70 million years, and are seen today in the red sedimentary stone at the base of some modern mountains.

Once again, wind, waves, and earthquakes beat down the mountains. Colorado turned flat and warm, and it became the age of dinosaurs. In Colorado paleontologists found the world's first *Tyrannosaurus rex* fossil, the world's first brontosaurus tracks, and the continent's longest dinosaur trackway.

Eighty million years ago the landscape transformed again. The Pacific Plate smashed beneath western North America and, for some still mysterious reason, crumpled up a vast range of peaks a thousand miles from the coast. These were the Laramide Mountains, which forced the oceans to retreat from Colorado for the last time.

Forty million years later, the Laramides had eroded away too. In their place, though, came an explosion of volcanic activity, with twenty separate calderas spewing out thousands of cubic miles of ash and pumice at speeds up to 100 mph. Vast piles of this volcanic material settled and consolidated to become the San Juan Mountains of southwestern Colorado.

Not long after in geologic time—make that about 26 million years ago—Colorado was wrenched apart by a long rift that dropped down the San Luis and Arkansas River valleys, and thrust up the Sangre de Cristo and Sawatch peaks, where I am today. Geologists still argue whether those mountains are still moving up faster than the forces of erosion are grinding them down.

One other result of this explosion in geologic activity: hot springs. Colorado has ninety-three of them, and the hottest one, flowing from the earth at 185 degrees, is right here at the Mount Princeton Hot Springs Resort. Built in 1879 with the proceeds of a gold mine won in a saloon knife fight, the four-story hotel and its soothing 135-degree hot springs became a turn-of-the-century tourism sensation. But the Great Depression plunged the resort into truly hot water, and the hotel never recovered. In 1950 a businessman stripped the grand structure of 1 million board feet of lumber and used it for the ultimate indignity—building a new subdivision in Texas.

Smaller versions of the resort had boomed and busted in the years since. What always remained were the calming waters along a snow-melt creek at the base of a 14,000-foot mountain. I had climbed Mount Yale earlier that day and was waiting for Gottlieb to arrive the next day for a hike of Mount Princeton. My legs were sore and my skin was sticky.

The hot springs are empty. I jump in. I moan with delight. I float on my back and watch the sun dip behind the Continental Divide. I moan some more.

Over my shoulder I hear giggles, female variety. Instinctively, I suck in my gut, but that just makes me stop floating. Don't whales ever bask?

I spin around and spot the source of the laughter. It's a gaggle of girls, four of them, lithe and tan and blond and maybe eighteen years old. I retreat to the opposite corner of the hot springs pool, but the gaggle has come with reinforcements. Soon I am surrounded in the pool by more than a dozen female hardbodies, all in jog bras or bikinis, and I am aghast. I should feel like I'm the star of every man's beer commercial fantasy—me in the pool with a traveling girls volleyball team—but the more they giggle and splash, the more I feel like Weird Old Uncle Pervy. I try to hide by dropping underwater, then realize they must think I'm checking out their legs.

When I surface, I expect the vice squad to be waiting for me with handcuffs. The reality is even uglier: Nobody has even noticed I'm in the pool. There is nothing more invisible to a group of young women than a lone middle-aged man. I leave unnoticed, lay out my sleeping bag in the back of my car, and read a book until I fall asleep.

Gottlieb drives up on time at 6 a.m., having left his house in Denver two-and-a-half hours earlier. He's drunk enough coffee to look bug-eyed, or maybe he's just shell-shocked over the swirl of the weather above us. The sky is a solid sheet of clouds. Though the maps say Mount Princeton is somewhere up there, we certainly can't see it.

I tell Gottlieb about my scary run from summit lightning the day before on Mount Yale. We both know that clouds before 6 a.m. are a poor omen for today, but there's no way I want him to have driven so far before sunrise without even attempting a hike. We move slowly upward fully expecting that we'll retreat swiftly downward.

We bounce in my SUV three miles up a surprisingly nonpunishing four-wheel-drive road, and park at 10,800 feet near some radio towers. There's mist in the air, and the clouds show no sign of breaking. We mutter about our bad luck, fiddle with our pack straps, and set off.

My bones creak. My joints ache. I'm just about ready to whine—how stupid am I, thinking I can do two Fourteeners in two days?—but Gottlieb knows me well enough to change the subject. He decides to show off his new hiking miracle cure, ski poles.

Ski poles? I didn't even know he skied.

Actually, he says, people call them trekking poles. They're really light and they collapse into three sections. They keep down the pounding on your body. Since he started using them, he hasn't even rolled an ankle. And he read somewhere that trekking poles make you burn 40 percent more calories.

Just what I need—something that makes me more tired.

Not that it would make any difference today. The more we hike, the less we see. There's more chill and more mist. It's as bad as the gloomiest day in London, but over 11,000 feet. My bet is we're hiking directly into the clouds. Visibility is less than forty feet.

From the eerie gray behind us we hear footsteps. The fog seems to intensify all sound, so it's hard to judge the distance, but the steps are steadily drawing closer. Bear? Deer? Another crazed elk in rut? We turn and brace for battle.

Through the mist our assailant emerges: It's a man, gray-haired and trim, wearing a T-shirt from the Pikes Peak Marathon, a 26-mile race up and down the famed mountain, and running straight at us.

Gottlieb and I are huffing and puffing just to walk. This guy is running without a sweat.

My jaw drops as he breezes by us. Gottlieb, however, has other ideas.

"One other good thing about these poles," he says, handing me one. "You want to shish-kebob that guy, or should I?"

We both laugh too hard to épée anyone. Besides, there's no way we can catch him. In the clouds we have seen Superman, without a cape.

At 11,800 feet we leave the jeep road and start hiking up a trail. There's a steep climb at first, and then something wild happens: The clouds vanish. How did they disappear without a wind to push them? We turn and see a startling truth. We are looking down on the clouds. It's the first time I've risen above the weather without the help of airplane wings, and the thrill of it all seems to turbocharge our feet. We're nowhere near as fast as the unimpaled runner, but we do manage to blast by scree and talus and lichens as if they were standing still.

Besides, we've got so much to talk about that the elevation seems to melt away. I tell Gottlieb about my invisibility with the young women in the hot springs pool; he tells me about the invisibility of his high school daughter, who has spent the better part of the summer trekking through Mongolia. (Could it be possible for an American teenager to find anyplace farther from her parents?) I tell him about my worries for our oldest son in middle school; he tells me about his worries about his daughter for college.

Not long ago his teenager's friend was returning home from a party with another friend who had been drinking. The closer they got to home, the more they could see the driver was drunk. They tried to take away the driver's keys. She refused. They tried to beat home their point by demanding to be dropped off immediately on the side of the road. The driver finally agreed, then floored the gas pedal. The result was heard from blocks away. Her car had smashed head-on into a tree. The driver was dead.

Though some people may win a confidence boost from climbing mountains, nothing strips it away faster than a parent returning to a home full of adolescence.

With the talk moving faster than our feet, we make the summit with much less pain than expected. We're thousands of feet above the clouds, basking in blue sky and sun above, and feeling more alive than ever.

I tell Gottlieb I had enjoyed soloing the other peaks, but nothing made the uphill pass as quickly, or with as much fun, as hiking it with a good hiking partner.

"Maybe someday you'll find one," he says.

"Up yours, pal," I say.

"Up yours too," he says.

We swap bad jokes the whole way down, and I secretly conclude that once again, my wife was probably right. Hiking solo is fun, but hiking with an old buddy is even better.

Chapter 4

The Monkey

CRESTONE NEEDLE 14,197'

HUMBOLDT PEAK 14,064'

MOUNT ELBERT 14,440'

GRAYS PEAK 14,278'

TORREYS PEAK 14,275'

The kids were in bed. My wife had just finished a glass of wine. The lights were low. The mood was right. It was now or never, and I was going for it.

"So what would you think if I tried the Fourteeners?"

"Who?"

"The Fourteeners—the mountains. What would you think if I tried them?"

"I thought you've been trying them."

"I've been trying some of them. I'm thinking about trying all of them."

"That makes me nervous. Isn't it dangerous?"

"Well, I've done the math here, and most peaks aren't. Most Fourteeners are Class One or Class Two. Class One means there's a trail to the top. Class Two means there's no trail, but there is pretty easy rock-hopping across talus. There's no such thing as an easy Fourteener, but the Class One and Class Two would have no real scrambling or rock climbing. Tough physically, but as long as I'm careful with the weather, no big danger. There are thirty-seven peaks like that. The majority of the Fourteeners."

"OK. So there are thirty-seven hikes. What about the rest? Aren't they dangerous?"

"Depends what you mean by dangerous. There are seventeen hard ones. Of those seventeen, twelve are Class Three. That means you're using your hands and feet for some sections. There's some exposure."

"Exposure?"

"Places you don't want to look down."

"Or fall down. I don't want you falling down."

"I don't want to fall down either."

"What makes you think you can do this? You're not a technical rock climber."

"One of the harder Class Threes is Crestone Needle. I did that one hung over with Gottlieb."

"Sixteen years ago. When you were thin and in shape."

"But I did it. And I wouldn't have to do it again."

"I want to support you in what you want to do. But this—it makes me afraid."

"There's a guy near Aspen named Lou Dawson. He was the first to ski all the Fourteeners. He said something I like: 'A mountaineer with no fear has no judgment.'"

"Since when are you a mountaineer?"

"I like the mountains. I have fear. I scared off a horny elk in my underwear."

"Does that make you a mountaineer?"

"No. But it's a start. I couldn't know unless I tried."

"Wait—you told me about the Fourteeners that you hike, and the ones where you use your hands and feet. What about the others? Aren't there more?"

"There are five more mountains. They're Class Four. I've seen pictures. They look bad. Don't know if I'd ever climb them."

"You don't know if you'd ever try them?"

"I might try them."

"Try them, but not climb them?"

"Don't know if I could."

"What are they? Where are they?"

"Three of the bad ones are out by Aspen—Capitol, North Maroon, and Pyramid. They've got rotten rock. People say they're like stacks of dinner plates, fourteen thousand feet high. Another bad one is in southern Colorado—Little Bear. It has rotten rock and one section they call the Bowling Alley."

"The Bowling Alley? Does that make you the pin?"

"And there's another bad one out by Telluride, Mount Wilson. It has some exposure."

"It has some exposure. Is that like saying the North Pole has some snow?"

"I haven't been to either place."

"So that's fifty-four Fourteeners?"

"Fifty-four."

"How many have you already climbed?"

"Before we had kids I did five—Crestone Needle, Humboldt, Elbert, Grays, and Torreys. And I did seven more this summer. So I have twelve down, and forty-two to go."

"And you want to do them next year? Is it even possible to climb forty-two mountains in a year?"

"Some people have done it. I don't know if I could. I'd like to try."

"Well, I don't want you climbing in the winter. That doesn't seem safe."

"I'm not too sure about the winter either. I'd wait until the high country really started melting out—probably after Memorial Day. So I could start in June. And then it starts snowing again up high after Labor Day."

"After Memorial Day and before Labor Day—you could do forty-two peaks in three months—forty-two peaks in ninety days?"

"I'd like to try."

"You'd have to get in shape."

"I lost eight pounds hiking this summer."

"Really?"

"Then I gained it all back."

"You'd really have to train this winter. I've heard you tell people that if you can run a mile, you can hike a Fourteener, and if you can run a 10K, you can do a Fourteener pretty easily. Can you run a 10K now?"

"You know I hate running."

"Forty-two peaks in ninety days—you'd need endurance. How are you going to get endurance without running?"

"I could start at the gym this winter."

"And if you try any of the hard mountains, I want you going with somebody who knows what they're doing. Like a guide."

"I could look into that."

"And I don't want you hiking alone. Ever."

"Ever? I'd have to find hiking partners for everything?"

"Every mountain. You have three children. You have a wife. I don't want to become a widow because you sprained an ankle alone in the mountains."

"I don't know anybody who could climb forty-two mountains in a summer. I don't even know anybody who'd *want* to climb forty-two mountains in a summer."

"You're not going to climb alone."

"But I don't know anybody."

"You're not going to climb alone."

"But—"

"No."

"No?"

"If you really want to do it, find somebody to do it with you."

"How?"

"If you can climb a mountain, you can find a friend. Listen, this seems like something you really want to do. You really seemed to enjoy it this summer. It's something you'll have for the rest of your life. But none of this is worth dying for. Right?"

"But I don't know anybody."

"Right?"

"How am I going to find partners for forty-two mountains?"

"Right?"

"All forty-two mountains?"

"Right?"

"I can try."

"Right?"

"I guess so."

"Right?"

"Right."

And so I entered the winter of 2006 with a two major problems—too many pounds and too few friends. The main obstacle to my weight problem was my willpower. The main obstacle to my friend problem was my personality. Concluding it would be easier to lose forty-five pounds than to be nice with strangers, I launched my quest to become fit. I tried to make a game of it by starting in a basketball gym.

When I worked downtown, I belonged to the YMCA across the street. There were mice, homeless guys, and, one day, condoms on the floor of the shower, but it still had the best lunchtime basketball game around. Three days a week for eight years, I had guarded the same man, who was seven inches taller than I, but twenty years older. To even out our differences, we banged bodies relentlessly in the low post. After our first ten games, we had matching bruises. After our first hundred games, we knew all of each other's moves. After our first two hundred games, we knew all of each other's insults. After our five hundredth game, I told him I probably knew his body as well as my wife's. He felt sorry for my wife.

Our game, like the newspaper business, eventually fell apart, so I had to search for a new court. I found it at the local Jewish Community Center, where a bunch of Realtors, bartenders, professors, and self-employed lawyers met weekday afternoons for hoops. Some cultural differences between the Y and the J were striking: At the J, nobody spit on the floor or screamed "Jesus" at a Hail Mary shot. And then there was that mysterious, steamy room in the back corner of the locker room, where I once saw sweaty men whack each other hard enough with sticks to make them speak Russian. I stood ready to rescue, but learned that schvitz happens. I retreated in fear.

Ultimately I stopped playing at the J because I never quite fit in, which is a polite way of saying that other players didn't enjoy being bounced around by a guy with a lumbering butt. Most of the other J players had grown up together—or, more accurately, had gotten older together—and argued foul calls with the ferocity and relentlessness of a couple in the dying days of a bad marriage. The best part of my game, my left elbow, was as welcome as a soon-to-be-ex-mother-in-law.

To find another game I had to find another religion. Luckily, a bunch of Catholic dads had scored the key to the Good Shepherd school gym for regular weeknight romps. After putting our kids to bed, we gathered under a crucifix and played like hell. Some players had game and some players had gab, but everyone had a hankering for that magic postgame potion of yeast, hops, barley, and malt.

My wife couldn't figure how, after five hours of nighttime alleged basketball, I was still keeping my twelve-pack abs. The truth was, I was playing for the tie—burning hundreds of calories on the court while gaining hundreds of calories in the bar. Basketball was fun, but it wouldn't get me up forty-two peaks in ninety days when the snow finally melted. I searched for something else.

I found it around the corner from basketball gym at the J, in a room filled with stationary bikes, loud music, and women of a certain age who genuinely enjoyed each other. A morning spin class, starting just after I had dropped off the kids at school, became part of my weekday routine. I could sweat like a pig and swap domestic war stories with people who, like me, could change a diaper with one hand and recite *Goodnight Moon* from memory. Boredom had always been my nemesis in gym workouts, but the anthropologist in me found it strangely interesting to hear tales of menopause between blasts of Nirvana and Evanescence. Best of all, the women in spin class looked out for me. I was rarely able to skip a few classes without hearing about it from someone. One powerful lesson: Never disappoint women in the throes of hot flashes. I learned to adjust the wall fans for them.

One had climbed Fourteeners before. She recommended doing exercises that simulated hiking. I could either heed her voice of experience or follow the bellowing voice in my head of my long-lost high school football coach. As if that were any contest—I naturally bowed to my fears. The result for me that winter was an impressive bench press—I could push more than my body weight for the first time in nearly three decades—but legs that still turned to fettuccine after two miles of running. I finally listened to the wise menopausal counsel and started doing things that looked weird but made me stronger: walking 3.5 mph on a fully inclined treadmill; walking backward 3.5 mph on a fully inclined treadmill; taking on a rotating torture device/stair-climbing machine nicknamed the Gauntlet; and, for extra mental toughness, taking on the Gauntlet while watching Elisabeth Hasselbeck and *The View*. By the end of winter I could climb two hundred floors on a stepmill after an hour-long spinning class, but only if Rosie O'Donnell stayed out of my face.

What I really needed, however, was Oprah to manage my diet. My problem: The more I exercised, the more I ate. Green chile cheeseburgers, barbacoa burritos, cookie dough ice cream—I could just work it off the next morning, right? Wrong. With spring approaching, I found myself in a strange state: fat, but with endurance. Though the classic body type for a climber was a gazelle—thin, limber, and quick—I looked in the mirror and saw a potbellied ox. I started the winter weighing 210 pounds, and ended it weighing 208. My oldest son, ever observant, attributed the loss of those two glorious pounds to male-pattern baldness.

Like my hairline, my chances of finding a hiking partner for the summer were also receding. A plea to our Christmas card list came up empty. The women in spin class weren't interested. Neither was the instructor. Personal trainers at the gym had a fear of heights. Everyone at basketball had work commitments, family commitments, or personal aversions to spending long hours on a trail with me. Parents

of kids I had coached at soccer preferred golf. I tried to soften up the
neighbors by shoveling their sidewalks, but when they saw me on the
roof, stringing up Christmas lights in the highest, most precarious
places—I wanted to see how I would do with exposure—they all had
other things to do. The one glimmer of interest came from an old college buddy called the Prince of Inertia, who was best known around
campus for his George Hamilton tan. The Prince said he might be
able to swing a week in Colorado. Another college friend expressed
vague interest, too, but the last time he had climbed a serious mountain, people got hurt.

I pleaded with Merrill for mercy from her no-solo rule, but she
wouldn't back down. I was lonely. I was desperate. I didn't know
where to turn.

So I sought help from strangers on the Internet.

At a fledgling Web site called 14ers.com, I found detailed route
descriptions, with pictures, of all the peaks. Set up as a labor of love
by Bill Middlebrook, a software guy who hit it big during the dot
.com boom, 14ers.com offered up-to-the-minute mountain weather
forecasts, detailed driving instructions to trailheads, regular updates
on trail conditions, no advertisements, and, best of all, an online
forum full of hikers obsessed with the mountains.

One 14ers.com regular, a student pursuing a PhD in astrophysics,
scaled technical rock faces in Boulder with a pet macaw tethered to
his shoulder. Another was an electrician who had swapped a dependence on drugs with a dependence on climbing. There was a Cambo-
dian concentration camp survivor who now specialized in American
national security issues, a TV weatherman from Albuquerque, a soils
engineer for McMansions around Aspen dressed as a caped McDon-
ald's Hamburglar, and a female guard at the Supermax ultrasecurity
federal prison, plus the usual assortment of doctors, lawyers, chefs,
house framers, pilots, students, and video game designers—and lots
of Texans. (It didn't seem to matter what people from the Lone Star
State did for a living; first and foremost, they were Texans.) Some

people on the board had climbed Mount Everest; others still dreamed of their first Colorado summit. Though they argued mightily about God and atheism, guns and dogs, Rockies and Red Sox, campfires and backpacking stoves, and the Grateful Dead 6/9/77 vs. Grateful Dead 9/3/77, they all seemed to share a singular love of the mountains. And the undisputed king of this glorious mess was a man who called himself the Talus Monkey.

I first ran across the Talus Monkey when he had summited his final Fourteener. He did it in a purple velvet pimp suit, with leopard trim and bling. According to his online reports—and there were hundreds— the Monkey had climbed all the Fourteeners in little more than a year. What's more, he did them with style. On some summits he cracked open a celebratory Colt 45 malt liquor; on others he dangled on one foot and swilled a shot of Captain Morgan rum. For summits with women he brought along a can of whipped cream. For an audacious joke, he chucked down rocks from the summit of Sunshine Peak, elevation 14,001 feet, with hopes of converting the Fourteener into a Thirteener. On a Web site where most people chose an avatar—a small photo accompanying all online posts—of themselves on a mountain, the Talus Monkey announced himself with Smilin' Bob from the Enzyte penile enlargement ads. Though he had an opinion on almost everything, most centered on the three G's—guns, gear, and girls. In general, he liked them all, but never seemed to have enough.

Still desperate for climbing partners, I contacted the Talus Monkey with hopes of hooking up for hikes in the summer. He was friendly enough, but made it clear that I had hurt my chances by not being female. He had his eye on one.

If the Talus Monkey was the undisputed king of the 14ers.com board, then USA Keller was the princess. A goalkeeper for the University of Colorado women's soccer team, she was young, blond, and the main subject of a post that asked,

What's with all the hotties posting lately?

Like the Talus Monkey, she was both a voracious climber and a voracious poster. While thousands watched, the Monkey and USA Keller—her screen name was a tribute to the World Cup goalkeeper Kasey Keller—bantered online and flirted online and sassed online. When they returned from their first hiking trip together, they posted photos of themselves atop two summits, she with an ear-to-ear smile, he trying his hardest to suppress one. Another picture showed the Talus Monkey with one hand on the shoulder of the girl, and the other hand near the barrel of his holstered pearl-handled revolver.

Through the winter the public courtship continued. There was a posted picture of him firing a shot of canned whipped cream into her mouth, and a series of shots of the two of them engaged in extensive personal research into this allegedly scientific topic: "Thermal efficiency of mated sleeping bags?"

Then one April day, as the spring sun began to warm the snow and hormones of the Rockies, some nosy climber posted a question under the heading *3 Mile High Club* and asked,

I was wondering if anyone has (or will admit to) making love at the top of one of these bad boys.

The reply from USA Keller came soon after:

Hmmm . . . great question! I have not, but it's definitely on my top 3 list of things to do on a 14er and something I've thought about for awhile!!

Some PG-13 banter ensued. When a criminal defense lawyer from Texas asked USA Keller for the other two items on her Top 3 list, she replied:

I also really want to:

Do a night ascent to watch the sunrise from a summit,* and

Camp overnight on a summit*

*Both may not be as exciting as the subject of this thread though!

But, I think that combining all 3 into one trip would be the ultimate experience!

    The Talus Monkey responded—and was not shy about his intentions:

USAKeller! I'm looking forward to that overnight camp on the summit of Humboldt next month that we've been planning all spring . . . We can watch the sunrise the next morning . . . and mark all three goals off of your list and mine . . . We'll be in the 2.65 mi high club, or, as I like to say, the "4,267 meter club"!

Your Monkey

    Online, hundreds tittered.

    Not much was heard about the big trip up Humboldt Peak for a few weeks. On May 6, however, a new post on 14ers.com carried an ominous warning:

Climber injured and stranded on Humboldt Peak.

A brief accompanying story from a Denver TV news station reported that a thirty-eight-year-old man, hiking with a female companion, had broken his shoulder and hip, and was stuck on the peak above 12,000 feet after dark.

    The post triggered two immediate responses: (1) My God, could that be the Talus Monkey and USA Keller? (2) Is the Talus Monkey really thirty-eight years old?

    Hungry for updates, I pounded the refresh button on my laptop for the latest posts. Two friends reported that USA Keller and the Talus Monkey weren't answering their cell phones. Dread spread.

    Then the Talus Monkey's best friend, posting on 14ers.com from North Carolina, confirmed the fears: He had spoken by phone with

USA Keller, who said the Talus Monkey had been hurt badly while descending the mountain. After wrapping him in two sleeping bags, she had rushed back down to town to call for help, but search-and-rescue crews couldn't reach him before sunset because of increasing snow and worsening avalanche dangers. The Monkey was stranded alone at night with broken bones in a snowstorm above timberline.

And one other thing: The Talus Monkey's real first name was David.

It was life vs. death in the highest reaches of the Rockies, with minute-by-minute updates on the Internet. Horrified and transfixed, I stayed tethered to my computer. So did thousands more.

Well-wishers posted their hopes and prayers for the Monkey. Many posters wanted more information. The Monkey's buddy from North Carolina, OBX Fisherman, relayed details from his phone call with USA Keller:

She said David was "glacading" (sp?) down a section of mountain and picked up too much speed and could not stop due to no ice ax and went over an edge and landed on some rocks. She said he could not move one arm and one leg.

If done properly, glissading is the most fun a grownup can have in the mountains while flat on his butt. The idea is to slide down a snowy slope with a specialized piece of mountaineering equipment called an ice axe. If you start sliding too fast, you jam the axe into the snow to cut your speed. In icy conditions, glissading without an axe is like driving a car downhill without a brake.

Through the night a late-season blizzard pummeled Humboldt Peak. The Monkey had two sleeping bags, no tent, and a body racked with cold, pain, and broken bones. Online people posted more prayers.

The next day, at 7:17 a.m., USA Keller logged onto the Web site and posted a brief report, which read, in total:

I did not glissade—the snowpack was too hard and I wouldn't have felt comfortable doing it.

I was unable to locate our snowshoes/skis so if anyone will be up in this area soon, would you mind helping us out and finding them? I have the GPS coordinates for our stash as well, but I can't hike because of bad blisters from my AT boots. But it will mean the world to me if you can help us out getting back some of our gear.

Lastly, THANK YOU to everyone who's said prayers—keep praying please.

Her note made me feel better. If the Monkey's girlfriend was worried about retrieving lost gear, then the injuries on the mountain couldn't be that serious, could they? One responding post summed up what many others felt: I've never met the Talus Monkey or USA Keller, but I feel like I already know them from all their posts online. Wishing them the best!

Newspaper and television Web sites reported that alpine search-and-rescue crews were converging at the base of Humboldt Peak at dawn. The overnight storm had dumped sixteen inches of wet snow, and crews were racing to gain the two thousand feet of elevation to the Talus Monkey's last known location. On 14ers.com, hikers frantically hit the refresh button for any and all news updates.

Three hours later, Jordan White, a college-age friend of the Talus Monkey and USA Keller, posted some fantastic news:

Just talked to Custer County Sheriff.

Quote: "He is alive, he is well, they are with him."

The board exploded with dozens of elated messages. The Talus Monkey was alive! All hail the Monkey! Surviving a night alone at 13,000 feet in one of the worst snowstorms of the year—wow. Could the legend of the Talus Monkey grow any larger?

With the Monkey alive and well, cheers and elation gave way to cooler analysis. What really happened up there? How did he get himself in such a fix? Were there lessons to be learned? As one climber posted,

Truly a reminder that even the most experienced among us can be made a victim in the mountains. I'm shocked.

Others weren't. Though no one disputed the entertainment value of the Monkey and his bawdy trip reports, some had questioned his mountaineering judgment. Yes, it was a major accomplishment to have summited all the Fourteeners in little more than a year, but the Monkey had done it in a drought year with relatively little snow and some of the easiest possible climbing conditions.

One of the Monkey's first hiking companions, Sarah Thompson, a laser physicist from Boulder who had also summited all the Fourteeners, wrote:

I'm not trying to provoke anything, but just wanted to speak my mind regarding this tragic event. I mean no disrespect to anyone. Talus Monkey is one heck of a guy, passionate about the mountains, a great friend and hiking buddy, but he is not one of the most experienced people around here. That's just the plain truth. I am not trying to be negative, but a lot of more inexperienced folks here need to realize that the most popular people on the forum aren't necessarily the most experienced. Hiking the 14ers in summer does not qualify someone as an expert, especially for hiking during the winter/spring seasons. This horrible accident could have been prevented with more experience leading to better judgment. It sucks having to learn the hard way.

I am no expert myself, but I've been noticing around here lately that younger, less experienced people have been taking big risks and getting lucky. That encourages more inexperienced folks to try similar things. Just last week I was mentioning this to a few 14ers.com members and I expressed my worries that it was going to take a bad accident for folks to realize the seriousness of their endeavors. It totally sucks that this happened to our beloved Talus Monkey and I was totally creeped out this morning when I heard the news and thought about what I'd said last week. I had no idea that in just a few days this would happen to a friend of mine.

I guess I just want to urge people to BE CAREFUL out there and realize the risks they are taking . . . Sorry for the lecturing, but I have felt strongly about this lately and this latest incident finally prompted me to speak up. If you disagree, feel free to send me nasty e-mails. I only have the best intentions.

For three hours the board fight was on: Some climbers wondered whether the Monkey was too cavalier about mountain safety. Others defended his patience and guidance for newcomers. A few questioned the propriety of this kind of debate while search-and-rescue was still trying to remove the Monkey from the mountain. Meanwhile, messages from well-wishers poured in. Record traffic was clogging the Web site—three million hits for the real-time alpine rescue.

At 7 p.m., however, a new post jolted the board. A member of the search-and-rescue team had talked on a cell phone with his brother at home west of Colorado Springs. The brother posted an alarming update:

GUYS, PRAY NOW FOR TALUS MONKEY. HE WAS STRUGGLING AT THE END OF THE RESCUE.

Josh Friesema—screen name, CO Native—was a volunteer member of the alpine crew on Humboldt Peak. With four others, he had lugged sleds, medical gear, and six hundred feet of rope up a 40-degree slope caked with sixteen inches of fresh snow. It was a brutal race against the clock, and Friesema feared they were losing. With all the heavy equipment, the crew had needed two hours just to climb the first thousand feet. According to USA Keller's GPS coordinates, the Monkey was a thousand feet higher.

At age thirty, Friesema was the youngest and fastest member of the rescue team, so the others told him to speed up the mountain by himself. He knew the Monkey had been on the mountain for twenty-four hours, much of that time in a blizzard. Friesema tried to blast up the steep couloir without stopping, partly because he was racing to save a life, but also because the last time he had stopped, a ferocious avalanche had tumbled down the other side of the valley. Better not to worry about that, he thought, while plowing another step up through the knee-deep snow.

By the time he had reached 12,700 feet, Friesema knew the Monkey must be close, but there was still no sign of him. A cloud wafted in and spit more snow. Friesema could see only 20 feet. He radioed for help and directions from the crew below, but cliff bands blocked his signals.

All was quiet. All seemed lost. In his professional life, Friesema was an accountant for the Colorado Springs evangelical powerhouse Focus on the Family. He knew how to ask for help. So he sat and prayed. "God, I can't do it. I can't find him. I need you."

Through providence or luck, the clouds broke. Friesema could see again. Fifty feet above him, at the base of a jagged band of cliffs, he spotted a purple sleeping bag.

He yelled. A hand waved back.

Friesema climbed as fast as he could and found a man sprawled on the snow, out of his sleeping bag, out of his jacket, and out of his gloves. In the final stages of hypothermia, victims often become delirious and start shedding clothes.

"My name is Josh," Friesema told him, testing the victim's awareness. "What's your name?"

"Talus Monkey."

Friesema laughed. Good thing Friesema used the Web site, too, or he might have thought the man he was rescuing had lost his mind. Even so, the Monkey was clearly in bad shape. As Friesema put it, the Monkey had plunged 200 feet through a series of jagged cliffs, and he looked like it. He had spent the night in a blizzard at 13,000 feet, and he looked like that too. The Monkey was so out of it that he couldn't give his real name. He did, however, keep asking for warm Mountain Dew, which he called the Nectar of the Gods.

There was no Dew on this mountain, but Friesema did have Gatorade, which the Monkey gladly downed. Friesema bundled the Monkey back into his clothes and sleeping bags, and watched his colleagues do their best to rush a thousand feet uphill with seventy pounds of lifesaving gear on their backs.

Meanwhile, Friesema's brother had reached the rescuer again on his cell phone, and started posting live updates on the Web site. When the Monkey had turned coherent enough to start joking again—he was needling his rescuer about his ascent time—Friesema told his brother that the search operation looked like a success.

At 12:30 p.m., or twenty-six hours after the initial accident, the Talus Monkey was moved onto a spine-saving sled, bundled up, and ready to go. A Flight for Life helicopter was on call, but could land only on a slope no steeper than 10 degrees. That meant search-and-rescue had to drop more than 2,000 vertical feet back to the valley floor to meet the chopper.

It was a daunting feat: lowering a heavy sled with a crippled man on bottled oxygen through an avalanche chute split by three separate sets of cliffs, all down an icy slope about the same steepness as the Red Pyramid of Egypt.

While two rescuers walked down the roped-up sled, another crew remained higher on the mountain to safely feed out more line like a leash. Though they had a six-hundred-foot rope, the slope was so long that they needed four of these belay stations.

The descent took three hours. Toward the bottom the Talus Monkey slipped into and out of consciousness.

Rescuers ran with all their might for the waiting helicopter. Friesema hoped for the best, but feared the worst, and told his brother so.

On the Web site, climbers argued the ethics of dissecting the rights and wrongs of this mountain accident. More well-wishers urged on the Monkey. Somebody arranged to take care of his cats.

After thirty-one hours on the mountain, the Talus Monkey was flown to a hospital fifty miles away in Pueblo.

Soon after the helicopter lifted off, a new storm moved in, bringing enough fresh snow and wind to erase all signs of the frantic rescue. As many as thirty people had given their all on Humboldt Peak to save one man's life. They were spent. Their footprints were gone. The mountain didn't care.

At 9:29 p.m., the Talus Monkey's best friend, OBX Fisherman, signed on to the 14ers.com Web site.

It's with a very heavy heart that I must tell you that David did not make it and died tonight.

Days afterward, while mourners were still posting their grief online, and while others who had never met the Talus Monkey were attending his memorial service, I was reeling with questions. Who really was the Monkey? Why did he have such an effect on people? What actually happened up on that mountain?

Answering the last question was easiest. Three days after the Monkey's death, USA Keller posted a trip report with pictures and written description of their climb of Humboldt Peak. It was a heartbreaker.

The real names of the Talus Monkey and USA Keller were David Worthington and Caroline Moore. He was an accountant for the Minerals Management Service of the federal government; she was a few credits shy of graduating from the University of Colorado. They had struggled through the snow to find a route up the mountain that avoided avalanche danger. Neither Worthington nor Moore had much experience with winter conditions. It was her first time attempting a peak with ski gear, and her feet blistered in the awkward plastic boots. She slipped and fell in a creek with freezing water. She still managed to beam a brilliant smile for his camera.

At timberline they were confronted with a wind blasting steadily at 30 mph. She was uncharacteristically tired. To save weight, he stashed his snowshoes, and she her skis, before continuing with the last push to the summit. He hiked ahead and told her how unusually slow she was hiking. She felt like quitting; he urged her on, noting they had listened in the car to the song "Hope" by the reggae dance-hall singer Shaggy. "Caroline, remember that song you played for me in the car about never giving up?" he asked her. "I brought you here to challenge you. Don't give up."

She summited a half-hour after him at 9:15 p.m. and cried. He fell to his knees, grabbed her shoulders, and told her, "Do you remember our first climb up Handies Peak together? I know I didn't know you at all, but when we were on the summit, I told you that there was nobody else I would rather be here with than you. That's exactly how I feel right now."

In the dark and the wind they struggled to put up their tent. The wind hurled a pole over a cliff. They decided to spend the night in a partially erected tent that flapped relentlessly in the wind. They slept little, but the morning sunrise was spectacular. They crouched together on the summit for a wonderful photo in the warm honey light of dawn. The wind stopped. His hand was on her arm. They looked proud.

Tired and dreading the descent, they decided to take a different, more direct, route back down the mountain. She posted a photo of him, with backpack and trekking poles, waiting for her at the top of a steep gully.

Underneath that photo in her trip report, she wrote,

For obvious and appropriate reasons, I will stop there.

David, I was thrilled to climb with you again. Thank you from the bottom of my heart for fulfilling a dream I had of camping and watching a sunrise from the summit of one of Colorado's Fourteeners. I couldn't have imagined any better of a place to do this than in the

Crestones with anyone else other than you. It will be an experience I will never forget. I hope you enjoy my trip report.

Ski descent information: you can definitely ski from the summit. There are a few rocky areas near the top, but both of the couloirs (especially the one we began our descent in) looked like a great ski.

I clicked on the bottom of her trip report page and shuddered. This was my first trip into a new online world with no clear line between public and private moments. I couldn't imagine any of my friends doing a similar report on my death, but I was a middle-aged dad whose only real contact with Facebook or MySpace was trying to police our twelve-year-old's interest in it. I wanted to learn more. I called Caroline Moore.

As a mountaineer, Moore said she felt an obligation to be public and truthful about Worthington's death. She didn't want anyone to repeat the couple's mistakes. At the top of the couloir, just after Moore had snapped that final photo, Worthington saw a thirty-foot stretch of snow and tried skating on his boot soles like a schoolboy on a slippery sidewalk. He lost control, plunged like a rag doll over a series of cliff bands, and finally stopped himself two hundred feet later. He screamed. The slope was so treacherous it took Moore twenty minutes to reach him. Worthington couldn't move either leg. Every time she asked about his condition, he apologized. I'm so sorry, he said, for doing that. I'm so sorry, he said, for putting you in this situation. I'm so sorry, he said, for my stupid mistake.

She spent an hour moving him fifteen feet to more stable ground. She packed him into their two sleeping bags, and left for help. It was her first solo hike. She was terrified.

"He was an addicting person to be around," she told me. "He was fast and he was funny. He made me laugh. We both loved being in the mountains."

In the mountains, Worthington had found something that had eluded him for years—a sense of community. For reasons none of his friends clearly understood, he was largely estranged from his parents, who were divorced. His father was a sergeant in the army; his mother was Taiwanese. Though he struggled to settle on an occupation—he had worked as a shoe salesman, electrician's apprentice, Christmas tree cutter, and firefighter in North Carolina, a banker in Wyoming, and a government accountant monitoring oil leases in Denver—he remained consistent in one thing: He loved to stand out and be noticed.

His best friend, Gary Rohrer, the OBX Fisherman, remembered Worthington in his North Carolina high school as the scrawny little Asian kid with glasses and stick arms who loved to play Dungeons and Dragons. In college, Worthington started lifting weights and transformed himself into a five-foot-eight muscleman who weighed 230 pounds and bench-pressed 300. He loved the new body. He wore a pink sleeveless shirt while driving his pink Geo Metro convertible to gun shows in the South. Worthington owned thirty guns, but was especially proud of his two AR-15s, the civilian version of the army assault rifle. He was blunt, honest, and flamboyant. "I used to tell him, 'Dude, you're an attention whore,'" Rohrer said.

While his friends married and started raising children, Worthington moved to Greybull, Wyoming, population 1,815, with hopes for a fresh start. He ended up bored with his job at a small-town bank. He moved again, to Denver, where the work was more interesting but his social life was not. Lonely, he clicked on the 14ers.com Web site and found hiking partners who became friends. Most were at least a decade younger than he; few even guessed at the age difference. He liked to ogle the waitresses at Hooters and did a mean impression of MTV's Beavis and Butthead. On the phone and on the trail, he rarely called people by a real name like Dave or Scott. Instead, he used CO Dave or Wyoming Mountain Man, their Web site screen names.

Worthington had spent hours swapping e-mails and talking with Moore before she finally asked, David, how old are you? He asked: How old do you think I am? She was off by ten years, but didn't care. He was strong. He was silly. He was fun. He was going to help her finish the Fourteeners.

Though the Fourteeners can be summited by the fit and the fat, the newbie and the gnarly, one sad fact unites every peak: They are unforgiving killers of people of every shape and size.

There is no central repository for information about deaths on Fourteeners, but it's clear that dozens, and likely hundreds, have lost their lives on the tops of the Rockies. At the time of this writing, one Web site, listsofjohn.com, reported 168 deaths on Fourteeners. The compiler conceded that his list was not complete; my own cursory check found a dozen deaths that weren't included on his dark tally. John's list also does not include any nineteenth-century miners who almost certainly perished while searching for gold and silver on the mineralized peaks. My own conservative hunch is that the fifty-four peaks have claimed the lives of at least two hundred, a number that, coincidentally, is about equal to the number of lives lost on Mount Everest.[*]

Everest, of course, is vastly more dangerous than any Rocky Mountain peak with just half the elevation. But the world's tallest peak also can't be seen from an interstate, Holiday Inn, or national park campground, and thus has never suffered the indignity of post-cheeseburger summit attempts by tourists in blue jeans, T-shirts, and flip-flops.

A twenty-six-year-old man once defied the National Park Service's warnings about icy conditions and climbed Longs Peak in September in jeans, tennis shoes, and a cotton hoodie; he died of hypothermia on the summit when a snowstorm blew in. An eighty-seven-year-old woman, too stubborn to accept a car ride home from the top of Pikes Peak, insisted on hiking back down the mountain by herself despite

---

[*] About 3,000 people have reported summiting Everest; about 1,200 have reported summiting all of Colorado's Fourteeners, though that number is certainly higher in reality because not all successful finishers report their feats to the Colorado Mountain Club.

an approaching storm; her body was found eleven days later. A father and daughter pushed on to the summit of Quandary Peak despite an approaching thunderstorm; their lightning-scarred bodies were found the next day. On a day when the Colorado Avalanche Information Center warned of high snowslide danger, a twenty-five-year-old skier set off alone into the backcountry without telling anyone where he was headed; four days later, on Christmas Day, his leg was found sticking out of the bottom of an 1,800-foot avalanche chute on Quandary Peak.

The vast majority of victims, however, were not ones who ignored obvious warning signs. They succumbed to the unrelenting foe of mountaineers everywhere—gravity.

About six of every ten Fourteener deaths result from falls. What's amazing is how little the plunges have in common. One man tumbled seven hundred feet on Longs Peak and broke only a leg. Another fell fifty feet on the same peak and died.

A fifty-one-year-old lawyer, hiking alone under a full moon on Quandary Peak, relied on a weed as a handhold to lower himself onto a six-inch ledge. He fell thirty feet, was knocked unconscious, but lived to tell other climbers on the Web how the experience made him "love the rush of being on the edge of danger." Two years later, on a traverse between two other Fourteeners, the same lawyer hiked solo, dropped a thousand feet, and died.

The grand champion tumbler, though, was Brian Smith, a fifty-four-year-old hiker from Santa Monica, California. On a snowy scramble across Kelso Ridge of Torreys Peak at 3:40 p.m.—hikers are usually cautioned to avoid steep spring snow in the afternoon after the sun warms it—Smith crunched through a snow cornice and cartwheeled down the aptly named Dead Dog Couloir. Rescue crews figured he fell more than a thousand feet, or about the height of the Eiffel Tower. Smith survived with broken bones.

On Fourteeners, there have been roughly equal numbers of deaths from the age-old mountaineering dangers—avalanches, rockfall, lightning, and hypothermia. Some deaths, however, have been more of a reflection of their times. In 1889, just below the summit of Longs Peak, an Iowa boy named Frank Stryker was killed by a gunshot. Though the circumstances are unclear—he was hiking with his father and cousins; some say there was alcohol involved; others say the shot was triggered by an accidental fall—the revolver was apparently his own. Guns have since been banned by the National Park Service in Rocky Mountain National Park.

In the past decade, though, there has been a rise in a new kind of Fourteener malady: death by snowboard. These accidents so far have taken place on Pikes Peak, which has easy road access to terrain that may look less challenging from the top than it actually rides in the middle.

Promise to my wife: I will not climb mountains with a gun or a snowboard.

Chapter 5

Man-Date

MISSOURI MOUNTAIN 14,074'

According to his posted Internet profile, he was trim, athletic, and looking for adventure. He enjoyed fishing and drag racing. He was a native of Amarillo, Texas, but now lived in a tract-home suburb of Denver. His online screen name was KirkT. I had never heard the sound of his voice—nor he, mine—but through the magic of the Web he was about to become something very special.

My first man-date.

Ever since Merrill put the kibosh on my attempts to hike solo, I struggled to find friends, neighbors, or acquaintances, or even friends of neighbors and acquaintances, who would hike with me. In general my conversations with all these people went like this:

"Hi, you don't know me, but a mutual friend said I should call you. He said you might be interested in hiking a Fourteener with me."

"A Fourteener? Oh, yeah—I did one of those about ten years ago. I still remember that splitting headache. It took a long time for my toenails to grow back."

"But wasn't it beautiful? Didn't you feel like you accomplished something? Want to try one again?"

"No."

In desperation, I turned to the 14ers.com Web site, which always seemed full of hikers trying for high-altitude hookups. One posting, by KirkT, in particular caught my eye:

I am planning on climbing Missouri on the 25th. Anyone is welcome to join us.

His words made me feel like a schoolboy before a homecoming dance. What did he mean by "anyone is welcome"? Does that include fat old farts? What if he doesn't like me? What if I'm too slow for him?

I circled nervously around my computer for what seemed like hours before I worked up the guts to click out an e-mail. (Thankfully, unlike high school dating, there was no way for a father or older brother to intercept my earnest message.) I waited for an answer. And waited. And waited.

At lunchtime the next day he responded: Yes.

Yes! (No way I was pinning any corsage on his chest, though.)

The plan was to meet Thursday night at the trailhead for Missouri Mountain. We'd sleep in our cars, then set out before dawn for the five-mile trek with 4,500 feet of elevation gain. And one other thing: KirkT was bringing a buddy. His screen name was Shad.

The good news was that Shad had summited Longs Peak, the monarch of the Colorado Front Range, a total of five times, including a solo bivouac climb of the dicey 14,259-foot peak in the dead of winter—a serious mountaineering accomplishment. Shad was experienced. I instantly felt safer.

The bad news was that Shad was in seriously great shape. He had completed three marathons and fifteen triathlons, most recently the Escape from Alcatraz race, which demanded a 1.5-mile swim from the infamous island prison through the shark-patrolled waters of San Francisco Bay, followed by an eighteen-mile bike ride and eight-mile hill run. Last weekend, just for fun, Shad had run twenty-three miles through the foothills of Boulder. In other words, there was no way in the world I could keep pace with him.

Just what I needed on my first man-date—performance anxiety.

Our e-mail plan was to meet at the trailhead parking lot on the night before the climb. At 10 p.m., eight miles from the nearest paved road, I wheeled into the lot and realized I had no clue what either of my man-dates looked like. How could I find them?

Luckily, others had the same problem. As soon as my headlights brightened the trailhead, three different men popped out of their own cars to meet me.

"Are you KirkT or Shad?" I ask.

Nope. They all seem nice enough, though, and they all want to know what I'm hiking tomorrow. When I reply, "Missouri," one says, "I hear there's a lot of snow up there." It's so cold there's steam coming from his mouth. His buddy just grunts and shuffles his feet. By the time I pull into a parking spot, they're gone, but another man remains.

Name's Craig, he says, from Aurora, a suburb about ten miles from my home. He's here to climb Mount Belford, which uses the same trailhead, for the seventh time. He'd told his girlfriend there'd be times when he just had to get away from any and all people, so he was planning to hike solo.

And then his mouth is off to the races: I get a detailed description of each of his prior Belford climbs, including the time he sat cross-legged on the summit for an hour because no one else was there and no one else was coming and that was just one of the things his girl-friend needed to understand about him, OK?

OK, I say, but can't help wondering why a man who needs to be solo is spending so much time talking to a stranger in the dark. It feels like a bar for lonely hearts, outdoors, without alcohol, at 9,700 feet. I wish him luck, then dive into the quiet refuge of my family station wagon's folded-over backseat. I lock my doors, wriggle into my sleep-ing bag, and try to fall asleep.

Not for long, though. Rumbling in next to me is a pickup truck with two men. I give them the once-over. They give me the once-over twice. My blind dates have arrived.

We shake hands through their pickup window and proceed to

have a perfectly normal conversation about our plans for the next day. Shad is about my height, with wire-rim glasses and a shaved head; KirkT comes to about my nose, and talks with a Texas staccato that makes me imagine he's H. Ross Perot's son. Not that any true scion of a billionaire family would ever take seriously the concerns of a paunchy man in tube socks and long underwear pacing a dirt parking lot in a remote nook of the Rockies.

The agreement is to rise at 4:30 a.m., but there's so little sleep in either vehicle that we all flick on headlamps and start dressing a half-hour earlier. I finish a Hershey bar for breakfast, and I head to the outhouse in the dark. Just as I sit, a mouse darts between my naked legs. I am now fully awake.

KirkT and Shad plan to camp tonight at a high basin at 11,500 feet, so they're lugging heavy backpacks. I try to make things fair by jamming my daypack with enough food for a Thanksgiving dinner, plus snowshoes and the shiny new mountaineering ice axe I purchased after the fall of the Talus Monkey.

At the trailhead there's a moment of awkwardness while everyone decides who should go first. In my mind, I know I'm riding caboose, but I fear that admitting this at the outset would turn me into an instant outcast. Still, my winter training regimen was pretty good, wasn't it?

Not good enough to hesitate this long, it turns out. KirkT bounds up the trail like a rabbit, which leads Shad to do his best greyhound imitation. It's an hour before sunrise, and these guys are practically sprinting up the dark timber. I try to catch them; my Hershey bar makes a return visit. Luckily, I'm so far behind that no one hears the hurl.

"You OK back there?" Shad calls.

I assure him that I'm just a slow starter. Shad and KirkT are nice enough to wait for me, but peel off at the same blistering pace as soon as they hear my gasps subside. The pattern repeats: They go, I gasp. One winter of spin class and the Gauntlet and I can't even keep pace on the first quarter-mile of the first hike of the season? I am totally and utterly demoralized.

Just as I'm ready to quit, or at least die, KirkT decides to wait for me. I struggle to find enough oxygen to form the word "thanks," but I notice something strange. KirkT is breathing heavily too. We stop at a switchback. My lungs have a blow.

"Sorry I'm so slow," I tell him. "You don't have to wait for me. Go on ahead."

To my dismay, he does. Like a jackrabbit all over again. Somewhere up in the dark is Shad, but he's so far ahead I can't even see his headlamp. Looks like I'm soloing after all.

At the next switchback, though, KirkT is waiting again. I tell him he doesn't have to stop for me, that his pace is stronger, that he should keep going, but he lets me lumber on by. Then it hits me: He's gasping too.

My biggest neurosis—that I'm too fat and old to be doing this—melts away. The thirty-seven-year-old furniture salesman from Amarillo is as slow as I am, maybe even slower. My feet fill with adrenaline. I tell KirkT I have a different pace, slow but with fewer stops, and I hope he doesn't mind if I keep plugging along. I chug ahead to catch Shad while KirkT continues with his blow.

Shad is in such great shape that he can actually talk while hiking. This is a wonderful thing. As long as I can grunt out an occasional question, he's content to make the time pass by telling me stories. Problem is, I ask the wrong first question.

"So I have some friends on the East Coast who love to go fishing for shad. Do you fish too? Is that how you got your screen name?"

No, his real name is Shad. Nothing to do with fish. It's just his name—Shad.

I offer Shad the chance to reciprocate by making fun of my last name. No more tit for tat, he says. He's been working hard to get over that.

In his senior year of high school, Shad lost all his friends when his parents moved from Nebraska to Fort Collins, Colorado. Though he was talented enough in Nebraska to start as a sophomore on his varsity football team, Shad was shunned by his new teammates in Colorado. He quit football. He took jobs at Kmart and Pizza Hut to help pay the bills, but fell in with an older crowd that valued drinking more than working. For Shad, a twelve-pack of Keystone or Black Label was just the start of a night.

Shad's parents divorced the year after he started college. He took up with his best friend's girlfriend, and he married and became a father before he got his diploma. The marriage busted up when his son was five, and the boy took it hard.

Shad was miserable too. He had no college degree. He had few friends. He was six feet tall, 230 pounds, and breathing heavy when he walked from the sofa to the refrigerator. He finished off a tin of Copenhagen chewing tobacco every day.

When Shad's misery spiraled into anger—arguing at work, snapping at relatives—an uncle challenged him to run a five-kilometer race. Shad survived. His uncle was thrilled. The same compulsive drive that had forced him to finish every twelve-pack and every tobacco tin was now turned toward exercise.

It wasn't easy. Shad knew people who could drink, not run. He joined an online singles group for a hike up 14,271-foot Quandary Peak. When he stood atop the summit, he couldn't believe his view or his accomplishment. He learned that Colorado was home to fifty-four Fourteeners. He could make a list. He could start hiking them. He could finish them off. "The mountains," Shad tells me, "became my place for anger management."

Today Shad is down to 165 pounds, a loss of 40 percent of his body weight in four years. He asks me about my wife, and my kids, and our dog, and my life, and my work.

And as he kicks my butt up the Missouri Mountain trail, I'm thinking, This is going pretty well for my first man-date. I've had dates with women with a lot less shared information. Clearly, something is going on here. Men don't talk like this when they're sober. Is altitude an intoxicant?

All the talk has made the time pass quickly, and before we know it, we've climbed to timberline. The sight is both spectacular and daunting. Spectacular because we're flanked by two massive ridges, one with bighorn sheep atop it, and daunting because everything as far as we can see is covered with snow. It may be Memorial Day weekend, but at 12,000 feet in the Rockies it still looks like the dead of winter. We're in for a snow climb.

I double-check with Shad to make sure that he really, truly had summited Longs Peak in winter—he had—and he assures me we'll turn back if avalanche conditions are too dicey. Just as I start considering the prospect of being pitched 2,000 feet down a chute by an avalanche in May, up struggles KirkT. Though Shad and I are in full winter regalia of parka, snow pants, and gloves, KirkT wears only shirtsleeves. The thermometer on my backpack reads 35 degrees.

"It's the heat that's killing me," KirkT announces. "That, and this beast of a backpack."

KirkT has packed so much gear and food that his pack weighs forty pounds. The only reason I beat the diminutive KirkT up the mountain was because he lugged nearly one-third of his body weight on his back. He lops off his pack; my spirits sink. I console myself with the truth that his heavy pack weighs less than my own spare tire. The difference is, he can drop his pack. So he does.

We survey the trek ahead and agree it's best to avoid the summer trail, which crosses several avalanche chutes, and grind straight up to the ridge. Shad asks if it's OK for him to go ahead. Neither KirkT nor I are in any position to say no. Besides, Shad seems excited by the prospect of gaining nearly 2,000 vertical feet of steep climbing through ankle-deep snow. Instead of spending energy kick-stepping our own way up the gully, we are grateful to follow in his footsteps.

Shad starts climbing and I stop trying to trail him after a hundred yards. He is three times faster than me. I pause a few minutes for my lungs to drop from my throat and wait for KirkT. My boot tracks are shorter than Shad's, and KirkT's are shorter than mine, but we make do anyway. From here the upper ridge looks like it may as well be on the moon.

Neither KirkT nor I have any oxygen to spare for talking. After two hours of brutal grunt work, my breath is taken away by sight of what comes next: a traverse through a gully topped by a five-foot snow cornice. It is prime avalanche terrain with a fat snow ledge that, at some point this spring, will be ready to rumble. Shad waits for us here.

So far the snow is in good shape, Shad tells us, but it's safest to do the traverse just one at a time. While one crosses, the other two will wait and watch, just in case.

Just in case of what? Death? Maiming? Being swept away by a 200-mph avalanche that deposits me upside down on the jagged teeth of talus below while the snow around me hardens into a white coffin? I don't bother asking.

Shad crosses without a trace of nervousness. I follow with my axe, setting the point firmly into the deeply packed snow before kicking in my next step. The traverse is only about forty steps, but time passes at its slowest rate of the day. KirkT follows with his ski poles. Luckily, the worst thing about this traverse is only my nerves.

And then we're all on the ridge. Up here it's a different world. Down low, sun reflecting off the snow had been basking us in warmth; on the ridge the wind rips at 20 mph, with some gusts twice as strong. We shout to be heard.

Missouri Mountain is more of a long ridge than a mountain. Unfortunately, the highest point remains a long slog in the distance. There are five false summits along the way; Shad collects them all, but KirkT and I try to waste as little altitude gain as possible by bypassing most. The wind strengthens.

Grinding to within one hundred vertical feet of the summit, we all see something that stops us in our tracks: the crux of the route. There's a ten-foot downclimb through a rocky notch, then a sidehill of several hundred yards across a snowpacked 40-degree slope that yawns below a sawtooth ridge. The price of a mistake: a thousand-foot slide into a man-eating gnarl of rock at the bottom. I can't help but think of the Talus Monkey.

What makes me think I can climb this? Why do I even want to? Am I chicken if I don't?

Shad reads the queasiness on my face. "Only you can know what's comfortable for you and what's not," he tells me.

I tell him I'm just not sure.

"The mountain will still be here in the summer," he says. "It will look a lot different then. A lot easier."

With that, Shad is off—through the notch and onto the traverse. The only way to conquer my fears is to confront them, I figure, so I follow behind. One step past the rock, though, and my boots tell me something that my eyes had missed: This slope is even worse than I guessed—two inches of Slurpee snow atop a sheet of ice. My heel slides an inch. I grab the rock behind me with all my might and refuse to commit to the traverse.

Over my head, though, KirkT is waiting for me to move out of the way. His eyes betray no worry, much less fear.

"What do you think?" I ask him.

"I haven't been on a mountain yet without summiting," KirkT says.

"But this traverse—what do you think?"

"I'm OK with it," he says.

Then I feel it all—fear, shame, cold, nausea. "I think I'll stay here and watch you guys," I say.

"Best to stay with your comfort level," he says. He drops down from the rock, and sidesteps past me. I clamber back atop the outcropping. The wind may be howling, but my face flushes hot with embarrassment. I watch Shad and KirkT move slowly, steadily, toward the summit.

Then the shock: Shad slips.

Right foot out, left akimbo, on his side, arms reaching, leg digging, body sliding, kicking, trying to jam something, anything, rolling, accelerating—hitting a rock. It's a jagged boulder, and it has blocked Shad's plunge. He plants his ice axe and props his back against the rock. He sits up. He waves. He has slid twenty feet, but he's OK.

Shad pulls off his backpack and fishes inside, pulling out two steel-toothed contraptions that fit over the heels and toes of his boots—crampons. He straps them on and stands. He looks back toward me, then turns to the summit.

KirkT, meanwhile, pushes onward. Unlike Shad, who carried an ice axe to stop his fall, KirkT has only ski poles for balance and self-arrest. Each step sends a small cascade of snow, or slough, down the steep slope. His feet sashay a few inches sideways every few steps.

Then the next shock: He twists awkwardly. One pole slips from his hand, and down, down, down it slides. After more than twenty years of resort skiing in Colorado, I had never seen a slope so steep and unstable to make someone lose a pole. This is it.

KirkT stands frozen. From my perch fifty feet away, I can't tell if his stillness is from panic, fear, or determination. My stomach, however, is anything but quiet. I turn so neither Shad nor KirkT can see me and then I retch.

What to do? Call search-and-rescue? Go for a helicopter? One point I remembered from the Talus Monkey tragedy: Flight for Life can land only on flat ground with a slope of less than 10 degrees. Unfortunately, the closest flat landing spot is thousands of vertical feet below. The hike alone would take hours, even without a full body litter.

I fumble through my backpack and pull out my phone. No cell coverage. Even worse, I have no clue what I would tell 911. I'm ashamed to admit I don't even know the last names of my mandates.

Beyond me, however, a cooler head has prevailed. Shad works his way back to KirkT, kicking steps in the snow with his crampons and chopping them deeper with his ice axe. After a few minutes of work, Shad reaches KirkT. They look to me, and I howl through the wind, "I'm staying here." They wave. KirkT strips the plastic powder basket from his one remaining trekking pole, which makes it look like a long ice pick. They turn toward the summit. Shad kicks and chops more steps in the snow for KirkT to follow. In less than ten minutes they're standing atop the mountain. They wave again, and I wave back. I shout my congratulations, but the wind drowns me out. We flash each other thumbs-ups.

Inside, though, I'm all thumbs-down. Shouldn't I have trailed along? They made it look easy. I even had an ice axe; KirkT didn't. Seeking comfort for my misery, I move back and forth on the ridge, trying to find a cell phone signal. About fifty feet back, I get two bars and call home. My wife answers on the second ring.

She can barely hear me between gusts. I tell her I tried hard, climbed to within a hundred feet of the summit, and stopped short because of conditions. My partners are up top now, though, and I feel like a weenie. On the summit, buffeted by a 30-mph wind, with a thousand-foot precipice over his right shoulder, KirkT is doing a headstand.

My wife tells me several times that I made the right decision, but can tell that I'm feeling neither smart nor right. By the way, she says, how are those guys going to get down?

Good question.

I promise her again that I'll stay safe, then turn my attention to the strangers I feel responsible for on the mountain. For the descent, Shad is starting to retrace his chopped-in snow steps. KirkT, however, opts for a new route: directly over the top of the sawtoothed ridge.

This feels like a slow-motion accident. The ascent slope may have been icy and steep, but at least it was a slope. The other side of KirkT's descent ridge is just a freefall. I remain fixed to the spot that offers me the strongest cell phone signal.

KirkT, however, turns out to be an extremely nimble scrambler. He reaches a ridge dip ten feet above me just as Shad finishes retracing his footsteps from below. Shad and I look up; KirkT looks down. The problem is the last ten feet from KirkT's ridgetop to our slope below. It's sharp, glazed with ice, and straight down. Shad plants his crampons at the very base of the rock, and motions up to KirkT, who lowers himself slowly and then jumps into a bear hug from Shad. Everyone is safe. KirkT sees the dazed look on my face and says, "I've always had a little daredevil in me."

I snort, but instantly regret my rapid waste of oxygen.

On our hike back down, KirkT, whose real name is Kirk Tubbs, confides that he was a competitive diver in high school who qualified for the Texas state championships. He prides himself on his continuing ability to perform a standing backflip. His goal is to perform a headstand on the summit of every Fourteener. As for his interest in drag racing, I misunderstood his Internet profile. Kirk is not a drag-racing fan. He actually drag races. He rebuilt his own '69 Mustang and hit 144 mph doing a quarter-mile in 9.5 seconds. When he's not defying death on a drag strip or mountain, he sells oak furniture.

I confess my fears on the mountain, and Shad—real name, Shad Mika—admits that while slipping his main thought was simple: Oh, shit. If the boulder hadn't stopped his fall, Shad felt confident he could have braked himself by self-arresting with his ice axe.

KirkT says he was grateful for Shad's help. If Shad hadn't kicked those steps in the snow, KirkT might not have kept alive his streak of summiting every peak he has attempted. "That's the closest I've ever come to stopping," he says. I tell him I hope I never try climbing any-place that's bad enough to make him stop, and we all have a pretty good laugh. Surviving the worst that a mountain can throw at us make us feel punch-drunk. We giggle and skip and tell bad jokes.

Atop our last descent ridge, Shad pulls me aside and shows me how to kick steps into ice and snow with crampons, and how to chop them deeper with an ice axe. I tell him I'm grateful for the lesson, but he tells me it's for a reason. What reason? He points down. We're at the top of the last ridge of the descent, and there's a long gully below. It's filled with slushy snow.

Either we can spend a lot of time slipping and sliding down that gully, Shad says, or we can just ride it down on our rear ends—glis-sading. Use the spike on the end of your ice axe to control your speed. Like this.

And with that Shad plops himself on the snow and starts sliding down, using his butt as a sled and his feet as steering levers. After several minutes of whoops and shouts of glee, he hits bottom and urges me on.

I drop in and enjoy the first, and most thrilling, snow enema of my life. In five glorious minutes, I blast down several hundred vertical feet and start to believe that I'm eight years old again. By the time I reach the gully's bottom I've lost all contact with my own bottom; it feels like I'm sitting atop a massive shot of Novocaine. This is the rush that the Talus Monkey was seeking.

As I turn uphill to watch KirkT's glissade, I realize I may finally have found my calling: My fat behind has plowed out a plush luge run. As KirkT rockets down my track with a smile as wide as the mountain, I realize I've learned a few valuable lessons—and even, at last, contributed something worthwhile to this trip.

Chapter 6

Panic

MOUNT ANTERO 14,276'

"If you're relying on me for mountaineering skills, then we are both in very deep shit."

I didn't mean to rattle the nerves of my latest man-date, but I did owe him the truth. We were high on the mountain at 13,000 feet. The temperature had just dropped 20 degrees. A storm was moving in. We were stranded on the wrong side of a frozen avalanche chute three miles from our car, and he had just slipped and stopped himself just short of a thousand-foot runout with sharp rocks at the bottom.

Yes, despite four inches of fresh snow and a blasting wind, we had successfully summited Mount Antero. That was the (relatively) easy part. Since then, however, the wind and cold had conspired to convert all that powder—the soft snow that had given us secure footing on the way up—into a vast frozen banana peel. Navigating it was threatening the basic sanitation of our underwear.

Still smarting from my lesson on Missouri Mountain with Shad and KirkT, I came loaded for bear on this peak, Mount Antero, with an ice axe, poles, and spanking new crampons. My man-date did not. What he lacked in equipment, though, he made up with a fully loaded personality.

His name was Matt, but I knew him better on 14ers.com as Del

Sur, the stickler for grammar who once barreled into an Internet flame war by quoting Lao Tzu: "Those who talk do not know; those who know do not talk." Before sacking up in our sleeping bags at the trailhead the night before, he introduced himself to me as a self-diagnosed, nonmedicated sufferer of attention deficit disorder. He quoted the Dead Kennedys. He practiced tai chi. He worked as a pharmacist in Shiprock, New Mexico, and specialized in epilepsy medicine for Navajos on the surrounding reservation. He talked fast.

He liked to listen, too, and what he wanted to hear most were stories about my wife and kids. He was thirty-two years old, and really, really, really wanted a family of his own. He had tried looking for love on the online dating site Match.com. When he posted his height—five foot six—he attracted little interest. When he posted his tall salary, he attracted plenty of the wrong kind of interest.

When he finally got lucky and met someone who was smart and cute and fun, there always seemed to be some land-mine deal-breaker. He stopped dating one woman after learning that she worked for the ACLU. Del Sur was a devout Catholic, and had a hard time forgiving himself for buying dinner for a lawyer who had shut down city Nativity displays.

Still, he was the first to admit that his methods of finding a date were less than traditional. On the 14ers.com site, Del Sur advertised himself with an avatar, or icon, that was a mug shot of a Korean pimp with a pencil-thin mustache, a bulletproof mullet, and an avocado smoking jacket. When a breathtaking young blonde appeared on the site calling herself a Fourteener virgin, Del Sur rode to the rescue by asking her, "Since my avatar is obviously a pic of me looking good, can you say the same?" She didn't answer; no date for him. Again.

So Matt, like William Henry Jackson and thousands of men since, decided to channel his frustrations into the mountain. He had climbed two dozen Fourteeners, and was angling to finish them off soon. Just as he started ticking peaks off his list, though, his ADD would kick in with a vengeance, and Matt would be sidetracked—trips to climb the

Navajos' four sacred mountains, epic snowboarding runs to Silverton, a St. Louis Cardinals pennant run. What's important is not the destination, but the journey, he would tell himself, while still regretting that it was taking so damn long to climb those fifty-four mountains in Colorado.

Of course, our problem on Antero wasn't the climb. It was the descent.

With a miner's jeep road that stretched to within four hundred vertical feet of the summit, Antero was supposed to be one of the more straightforward Fourteeners, but all the freeze-and-melt cycles of the past days—no, past hours—had converted our descent route from straightforward to straight downward.

The issue at hand: an old avalanche that had run from the top of one ridge, across the jeep trail, to the bottom of a thousand-foot gully. Crossing it means sidehilling over a snow mound as big as a house, with a roof more slippery than snot. One misstep had already dumped Matt at the very edge of the icy precipice.

"Scary," he says, in the understatement of the day. This leads me to repeat my gallows humor on my lack of winter mountaineering skills. My confession is no surprise—we discussed it before even beginning our hike—but for some reason I feel better repeating it.

Matt mutters something about not wanting to spend the night on the mountain. Over our shoulders the storm clouds darken and draw nearer. Now is the time, I tell myself.

On the way up the mountain I had donned crampons for the first time, mostly to practice with my new gear, but also for safety. Besides, they let me climb like Spider-Man. Slopes that Matt had to hop and peck and squirm around, I just sauntered straight up. The twelve sharp steel teeth strapped onto each hiking boot may as well have been superglue; they stuck to anything, and I beamed like a boy with his newest, favoritest Christmas toy. I felt safe. I felt strong. I even felt a little bit of an even rarer commodity—confidence.

Remembering Shad's lesson from high atop Missouri Mountain, I chop flat steps in the avalanche path with my ice axe and kick them deeper with my crampons. I'm huffing and puffing, but still making clear progress.

First five steps, then ten; after fifteen minutes of heart-pounding work, I'm safe on the other side. I cross back to Matt's side and offer my help. He asks for my axe. I lead the way with my crampons and ski poles, and hear Matt behind me thrashing the sharp steel into the mountain like Norman Bates at a Hitchcock motel.

Am I the Pied Piper of Death? I can't bear to look behind me, or down, or anywhere else, for that matter, except for my next forward step, which is no more than six inches ahead of my last. I reach the other side, and have an inkling of what Philippe Petit must have felt when he tightroped the Twin Towers in New York.

A few minutes later, Matt also crosses to safety, and blasts out a sigh of relief that's a match for the mountain winds. We can't help it; we hug. Not touching chests or pelvises, mind you, but still pretty advanced for our first man-date.

"If it weren't for you and that axe and those crampons, I'd be stuck up on the mountain in the storm all night."

Nonsense, I tell him, but my denial is filled with as much bravado as truth, and we both know it.

We're ready to turn off our brains and slog down the mountain, but Mount Antero has other ideas. It confronts us with another frozen avalanche chute, then another, and finally our fourth frozen obstacle of the day. We're becoming old pros at chopping steps. This wintery day is changing us from hikers to mountaineers, but I would have preferred a transformation by choice, not necessity. After clearing the last frozen obstacle, I'm more relieved than proud.

We start our slog down the easy parts of the mountain. The combination of having survived the worst the alpine gods could throw at us, plus the giddiness of hiking at 13,000 feet, leaves us both with a vibe for honest confessions.

I tell Matt the truth: Though he believed his stature limited his success with women, I had spent more than six hours with him and never even noticed his height. On the climb up, when I was stuck to my crotch in snowdrifts, or knocked off my feet by 50-mph wind gusts, or claiming we were lost and headed up the wrong peak, he just seemed like a guy with a big heart and a blind eye for stupid people.

Matt tells me his problem isn't just height.

"What do you mean?"

"Well, when I was a kid growing up in Missouri, there was always a word that rhymed with Matt."

The schoolyard teasing was so bad that, even today, he wouldn't say the word "fat."

He seemed destined to go through life as a beefy short man until a chance Colorado vacation trip a few years back. Like millions of tourists before them, Matt and a buddy headed for Rocky Mountain National Park, the crown jewel of the Colorado Front Range and the No. 6 most visited national park in America. (Strangely, though, Colorado tourism officers found the park is less popular with visitors than the Cherry Creek Shopping Mall in Denver.)

From a bar in the base town of Estes Park, Matt and his friend looked up, saw the domineering 14,259-foot Longs Peak, and decided to climb it. Park literature said Longs Peak had a trail. If a trail is in a national park, they figured, how hard could it be? Somebody in town advised them to hike early, so they were on the trail at 3 a.m.

One hour later, his buddy was keeled over and vomiting. Matt, however, was so surprised and delighted at his own ability to hold down breakfast that he continued onward. That lasted four hours. Then he, too, was keeled over and wobbly and dizzy and facing an awful dilemma: He was too far up the mountain to go down, and too far from the summit to go up. Though he didn't know it at the time, he had succumbed to a nasty bout of altitude sickness.

Luckily, two young women took pity on him, giving him food, water, and, best of all, encouragement to keep putting one foot in front of the other until all three summited at the same time. Then the women guided him back down.

At the trailhead Matt was so delirious he couldn't even remember the girls' names. He just kept looking up at that mountain and asking one question: Did I really survive that?

He had, and he was hooked. The more he hiked, the less he weighed. In the past year he had shed thirty-five pounds—the weight of a full winter daypack—and was hoping that his new 170-pound shape would help him get up more mountains this summer. "I don't look like I can do this, but I can," he says. Besides, few things focus his jumpy mind like a step-by-step negotiation of a frozen avalanche chute with a thousand-foot runout.

Still, like me, he was paranoid about his pace. He was hoping to hike with some new online friends this summer, but worried that he was too slow to keep up. When I confide that I had a hard time matching steps with him on the way up Antero, he stops dead in his boot tracks.

Really?

Really.

A small metropolis could be electrified with the power of his smile.

We drop another five hundred feet by arguing red vs. green chile, and snowboarding vs. skiing, and life in Colorado vs. New Mexico. After failing to find any consensus, we switch to the always-easy-to-resolve national health care debate. (He's worked with his share of arrogant doctors.)

From nowhere Matt suddenly interjects: "One thing I like about climbing is that you get to see people for who they are. When somebody is stripped away from their possessions and their business cards and their normal comfort zone, and nothing is preset and decided, and it's before dawn and it's dark and cold and you've got to figure out whether you can get up and down a mountain, you really get to see . . ."

He leaves his thought hanging, and I wonder: Do I measure up? Does he see me for what I am? How can he be so right about human character, but so wrong about his snobbery for New Mexican chile?

Then I see the reason for his silence. At the switchback just down the trail stands a man who looks fresh out of *Deliverance*—tall, gangly, bearded, and with brown Carhartt overalls that haven't seen the inside of a washing machine since at least Y2K. Matt and I are hustling to beat a storm in full Gore-Tex climbing regalia; the mountain man wears only shirtsleeves. Strange, but now I'm the one with the shivers.

There's an awkward pause, and I fear we are about to be serenaded by an inbred boy with a banjo.

"What you been doing up there?" he asks.

"Just climbing," I say. "How about you?"

I wait for him to tell me I have purty lips.

No answer.

"I'm writing a book about climbing these mountains. You know much about this one?"

He looks me up. He looks me down. I'm hoping Burt Reynolds has got my back covered with his bow and arrow.

"I got ten thousand dollars of aquamarine here last summer."

"Here? Right here?"

"Devil's Backbone—that mess of a ridge before the top."

The place where I did my Spider-Man imitation in crampons. I tell him that the Devil's Backbone is icy and snowpacked without much rock exposed for mining.

He seems interested—until all hell breaks loose. From the cheap pup tent behind him emerges another hardscrabble man in Carhartts.

"Goddamn," he screams at his buddy. "What the hell you telling them?"

The second miner's eyes are bulging.

"Son of a bitch—can't you keep your goddamn mouth shut?"

"Why don't you just put a goddamn lid on it!"

Just to the side of the miners' tent is a gully that's not too steep, with snow that's not too hard. Matt and I are thinking the same thing: Let's get the hell out of here. We drop down onto our butts and glissade away from the screaming miners.

Whew.

Safely off the mountain, I poke around in town and find out that Mount Antero is North America's No. 1 source of aquamarine, a prized gem that's the pale blue cousin of emeralds. The gem lode on Antero is the reason why there's a jeep trail to 13,900 feet; a commercial operation bulldozed it in 1956 with a massive TD-14, though the danger of that construction feat became apparent when talus collapsed and sent the tractor tumbling hundreds of feet down the mountain. The bulldozer driver jumped to safety just in time, and the owner let juvenile delinquents from a nearby state reformatory spend the summer carting away the broken machine, piece by piece, to be sold for scrap metal. For the teenage criminals, it was a truly cruel and unusual punishment.

Because most of the mountain is public land managed by the federal government, amateur rock hounds can keep whatever they find. And they still do. Just three years ago, a New York prospector named Steve Brancato, relying on only a hammer, shovel, and crowbar, was smashing rocks about two hundred yards below our hiking trail when he detected a telltale hollow sound. From a rock cavity the size of a household oven he extracted a matrix of more than one hundred crystals of aquamarine—as blue as the Rocky Mountain sky, with even deeper color than gems from competing mines in Pakistan and Afghanistan—plus white feldspar, black quartz, and red garnet. One 37-by-25-inch aquamarine assemblage, the largest and finest ever found on the continent, was sold to a private collector for donation to the Denver Museum of Nature and Science, where it remains on display today. Brancato honored his mother lode by naming it Diane's Pocket, after his own mother. All told, Diane's Pocket yielded gems valued at more than $500,000, which explains why Brancato, as well as many other Antero miners, digs while packing a loaded handgun.

Good thing Matt and I glissaded away so swiftly.

We drive to the Arkansas River Valley town of Buena Vista for a celebratory late lunch of bacon double cheeseburgers, with fries and a chocolate shake. (Could this be a reason I'm still clocking in at 210 pounds?) We both agree that we've had such a good time that we want to do this again. Above us Antero and the tops of the Sawatch Range are buried in snow clouds. We got out just in time. We shake hands and pledge to keep in touch.

I ask for his contact information. He takes my reporter's notebook and writes in "Matt," along with his e-mail address.

"Hey, Matt," I tell him. "Do you have a last name too?"

No answer.

"I thought I saved your life. How about a last name?"

He takes back my pen and notebook and writes, "Ellis." And then he's off. He's got five-and-a-half hours to drive back home to Shiprock to help epileptics on the Navajo Reservation.

My own drive home is two-and-a-half hours. I pull up outside our house in Denver, where it's 65 degrees and sunny. Kids are playing on the sidewalk and neighbors are arriving home from work.

Exiting my car in full mountaineering regalia, I shoulder my heavy backpack, and, with as much macho as I can muster, swagger to our front door. Merrill stops me at the steps.

Our three-year-old has pooped in the yard. The dog ate it. And now he's running around and terrorizing all the kids on the block with his disgusting breath. I need to do something about it.

My first instinct is to reach for my ice axe, but I realize there's no way to glissade my way out of this mess. I run to catch the dog in my hiking boots.

Chapter 7

Shock

MOUNT MASSIVE 14,421'

Two hours after sunset, fifteen miles up a dirt road, I'm trolling for my latest man-date. It's supposed to be another threesome, this time with a guy named StevieTwoShoes and his older brother, Doug. I've never met them, never talked with them, never even swapped e-mails with them. Through a series of voice-mail messages—well, two, actually—we've arranged to meet in a dirt parking lot at 5 a.m. the next day. I fall asleep in the back of my car with the windows locked and wonder, Is this really going to happen?

It happens—big-time. At 5 a.m., up rolls a new Jeep Sahara blasting Ghostface Killah, the New York gangsta rapper, with the bass thumping so loud it rocks the shocks over the vehicle's oversized tires. The Ghost lays it down: *Yeah, what's the deal? What's the deal y'all? / I need y'all niggaz to buckle up one time / Fasten your seatbelts, I'm a take y'all on some real shit.*

Hmmm. Do I really want to get into this car?

Through the predawn gloom I see the Jeep's dome light illuminating the faces of two very white men—Steve and Doug Spannring, who busted straight outta the suburbs of Des Moines for new cribs in the northern Colorado towns of Greeley and Fort Collins. Not quite the 'hood. I do as Ghostface says and fasten my seat belt.

Though it's nearly impossible to shout over the throb of the rapper, I try swapping a few words with Doug, and conclude that he's pretty mild-mannered. He wears the classic skin yarmulke of a middle-aged man, while Steve, our DJ for the morning, has the shaved head of a hipster. I gravitate toward Doug.

Which is a good thing, because as soon as we slam the Jeep doors, Steve shoots up the trail like a greased bullet. Thankfully, Doug stays behind to humor me. He's an engineer married to a doctor and they have two kids, and he hardly ever gets to hike anymore, even though the Great Outdoors was one of the main reasons he moved to Colorado, which is a great place to raise a family. At least I think that's what he's saying, because I have to hustle so fast to keep up with him that I can't hear anything above the throb and wheeze of my heart and lungs.

At this point I realize Steve is a lost cause—illuminated by only his headlamp, he looks like a comet shooting over the horizon. Doug turns to me and asks how I'm doing. I tell him I'm going my pace, and if he needs to go his pace, he should just go. Luckily, he doesn't. He talks some more, and I do my best to listen, but it's hard to concentrate when all I can think of is one question: When I die of my heart attack, will two fans of Ghostface Killah haul my body off the mountain?

At a switchback, Steve stands waiting. He's been there for an unstated amount of time, though I presume it's a lot. He has legs like a giraffe and a voice that starts two floors below the basement. He's in such good shape that the pitch of his voice doesn't climb when the trail does. I conclude that he's a lung on two legs, and that this is the last I'll see of him.

Amazingly, it's not. Like professional wrestlers, the brothers Spannring have decided to tag-team me: Doug shoots on up the trail while Steve holds back for a talk. It's a good one.

After drinking and partying himself out of Iowa State University, Steve moved back home with his mother, and then spent another year drinking and partying. He worked part-time at the local Quik Stop, but spent much of his time hanging out in Mom's basement. On a typical night with his buddies, a six-pack was just a start. Though Steve kept bracing for it, his mom never yelled. She just "expressed disappointment." Months of quiet but persistent mom-guilt finally wore him down, and he enrolled in a local community college to try to get his grades up. Because of his lousy record at Iowa State, no four-year school would have him. Finally, though, at age twenty-one, when most of his high school friends were graduating from college, Steve was allowed to start as a sophomore student at the University of Northern Iowa. He cranked. When he graduated with a 3.5 grade point average, his mom wept.

He had decided to become, of all things, a teacher. Of seventh grade. Same grade as my oldest son.

Today Steve teaches American history and geography in the meat-packing town of Greeley, where his students are the children of migrants and millionaires, boys who are shaving and boys who are collecting Pokémon cards. At first he was surprised to see some thirteen- and fourteen-year-old students with gang symbols tattooed on their faces. Then he scheduled parent-teacher conferences, and met some dads wearing the same tattoos on their faces too. It's a messy stew of rich America and poor America, WASPs and Mexicans and cowboys and Indians, and the excitement I hear in Steve's voice is contagious.

The cool thing about thirteen-year-olds, he says, is that they're still excited to learn—and not always embarrassed to show it. Whenever one kid puts down another by calling him a brain, or a scholar, or a suck-up, Steve drops his voice as low as it can go and works mightily to put an end to it. He's fighting teenage hormones, AWOL parents, gangsta recruiters, meddling administrators, bulging class sizes, and a *Lord of the Flies* culture in the hallway during passing period. His job does not bore him.

He especially enjoys letting teens live the lesson. To start teaching the American Revolution, he extracts one pencil from every student as they enter his class. The next day, he takes a few sheets of paper. Then gum, then backpacks, then cell phones. He shouts when he hears a student whisper, and he sends kids to the principal's office for the tiniest infractions. After a week of his tyranny, when he has pushed all desks to the side of the classroom and forced all students to sit on the floor, Steve is invariably confronted by a group of sheepishly grinning students with a handwritten declaration that begins, "When in the course of human events it becomes necessary for one people to dissolve the political bands which have connected them with another . . ." The kids declare independence; the teacher applauds; lesson learned.

The same figure-it-out-yourselves philosophy helps him deliver memorable lectures on different forms of government—he's a jerk during dictatorships, one among equals during democracy, and a confiscator during Communism—but even Steve confesses to some squeamishness about one class. It can be very, very dangerous to let thirteen-year-olds teach themselves about anarchy.

When his classroom inevitably grows too rowdy, Steve always has his fallback warning: Keep it up, he tells his teens, and you'll end up like me—twenty-one years old and living in your mom's basement.

That usually scares them straight.

By the end of the school year in June, Steve is mentally exhausted, but his body is ready to go. He has the luxury of a summer off, but the limited financial reality of a teacher's paycheck. So most days, he hikes. He hails the opening of summer hiking season by shaving his head—during the school year he wears a blond Beatles mop—and lacing up his boots. He's six foot three, and has melted away seventy pounds in the mountains. Almost all of his hiking buddies have wives or kids or beer guts, so he finds himself hiking alone a lot. He likes the mind-clearing properties of a solo hike, but he's clearly a talker, and a thinker, and a reader. He ends all his posts on 14ers.com with a quote from the playwright Wilson Mizner: "I respect faith, but doubt is what gets you an education." The trail up the southwest slopes of Mount Massive may be steep, but StevieTwoShoes has made sure that the climb isn't boring. I wish he were my son's teacher.

We rise above tree line and find a steep gully filled with rock-hard snow. The couloir looks like Mount Antero, but bigger, and we're at the bottom looking up. Doug decides to traverse it. I, however, come loaded with crampons and axe, and decide to pick straight-up it. Steve and Doug look at me admiringly. What do they think I am, a mountaineer?

Armed with ski poles, Doug sets off on a sixty-yard traverse across the frozen gully. Steve, who carries an axe and knows how to use it, joins me for the pick and scratch directly up. Everyone seems safe and happy.

About halfway across the gully, though, Doug starts to falter. The snow is too bulletproof, and his nerves seem a little too shot, for him to keep sidehilling. Steve and I offer help, but he waves us off. Doug knocks small steps into the ice with his hiking poles, and, little by little, works his way toward the side of the gully, where a snow-free rock rib awaits. Steve and I steadily progress to the top of the six-hundred-foot gully. We sit on a rock and watch and wait.

Far below us, Doug is plopped on his butt. He bangs one step, tests his weight, scoots a little, bangs another step, tests his weight again, and so on, gaining on the mountain an inch at a time. A trekking pole is clearly not designed to cut steps in ice. It's slow and painful to watch. A slip would result in a four-hundred-foot slide down the mountain. At my side, Steve's brow knits with worry.

"If it was a friend down there, I'd be OK with this," Steve tells me. "But it's my brother. I can't help it. I don't like it."

I try to take Steve's mind off his brother's balancing act below by talking schools and mountains and movies, but Steve will have none of it. We just sit there and stare.

Finally, after a half-hour of banging and scratching and inching, Doug is off the slippery gully and onto solid rock. What a relief. Now there's a new problem: We can't see him. We assume he's climbing somewhere behind that rock rib, but what if he's stranded on another frozen gully on the other side? Steve and I continue on for a few minutes, but Steve can't take it any longer. He peels uphill at his regular, faster pace with hopes of making sure his brother is OK.

He is. Whew. The three of us gain the summit ridge, and see that the mountaintop is a quick jaunt from here. We light the afterburners beneath our feet, and then learn the hard way that our short ridge to the summit is actually a short ridge to a false summit. We stop atop it and curse. Then we pick up again and charge hard to the real top, until we find that this crest is another false summit too. From here I think we see the true summit above and beyond us, but at this point, I'm too demoralized to place any bets. It's a tough lesson: There is no summit that comes before you expect it.

Around us, the weather worsens. Up high, the puffy white cotton clouds begin to grow black bottoms.

We summit—finally!—at 10:30 a.m., snap a few photos, talk about the blackening clouds, and quickly start retracing our steps back down the summit ridge. We're still a long way above tree line, and ugly weather is moving in.

At the top of the gully, I feel something hit my nose. It's graupel— airborne frozen white stuff that isn't snow, sleet, or hail, but about the size of a pellet of Styrofoam. This, we know, is a formula for danger: Cold precipitation plus warm spring temperatures equals scary weather. The wind swells. I call to Steve and Doug, but they're ahead of me, out of earshot, hustling down the same rock-rib summer trail that Doug had ascended. I pick up my pace.

Now the graupel is really coming down, and it's starting to turn into hail. Ouch. The outer shell of my jacket sounds as if it's being assaulted by pop machine guns. I'm moving as fast as my weary legs can carry me—boot-skiing down scree, with each step plunging three feet before coming to rest. My heart pounds. My lungs sear. I struggle to keep my balance.

Then: *KABLAM! KABLAM! KABLAM!*

Three valley-rocking rolls of thunder, right above me. With lightning too.

I look sideways to the exposed rock rib, but can't spot Steve and

Doug. I gag, choke it back, vomit anyway, fling off my backpack, fumble with straps, rush to unfasten my ice axe, grab it with my right hand, bend over, and puke again.

At the top of the snow gully, I make like an Olympian and long-jump with feet in front and arms like wings. I land hard on my ass and start sliding, downhill and fast. I'm trying to glissade faster than lightning, and the wind whistles through my ears.

One hundred, three hundred, five hundred feet of elevation are lost. There's a rock band at the bottom of the run, but I dig my ice axe hard into the softening snow and stop just as my feet reach the rocks. Down safely.

I look back up the ridge, and see the brothers hundreds of feet above me. They are in a bad place—exposed on a rock rib with clouds threatening more lightning. Doug is struggling with shot legs and toasted nerves. Steve runs back uphill and shouts.

"Doug, we have to get down! Now! Not slow! Fast!"

Doug speeds up. He seems a little out of it. Steve's hand tenses around his metal ice axe, but he feels something strange—a tingling sensation. His axe is electrified.

He hurls his axe as far as he can and assumes the position—squatting down on the balls of his feet like a baseball catcher, trying to make his body as small a target as possible. The storm's electrical charge builds up in the air around him.

A few seconds, and still no lightning.

"Come on, Doug! Let's move!"

Steve retrieves his axe. Steve runs. Doug runs.

KABLAM!

Brothers fall back into a squat.

"Gotta get out of here!"

Steve grabs his axe again, but it starts to hum like an AM radio. Again he chucks it.

KABLAM!

They run. More hail, more graupel. I can't see them on the ridge anymore.

I jump into another gully and glissade another six hundred vertical feet. My butt is numb, and my arms are tired from using the axe as a snow brake.

The gully finally peters out and leaves me a few steps from the tree line. I'm safe, but I can't see or hear Doug or Steve. Surely, I figure, they must be far ahead, because everyone is always far ahead of me. Though there were five distinct thunderboomers, I never heard a scream. I'm hoping no one was hit. I wait fifteen minutes in the spruces, but still see no sign of Doug or Steve. I hightail it down through the trees to catch them, and, after several hours, finally reach Steve's Jeep.

No one is there.

I feel sick again. Where are they—hurt up on the mountain? I check my cell phone, but can't conjure a signal to call them. I decide to wait before doubling back on my tracks to find them. I don't know if I have the strength to head uphill again, but I have no choice.

I lean against a tree and wait. And wait.

Forty-five minutes later, they emerge from the woods. Neither is hurt. Both are tired. They tell me in detail what happened to them up high. They saw me glissade through the thunderstorm, and were jealous of my speed.

It's the first anyone besides a police officer ever put my name in the same sentence with the word "speed." I laugh and I can't stop. This, I tell Steve and Doug, is cause to celebrate. I'm buying lunch for all in that infamous little mountain town that knows near-death experiences better than most—Leadville.

On April 26, 1860, in the shadow of the peak that came to be known as Mount Massive, a hardscrabble prospector named Abe Lee dipped his pan into the black sands of the upper Arkansas River and found something bright. "Oh, my God," he shouted, "I've got all California in this here pan!" Lee fired four shots into the air and lit a signal fire. One year after a legion of miners had declared, "Pikes Peak or Bust," a new gold rush was on.

This rush faced major obstacles: Lee's valley was rimmed by the unforgiving 14,000-foot peaks of the Mosquito Range to the east, the Sawatch Range to the west, and no roads, rails, or navigable rivers in between. Within four months, however, the frigid valley had attracted five thousand fortune hunters.

They called their ramshackle settlement Oro City, after the Spanish word for gold, and it lived up to its name: In the first summer alone, $2 million of gold was extracted from Lee's California Gulch. Lee himself pocketed $60,000, or $1.5 million in today's money—not a bad take for a man with a pan, a pick, and a shovel.

Though some came to get rich quick by mining the earth, others found it easier to mine wallets. A shrewd Vermonter named Horace Tabor set up a general store to sell food, pots, and placer-mining supplies. If a prospector couldn't afford the supplies, then Tabor grubstaked him. The miner got tools and food, and in exchange Tabor got a third of the profits of any resulting mine. Though many were grubstaked, few amounted to anything.

Still, Tabor remained one of the most popular men in town, in no small part because he brought his lovely wife, Augusta, the first white female resident of the new mine camp. Lovesick prospectors were so thrilled to see a woman, any woman, that they built Augusta her own 18-by-32-foot log cabin.

The thrill was soon gone. Like dozens of mine towns before and after, Oro City went bust, and within five years the population plummeted to less than five hundred. Yet the Tabors stuck it out.

For ten years, prospectors tried but failed to scratch out a living from the valley's black sands. Augusta warned her husband that he was throwing away their money by grubstaking so many dead-end miners; Horace kept doing it anyway, no doubt because he enjoyed passing away the afternoons playing poker with them.

In 1876, two secretive prospectors, William Stevens and Alvinus Wood, grew so weary of the pan-clogging black sand in the valley below Mount Massive that they decided on a whim to have it chemically analyzed. The results changed Colorado.

The cursed black sand turned out to be lead carbonate, loaded with silver. A new boomtown sprang up around it, and, for the next decade-and-a-half, Leadville became one of the richest, fastest, rowdiest, and most wicked places ever invented by man. It's tempting to call Leadville the nineteenth-century version of Las Vegas, but Leadville's fortunes were more fantastic, its debauchery deeper.

In a matter of months, the population of Leadville exploded from 300 to 10,000, and at its peak, some say, 45,000, all fed by tales in national magazines of money ripe for the taking.

One story held that a hunter, after shooting a deer, saw the dying animal kick up a black stone. Assuming the rock was coal, the hunter pitched it into his campfire—and saw it melt into silver.

Another legend surrounded the Dead Man Claim. When a prospector named Scotty died in winter, his buddies hired a gravedigger for a proper burial. The digger disappeared for three days. Fearing the hired help had ditched them, the buddies put Scotty on ice in a snowbank and went searching for the missing gravedigger, who, it turned out, had struck silver after just a few spades into the grave. A nasty argument ensued, and the gravedigger and Scotty's friends spent the rest of the winter digging and filing competing mining claims all over the intended cemetery. Long forgotten, Scotty's body melted out with the spring thaw in April.

And then there were the Tabors. In the spring of 1878, Horace was minding the store when a German immigrant, August Rische, and his partner from Pittsburgh, George Hook, strode inside and asked for a grubstake. Busy with other customers, Tabor told them, "Yes, come in and get what you like, but don't bother me now."

The prospectors walked out the door with food, whiskey, a hand winch, wheelbarrow, and other tools worth a total of $64. A few weeks later they burst back through the doors of Tabor's store with big news.

"We've struck it! We've struck it!" cried Rische.

Indeed they had. Because of his grubstake, Tabor now owned a third of one of the richest mines on earth, the Little Pittsburg, which at one point was producing up to $10,000 a day (more than $200,000 a day in today's dollars). For Tabor, it was like drinking money from a fire hose. After a year of fabulous wealth, Tabor sold his share of the Little Pittsburg for an even $1 million, and, to the relief of Augusta, got out of the grocery business. He went on to build the city's largest bank and grandest hotel, and the biggest theater in the West. He then topped it all off by buying the redoubtable Matchless Mine, which paid him up to $3,000 a day. He was the King Midas of Colorado, but with a silver finger.

Leadville's riches were so great that Jesse James, bank robber extraordinaire, temporarily detoured from his life of crime to dig for silver in California Gulch. Soon after his arrival he was accused of three local stagecoach robberies, but subsequent investigation found the heists were actually the work of the captain of the Leadville Police Department.

In a town that, in the words of historian Duane Smith, "seemed to take pride in its depravity," law enforcement was a punishing job. When a cop shot and killed the city marshal in a drunken fight, Leadville replaced the dead man with a local tough named Mart Duggan, who, according to the Leadville *Herald Democrat,* was "a notorious bully and killer, openly boasting of seven notches on his gun." Even a killer cop couldn't keep the streets safe; Duggan was shot to death outside a poker hall.

Fed up with rampant violence and thievery, miners formed vigilante squads to hang suspected criminals. Two days before the opening of the Tabor Opera House, a mob busted into the city jail, wrestled out two accused bad guys, and hanged them from the rafters of the new City Hall down the street. On the backs of the executed were scrawled the names of eighty more men expected to leave town by sunset.

When those threats didn't work, Leadville turned to legal hangings, but with a gruesome twist: Instead of dropping the condemned on a noose to quickly break his neck, Leadville's new gallows raised a criminal slowly with a pulley and weights to make sure he suffered a drawn-out death by choking. More than 7,500 gathered to watch.

By one count, Leadville was home to more than a hundred saloons and poker dens. Men outnumbered women ten to one, and if ever there was a place that lived up to the romantic lament of even modern small-town mountain men everywhere—you never really break up with a woman, you just lose your place in line—the Cloud City was it. Of course, many men pursuing instant riches also wanted instant libidinal release. For them, Leadville had dozens of "sporting houses," full of "soiled doves" and "fallen angels." Though one dance-hall girl, Red Stockings, was said to have walked away with $100,000 of miners' nuggets, too many other women ended up in Stillborn Alley, where the bodies of unwanted babies were dumped and forgotten.

Most fortune hunters were too busy to care. In Leadville, Bavarian immigrant David May opened his first clothing store in the chain that eventually became the powerhouse national retailer that owned Lord & Taylor, Foley's, and Filene's. The Chicago retailer Marshall Field had a mine in Leadville, and Meyer Guggenheim, with initial help from J. P. Morgan and the Rockefellers, piled up a great fortune in the smelter business. When no hangings were scheduled on a Saturday night, miners forked over their silver dollars at the Tabor Opera House to see Houdini, John Philip Sousa, Oscar Wilde, and Buffalo Bill.

The entertainment wasn't enough for some. At age fifty-one, Horace Tabor found himself rich, powerful, famous, and bored—classic warning signs for a midlife crisis. Like Leadville, his was larger than life.

In 1879, Tabor met a woman who had come to Leadville, not as a miner of silver but as a gold digger. She was twenty-five, blond, blue-eyed, and had a face so fresh and cherubic that tongue-wagging men on the street called her Baby. Horace Tabor could not resist.

Tabor and Baby Doe carried on a very public love affair for months while the upper-crust women of Leadville, and America, rallied to the side of Augusta, his wife of twenty-three years. Public scorn, ridicule, and anger could not tear Horace from his mistress's sheets. He walked out on Augusta, but the wife refused a divorce.

A man of such wealth and influence would not be denied. A trusted business ally granted Tabor a secret divorce. Tabor and Baby Doe traveled to St. Louis and married.

Or so they thought. Months later they discovered that the divorce was not legal. One of the nation's richest men was actually married to two women at the same time. Oh, the scandal!

Augusta would not go down without a fight. In a nasty divorce proceeding, she amazed the world by listing all of Tabor's known financial assets. In just three years, Tabor had gone from mining-camp grocer to full-fledged magnate, with mines, banks, real estate, diamonds, investments, and factories worth $9 million—or $191 million in today's money. Embarrassed, Horace finally agreed to pay $300,000 to Augusta for a divorce.

By this time, Tabor was a newly appointed U.S. senator. He married Baby Doe again in an official ceremony on March 1, 1883, in Washington, D.C. President Chester Arthur wished them well.

The good times did not last. Ten years later, with banks failing and the nation plunging into economic depression, President Grover Cleveland stripped away massive federal subsidies for the price of silver. With the repeal of the Sherman Silver Purchase Act, which had forced the federal government to buy at least 4.5 million ounces a month, the price of silver collapsed. Almost overnight, Leadville's mines shuttered, businesses bankrupted, and thousands of men fled to search for work elsewhere.

For the second time in three decades, Leadville went bust.

Few people were hit harder by the implosion in the silver market than Horace Tabor. He lost nearly everything, and was forced to start work again as a postmaster in Denver. Before his death in 1899, Tabor was said to have told his scandalous trophy bride Baby Doe, "Hang on to the Matchless," the mine that once seemed to let him print his own currency. Thirty-six years later, Baby Doe, penniless, bundled in rags, and utterly alone, was found frozen to death in a shack outside the entrance to the moribund silver mine. The tawdry tale of the Tabors was the subject of dozens of books, a movie, and even an opera.

The fate of Leadville was almost as bad: For years it was mostly forgotten. Glorious old Victorian buildings fell into disrepair, and only a few thousand people managed to scrape out a living. Nearly two miles above sea level, Leadville remained the highest incorporated city in the United States, but no place seemed more down on its luck.

When the nation was most desperate, however, Leadville stood ready to help. Wartime gave America an insatiable appetite for lead, zinc, and copper, and the Cloud City boomed again during World War I, World War II, and the Korean War. For a time, the world's No. 1 producer of molybdenum, a gray mineral used as a hardening agent for steel, was the Climax Molybdenum Company, which was literally tearing down Bartlett Mountain just outside Leadville on Fremont Pass. The mine became a railroad station atop the Continental Divide, which allowed several generations of anxious fathers to have the following conversation with smart-aleck Leadville teen boys: "Where do you intend to take my daughter on your date tonight, son?" "Sir, I plan to bring her to Climax."

Nearly a billion dollars of silver, gold, lead, zinc, copper, and moly have been produced in Leadville, but there are few signs of those riches today. Though the Guggenheims amassed a fortune that created a magnificent museum in New York, they left behind heaping piles of slag and toxic waste in Leadville. After decades of mining abuses that killed most aquatic life in the Arkansas River, much of Leadville is now a designated Superfund cleanup site. Whole neighborhoods of Leadville have been reduced to serving as bedroom communities for the ski resorts of Vail and Copper Mountain, where a new wave of immigrants, this time Mexican, removes the trash and changes bedsheets for vacationing outsiders.

Tens of millions of taxpayer dollars have been used to clean up old toxic messes, but there's still plenty of resentment that so little of the wealth that came from Leadville actually stayed in Leadville. To paraphrase the old country song: Easterners got the silver mine; Leadville got the shaft.

Though it ended up working out for the best, my mooched Jeep ride with Doug and Steve to the Mount Massive trailhead convinced me of one thing: I needed my own manly vehicle. More than half the Fourteeners had trailheads up four-wheel-drive roads, and my city slicker station wagon wasn't going to cut it. Unfortunately, renting an SUV through the peak of the Colorado summer tourist season would cost more than paying our home mortgage through that season. My wife's advice: Just buy a beater truck and sell it at the end of the summer.

There was no telling who was more excited by my wife's advice—me or my sons. Buy a truck for the sole purpose of abusing it? That was almost as cool as having your own Xbox. (Our sons didn't, and often reminded me of that fact.)

As the father of three boys, I never really understood the whole mom-and-daughter-go-shopping-at-the-mall thing. But dad-and-sons-go-shopping-for-monster-truck? Now, that was a language I could learn. We didn't kick the tires. We pounded them. Cracked windshield? Badge of honor. The bigger the mud flaps, the wider our smiles. I did, however, have to draw the line when Cass, our oldest son, wanted to fill the trailer hitch with swinging rubber bull testicles.

The shopping gave me a better chance to see how the boys were doing in a summer without a stay-at-home dad. My wife had hired a college student, Amy, to help out, and the boys raved about her. She took them to the pool and zoo and library and movies and sometimes even on train rides to nowhere just for the fun of it. Part of me was glad, but part of me ached. Were they really allowed to have such a good time without me?

When I finally found a truck I liked, I brought our two youngest boys—Cass was away at summer camp—and Amy. While they turned the back of the pickup into a trampoline, I ducked inside the office to negotiate a price. I emerged a few minutes later with the salesman to find my boys dancing like fiends in the pickup bed with the radio blasting. Our three-year-old, Wesley, had learned nearly all the words—the non–swear words, at least—to the grinding song "Ferga-licious."

Our nine-year-old, Max, insisted on naming the truck, which was fire-engine red and lifted an extra three inches off the pavement with heavy-duty off-road shocks. What do you have in mind? I asked.

LaKisha, he said, just like the star singer on *American Idol*, be-cause the truck was big, loud, and had very, very large tires.

My sons were having a good time without me.

Chapter 8

Bulldog

MOUNT SHAVANO 14,231'
TABEGUACHE PEAK 14,162'

After weeks of begging and pleading, badgering and harassing, I finally figured out how to get my old buddy Gottlieb to hike with me again. I fell back on the time-honored method—bribery.

Specifically, I promised him cold beer and a warm bed. Though he did say yes, I still detected some reluctance in his voice. Truth was, Gottlieb had little experience hiking on snow and ice, and he was a little skittish because of it. When I told him about my misadventures on Missouri and Antero, his skittishness turned into downright dread. Fair enough, I told him, but the two peaks I had in mind for us were among the best for learning snow travel. Even better, the base for these mountains was the very cool railroad-and-smelting-turned-artsy town Salida.

Turned out Gottlieb knew Salida. He had fled it once under the barrel of a cop's gun.

While attending Colorado College years ago in Colorado Springs, Gottlieb was hanging out after classes on Friday when some buddies got the bright idea of hopping a freight train. (There was alcohol involved.) One thing led to another, and next thing he knew, Gottlieb was one of seven college boys sneaking into a local rail yard with hopes of riding the rails to a tiny Mexican restaurant forty miles away in Pueblo. (There was more alcohol involved.) They eluded the rail guards, clambered into an open boxcar, and were off. (Celebratory toasts.)

The *mole* in the Mexican restaurant—actually, a tavern, with four gas burners in the back—was fine, but the real attraction was the locally brewed Walter's Premium Beer, which put a higher premium on buzz than price. Weaving out of the tavern, one buddy jumped on the hood of a parked car; police threw all seven drunken college boys up against the wall, frisked them, and ordered them out of town.

They hopped another freight that seemed to be headed north to campus in Colorado Springs. (Jug bottles of Almaden Mountain Chablis.) A half-hour up the tracks, however, somebody noticed that the train was speeding up. (Wine jugs pulled away from lips.) They looked out the door and found a double whammy of movement—their heads spinning from the booze, their boxcar rocking from an accelerating locomotive. (Wine jugs set down on boxcar floor.) Luckily, someone was sober enough to remind everyone that it would be really, really stupid to jump off a moving train. (Toasts to lifesaving wisdom.) They settled in for a long night's ride and drank until they fell asleep, or, more accurately, passed out.

In the morning they woke in a boxcar roiled with puke, and a switchyard plopped in a desert moonscape. Helper, Utah, was in the middle of nowhere, and 480 miles from home. A real hobo told the boys that Helper was home to a notorious cathouse, but the boys wanted nothing to do with that. They hopped an eastbound train. The alcohol had run out. The hangovers had not.

They spent another night in a boxcar, and tried to dry out the next morning by sprawling in the sun on an empty flatbed. They rolled through the red-rock canyons of the Colorado River, the limestone caves and hot springs of Glenwood, and the snowcapped peaks of the Continental Divide. When the train stopped a hundred miles from home, in Salida, the boys stood to stretch their legs.

Two cops with guns drawn had other ideas.

"Get off the train! Now!"

For the second time in three days, the boys were ordered up against the wall by cops. It was a distinctly hairier feeling to be frisked with a gun trained at the temple.

Earlier that day there had been a breakout from the juvenile detention facility up the Arkansas River Valley—the same facility that forced teens to haul away the broken-down bulldozer from Mount Antero one summer—and police suspected that Gottlieb and his friends might be the perps on the lam. When the boys proved they weren't, the Salida cops were still mad enough to ban them from reboarding the freight.

Gottlieb had to bribe another classmate with several cases of beer to pick him up and bring him home to Colorado Springs. Except, instead of bringing him back to his campus room, Gottlieb's buddy took him straight to a Jerry Jeff Walker concert, where the country troubadour's anthem, "Up Against the Wall, Redneck Mother," took on a new and highly personal meaning.

So that's why Gottlieb is skittish about Salida.

Of course, he's telling me this story in Salida, from the next barstool, at the most infamous saloon in town, the Victoria Tavern. He mumbles something along the lines of, that which does not kill you makes you stronger; we order two more beers. We're hoping to summit two peaks tomorrow, and we're convincing ourselves that we need plenty of carbo-loading, liquid variety.

We're not the first to gird for battle over beers at the Vic, a bar that's a century old and feels it. The home-away-from-home for generations of miners, railroaders, bikers, and long-bearded loners, some with hair-trigger tempers, the Vic was the first place someone told me, "Nobody ever moved to a small town in the mountains because they like people." (The second time I heard this epithet was after a loner in another small town in the mountains, Granby, exacted revenge over a city zoning decision by fortifying his bulldozer with steel and concrete and demolishing much of the central business district.)

The last few years, though, Salida has changed. Where there once were hardware stores and pawnshops and empty storefronts, there now are art galleries, coffeehouses, and restaurants that serve green things that aren't just sprigs of parsley. And the Vic has tried to keep up with the times. When the state government banned smoking in almost all bars and restaurants in Colorado, the Vic needed ten full days to scrub out a century of smoke from its plaster walls, hardwood floor, and tin tile ceiling. There are still longbeards drinking alone at the bar, but now there's a new crowd too. "Before the [smoking] ban went into effect, a lot of people would look in and would walk away," the Vic owner told the local paper. "Now I see them look in, and they don't feel as excluded and offended."

No offense in the Vic? Gottlieb and I were both incredulous. The joint sure looked scrubbed down, but was it truly clean? On a break between rounds—another Vic patron reminds me that you can't buy beer, you can only rent it—I see what somebody has scrawled on the quarters-only machine for glow-in-the-dark condoms: "*In case of product failure, return baby here.*"

It would take a lot more than ten days of Mr. Clean to scrub the raunch from the Vic.

After solving all the world's problems but few of our own, Gottlieb and I ramble out of the Vic in search of some solid carbs. A few blocks from the bar I run into a neighbor from Denver who grew up in Salida. She tells us about a local tradition: Every year in her youth some teenager would drink enough to try to climb to the top of the town's 365-foot smelter smokestack, where, legend held, a gold coin was stashed.

Gottlieb and I eye each other. I tell my neighbor: What do we look like—teenagers? She laughs hard enough to make me hope she's laughing with us, not at us, but I wonder how long it will take for me to wash off the smell of the Vic.

The good news is, she knows the local restaurants. She points us toward a Mexican joint. It even has *mole*.

We roll out of the restaurant in time to see the sun set behind Mount Shavano and its renowned Angel of Shavano, a 1,400-foot snow figure with upstretched wings that, according to local legend, was formed when an Indian maiden sacrificed herself to the rain gods to spare the region from a crippling drought.

Beer, *mole,* and an angel—Gottlieb and I fell asleep in a friend's cabin hoping the exorcism of his old Salida demons was complete.

"Mind if I go first?"

"Actually, I'd kind of like to."

"You sure?"

"Yep."

"We'll take turns, then."

Silence.

Gottlieb and I are on the trail by 4 a.m., but already bickering like an old married couple. This is strange, because we hardly ever argue, even though I've known him almost as long as I've known my wife. Still, there is no debating the point each is trying to make: After last night's training meal gone bad, neither of us wants to be on a steep trail up a mountain behind the other.

Citing the old Cold War credo of mutual assured destruction, we spread out on the trail and grind ahead. It is steep, and cold, and dark, and steep. Luckily, we're both moving at the same pace, though I seem to be ducking into the trees more than he.

Which turns out to be the cause of a serious problem. On one sojourn into the trees we lose the trail. We backtrack, but can't find the trail again. Thinking we doubled back too far, we push forward again, and stumble onto the trail. Several hundred feet up a very punishing grade, we decide our trail isn't really a people trail, but an elk trail. We can descend again to look for the true path, or cling to our hard-won altitude gain and just push forward from here. The mountain always goes up, right? We push on.

Unfortunately, Mount Shavano pushes back. In the predawn gloom we've worked mightily to place ourselves in the middle of an incredibly muddy and steep blow-down of lodgepole pines—a vast swath of forest with logs dumped like a child's game of pick-up-sticks.

Sweat is poured. Thighs are burned. Foul language is exchanged.

After the sixty-seventh time I trip over a fallen tree trunk, I hear something. It's breathing hard, and it's just on the other side of a pile of logs. I raise my hiking poles as if they're sabers.

What emerges from the deadfall is something scary, but not on four legs. It's a hunchbacked man, in his sixties at least, wearing a pirate's bandanna and shorts on a morning when my car thermometer at the warmer, lower elevation at the trailhead read 28 degrees. He's hiking with a six-foot wooden staff that looks as if it was last carried by Moses, which is fitting, because right now we are all wandering lost in the wilderness.

"Are you on the trail?" he asks.

"Not that I know of," I reply.

"Do you see a trail?"

"No."

"Damn."

All three of us crash upward through the brush until Gottlieb trips, loses a pole, and watches it roll forty feet downhill. I'd walk back down to retrieve it, but I have another date with last night's dinner. Our new companion wisely continues climbing, and he moves at a pace I can only envy. My face should be turning red from being smoked up a snowy mountain by a Moses in shorts, but my heart has no blood to spare for mere color. I feel like I'm scratching and clawing my way up a wall, underwater, around and over a million track hurdles set in position by a bouncing tornado.

The deadfall gnaws my ankles, shins, and thighs, and I'm starting to feel sorry for myself. Ahead, though, I see the old guy bent over at the waist and leaning hard on his staff.

"You OK?" I ask.

"I'm handicapped," he replies. "My calves are messed up."

"Can I help?"

"Nah—go ahead."

So we do, still humbled by the fact that we were getting beat up the mountain by an old man in shorts with a physical disability.

After a couple hundred more vertical feet, the sun is finally high enough for us to turn off our headlamps, and we spot a well-crafted trail ahead. Gottlieb and I stop, blow out our lungs, and try to force down some trail mix for energy. During our pause, however, we hear a new sound below us: click, clack, click. It's the staff of Moses, banging into deadfall. We call out that we've found the trail, and in return hear a grateful grunt, followed by clicks and clacks that draw nearer. He catches up to us, but doubles over again to stretch his calves. Go ahead, he urges us, and we do.

We reach tree line, and the Angel of Shavano greets us with open wings. It's a marvelous sight—a snow formation on the flanks of a mountain as tall as the biggest skyscraper in America. I'm tempted to use my axe and crampons to climb directly up the angel's body, but Gottlieb doesn't have snow gear. When I tell Gottlieb about my wife's latest fear—that some deranged climber will whack me on the back of the head with an axe, then save my life to become a public hero—Gottlieb sets me straight: I know your friends, he says, and if I saved you, nobody would consider me a hero.

Just as I'm about to smack him with a hiking pole, we hear it again: click, clack, click. Up hobbles the old guy. I tell him I feel like Captain Hook being stalked by the clock-eating crocodile in *Peter Pan*. He laughs.

He's Michael Bodine, sixty-two, a Boeing engineer from Wichita, Kansas, better known to his family and friends as Bulldog. Twenty-five years ago the muscles in his calves and feet started wasting away, and doctors told Bulldog he had Lou Gehrig's disease, which is fatal. He got a handicapped-parking placard for his car and spent six years learning how to walk again. When he did not die, he celebrated by summiting eleven Colorado Fourteeners and the high points of thirty-one states. On flat sidewalks in town he still stumbles with a permanent limp, but the doctors have changed their initial diagnosis. Nobody knows for certain what's gotten into Bulldog's legs. He wore long pants once on a hike in January, but airs out the gams the rest of the year. He starts and finishes his climbs by attending Mass.

We hike together until Bulldog again stops to stretch his calves. He waves Gottlieb and me ahead, and we progress up the mountain in this strange pattern: Up two hundred yards, blow, click, clack, click, up another two hundred yards, blow, click, clack, click, repeat. Between gasps I dream wistfully of Peter Pan and his ability to fly to this summit. Gottlieb and I are hurting; Bulldog is relentless. There seems an easier way up looping around to our right, but Bulldog insists that straight up the talus is the way to go. We are too tired to argue with a man in shorts at 13,500 feet. Straight up it is.

The higher we go, the more we see that Bulldog is right. The stylish way to summit would be to hop higher from boulder to boulder, but we're so wiped out that we stagger like Frankensteins. In the last two hundred feet we're passed by two college girls. They look fresh. We look like we've climbed 4,600 vertical feet after four beers and a burrito. They summit first.

It's a spectacular day, sunny and calm, and we soak in the views. We can see a million snowcapped peaks, but there's no sign of Bulldog. Did he run out of gas? Turn around? Stop for a very extended stretch?

Gottlieb and I are too preoccupied with another problem to worry about the absent click, clack, and click. To the northwest is Tabeguache Peak, our intended second summit of the day, and it looks very scary indeed: flanked with forbiddingly steep gullies, filled with snow, and beneath a ridge lorded over by a fat and potentially unstable cornice. While Shavano looks ready for summer, Tabeguache keeps scheduling long and nasty playdates with Old Man Winter.

We talk with the two young women. They decide the trip to Tabeguache looks bad. I know they're right, but I don't want to hear it. It was five hard miles to reach the top of Shavano, and I'm nearly spent. If I don't go for Tabeguache now—an out-and-back trip of two miles and a thousand feet of climbing—I'll have to retrace all my painful bootsteps up Shavano and then to Tabeguache later this summer.

Hoping against hope, I point to the unclimbed peak and ask Gottlieb: Whaddya think?

"I think I don't want to die today," he says.

I put on my hurt-puppy-dog eyes, but to no avail. (Most puppy dogs don't have bloodshot eyes.) The women leave. Gottlieb and I plop our sorry butts on a rock, bask in the sun, and try to work up the energy to chew our peanut-butter-and-jelly sandwiches. I can't help but peek over at Tabeguache, and think about doing this all again after the snow melts. I cringe. Gottlieb edges toward a nap. For ten minutes we're the only ones at 14,231 feet, and the peace and beauty and quiet, combined with my sheer exhaustion, push me to the edge of tears.

Then the girls return with the force of a cavalry charge.

"You're back?" Gottlieb asks.

"We're going to Tabeguache," one replies.

"Tabeguache! You sure? What happened?"

What happened was, they met the man with the Moses stick. Bulldog told them about a route below the cornice that skirted many of the dangerous snowfields. It's not as bad as it looks, he told them, which is a fairly remarkable statement, because we learned earlier this day that Bulldog has never even seen Tabeguache. At this moment, he's somewhere on the flanks of Shavano, girding himself for not one summit but two.

The women take off. We wait for Bulldog.

He doesn't disappoint. When he reaches the summit of Shavano, he keels over so far on his rod that his forehead nearly hits his knees. We give him a minute, then interrogate him like cops on overtime: What do you know about this Tabeguache route? (Just what some guy in the parking lot told him.) Have you ever done it yourself? (No.) Where is it? (Below the ridge cornice.)

We look to Tabeguache. The girls have lost five hundred feet of elevation by descending the northwest ridge of Shavano, and have begun to cross the first snowfield of Tabeguache. They're making good time.

"Well, maybe we can head down and just eyeball it a little closer," I say.

Gottlieb agrees, but uses his deepest voice to add: No guarantees.

Bulldog takes off like a heat-seeking missile.

One hour later, amazingly, surprisingly, gratefully, we're standing on the summit of Tabeguache Peak. Neither Gottlieb nor I can bury our grins: We thought we were done, but we weren't. There is no greater thrill than to be shot at and missed.

Bulldog plants his staff in the snowy crown of Tabeguache and keels over again. I wait a few minutes for him to erect himself, then offer up my palm. I want to shake your hand, I tell him. If not for you, we wouldn't have done this.

Gottlieb tells him, "You are one tough SOB."

He smiles. We all know he's right.

Chapter 9

Punishment

MOUNT COLUMBIA 14,077'

Some mountains are regal. They tower over their surrounding valleys and dominate the landscape for miles around. Their summits are tiny, their shoulders steep. With snow up high and wildflowers down low, they inspire painters and poets, dreamers and troubadours. Tourists love to gape at them. Photographers love to shoot them. And, most of all, climbers love to scale them.

Mount Columbia is not one these mountains.

It is gray and lumpy, barren and broad, a dismal wart that rises unfortunately in a high-country neighborhood where the other peaks are majestic and muscling upward with style and grace. Though this peak had been discovered by white men about the time of the Pikes Peak gold rush, nobody bothered naming it until 1916, when a native son of Denver, Roger Toll, summited the skanky cobble pile and lacked the inspiration to bestow upon it any local moniker. Other peaks in the area had already been named by alumni after Harvard, Yale, and Princeton, so Toll continued the ignoble tradition and deemed his hulking heap Columbia, as if an ivied institution with faux Greek architecture on the tweedy side of the Hudson had any connection whatsoever to Colorado and the burly wilderness.

Calling a Rocky Mountain "Columbia" makes about as much sense as calling a hardscrabble Texas railroad town "Paris." Alas, both names have stuck around, though Toll decidedly did not, going on to serve as the trailblazing superintendent of the national parks at Yellowstone, Rocky Mountain, and Mount Rainier, which thankfully were not renamed Brownstone, Dartmountain, and Mount Penn.

All of which meant there was a lousy peak over 14,000 feet with a lousy name that we had to climb in Colorado.

I say we, because on this Columbia expedition there were two—me and StevieTwoShoes. We met at the trailhead at dusk and backpacked in four miles and 2,000 vertical feet to make summit day shorter and sweeter. He brought a tent. That night, on just our second man-date, we slept next to each other, which made me think the relationship was progressing swiftly, though we did set up our mummy bags so one man's feet were in the other man's face. I slept on my side to prevent any chance whatsoever of accidental touching.

Because the summit-day weather forecast called for nasty thunderstorms—what was it with StevieTwoShoes and airborne electricity?—we wanted an early start.

We launch in the early-morning dark and promptly get lost. After retracing our steps with headlamps, we find another trail, which turns out to be another dead-end spur. We slide across a narrow snow band, look up, and see it: 1,600 vertical feet of pain and misery. It's Columbia's notorious scree field. Rotten, slippery, and steep, a scree field is a mass of broken rocks, fist-size or smaller, that moves when you try to walk on it. Scree is what results when talus breaks down.

The larger chunks of scree make me slide; the tiny, sharper pieces wedge between my socks and boots.

I slip. I curse.

I fall. I curse.

I twist an ankle. I really curse.

StevieTwoShoes, however, with his size 13 hooves, just glides on up. He's in full rocketman mode, and there's no way I can stop him or even catch him. I struggle alone. I slip, again and again and again, and conclude it's a good thing there are no children around, because they would be learning all kinds of new and truly vile vocabulary.

Stevie is somewhere up on the ridge; I'm down here in agony. I could quit, but that would be stupid, because then I'd have suffered this far for no reason at all.

When I sit on a rock with hopes of regaining my composure, I slide downhill several feet. On top of the twisted ankle and the scabbed knees I now have a bloody ass. This mountain is really, really, really pissing me off.

I decide to grunt and bear it, training my concentration on the closeness of my next step instead of the distance from the far ridge. For every three steps up, I slide two back. This slope is made of greased marbles. If I could make my feet go faster, I'd lose less ground, but my heart and lungs and thighs aren't willing to go along with that deal. StevieTwoShoes is somewhere over the horizon.

Bloody, bruised, and battered, I finally make the ridge, and am grateful to see the summit just ahead. When I get there, though, I see it's just a lump on the ridge. Another false summit—just like the false summits StevieTwoShoes and I endured on Mount Massive.

And speaking of StevieTwoShoes—where is he? There's another false summit ahead, and he's not on it. Or on the one that follows. No way I could have passed him again, is there?

There's not. When I finally stumble to the true top, I find Stevie TwoShoes basking in the sun like a sleepy marmot. I ask how long he's been waiting. He says forty-five minutes, but I think he's lowballing me to make me feel better. We spend some time lollygagging on the summit—he, enjoying the day; me, giving my open wounds time to coagulate—and retreat down the ridge.

Back on the evil, nasty, ugly slope of loose rock, I try to ski the scree with my boots but end up glissading the gravel with my butt. Stevie, however, remains as nimble and sure-footed as a lumberjack in a logrolling contest. I am flabbergasted.

A hundred yards from the bottom of the worst stuff, however, TwoShoes trips and sends both shoes flying. I can't help but laugh. I apologize, and laugh some more. Luckily he laughs too.

We hit rock bottom at camp, and are grateful for the solid ground.

He decides to stay another night to climb Mount Harvard, which is in the same basin, but I want out of here. I give him my trail munchies, wish him luck, and reconsider my mockery of Roger Toll's 1916 nomenclature decision.

Hey, Columbia U.—you can keep your damn mountain.

Chapter 10

Blown Away

MOUNT EVANS 14,265'
MOUNT BIERSTADT 14,060'

The slippery-slide fiasco on Mount Columbia did considerable bruising to my ego—and my shin, and my hip, and my butt—so I looked for another climb that would build confidence. After searching maps all over the state, I realized I had no close and easy peak to do, and no one to do it with. My legs were finally growing muscles. I could use that newfound strength to mow the lawn, but I waited a few seconds to let that strange urge pass.

Sitting at home, spinning my wheels, I figured I could do the same thing in a more productive way. Bright idea: Mount Evans, on my bike.

The dominant snowcapped peak seen from downtown Denver, Mount Evans is home to North America's highest paved road. Like many mountaineering feats, the battle to build it resulted from a combination of jealousy and one-upmanship.

Though the first Colorado scramble for riches was routinely described as the Pikes Peak Gold Rush, the reality in the 1860s was that hardly any gold was found around Pikes Peak. Most of it was sixty miles north, in the shadow of another Fourteener, then called Mount Rosalie, where Denver, Idaho Springs, and Central City were becoming mining boomtowns. Nevertheless, Pikes Peak got all the fame, partly because it was so visible to wagon trains approaching from the eastern Plains, and partly because it was pumped up so much by local promoters. By 1888, Pikes Peak had a carriage road built to the summit. A cog railway soon followed. The Pikes Peak region may not have had much gold, but it was fashioning itself into a tourism magnet.

In 1891, as the gold mines around Mount Rosalie had started to play out, prospectors hit pay dirt just southwest of Pikes Peak. That lode in Cripple Creek became the richest in Colorado history, and Denver's rival city to the south, Colorado Springs, was suddenly flush with wealth—and searching for something unique to spend it on. This was no easy task. Colorado's best opera house was already in Denver; the best debauchery was already in Leadville; and the best new invention, electric power, was already running a mine in Telluride, thanks to the joint work of Nikola Tesla and George Westinghouse.

So in 1915, mining magnate Spencer Penrose decided that the bragging rights for Colorado Springs would be the best, or at least the highest, road for an automobile in the world. A year and $500,000 later, Pikes Peak had its highway.

Denver would not concede such glory so easily. It was bad enough that the state's Second City was successfully mining so much gold. Denver didn't want it to successfully mine so many tourist wallets too. As the leader of the state's most populous city, Denver mayor Robert Speer persuaded lawmakers to ante up the money for an automobile road up its backyard peak, which had been renamed Mount Evans after the second territorial governor of Colorado.

The Pikes Peak road reached its summit at 14,115, but the Mount Evans Road topped out at 14,130 feet, meaning Denver had won the claim to the highest paved road by a full 20 feet. Nanny-nanny boo-boo!

Today the dirt road up Pikes Peak draws ten times more drivers than the higher, paved highway up Mount Evans. With the price of popularity, however, came more regulation. Pikes Peak bans uphill bicycle traffic; Mount Evans doesn't. Sounded like an opening to me.

An instructor in my winter spinning class—a gray-haired man older than I—had pedaled up Mount Evans in less than three hours. During our hardest spin classes, I had always wondered whether the instructor was secretly slacking off by turning down the resistance on his wheels while urging us to friction up. How else could he talk so easily while pedaling so swiftly? A ride up Mount Evans would be my way to find out.

The spin teacher had always started his rides down the highway at Idaho Springs on a skinny-tire road bike. My mountain bike's tires are so fat and so knobby that I grant myself permission (well, an excuse) to cut out thirteen miles of road and 3,000 feet of climbing by starting instead at the base of the Mount Evans toll road, near Echo Lake.

First, of course, I need to beg an exemption from the no-solo rule. I tell Merrill the truth: It's a road, there are lots of people, the trailhead is only about an hour from home, I'll be back in time to grocery-shop and cook dinner for the family.

Shop and cook dinner? Bingo.

And so I'm off.

The first two miles are absolutely wonderful. At 7 a.m., I have the road to myself. From the spruce forest on my left buzzes a raspy chorus of *chicka dzee dzee dzee*—mountain chickadees—while my right bubbles with the boisterous sopranos of *CHEESEburger CHEESEburger CHEESE*—ruby-crowned kinglets. I can't imagine a prettier morning serenade. It all seems too easy and too fun. If I were hiking, I'd assume I was lost, because this path is far too gentle for any real Fourteener.

Just as I settle into a pleasant cadence I notice that the treetops are swaying. Though I'm all warm and cozy down here among the pine boughs, I wonder what the weather is doing above me. No clouds anywhere. A sweat-free Fourteener at 10 mph—it feels too good to be true.

It is. Twenty pedal turns before timberline, I see the spruces bending and twisting. I reach the last tree and brace myself, but learn the issue isn't mere wind. It's a gale, and it slams me. I jam my right foot to the ground just to keep from falling over, except that I do anyway, and the top tube of the bike rams me in the crotch on my way down. I can't breathe. I'm assuming the wind has been knocked out of me, but there was never much oxygen to start with at 12,000 feet. I fold like a taco. I still can't breathe. I point my head into the wind, open my mouth, and let the wind force open my lungs and jump-start the CPR. If only there were some straightforward way to stop throbbing in the nether regions.

As I stand on the side of the road, mouth agape and wind blasting two streams of tears sideways from my ducts and directly into my ears, two men on road bikes pedal by.

The front rider asks: You OK?

I nod.

The trailing rider asks: You sure?

He whizzes by before I can reconsider.

By the time I can breathe freely again while still standing upright, I notice an unexpected change: That gale has relaxed into a mere stiff wind. I saddle up, hop off the bike seat from pain, wait a few more minutes for the throbbing to subside, and hop on again. What knocked me off before was a sudden gust, but now it's all a steady 20-mph blow. My balance is fine. My endurance is not. I hadn't been counting on a headwind while pedaling uphill. The nice thing is, one of my worst pet peeves for biking—sweat running down my frictionless forehead and stinging my eyes—is not an issue here. The wind transports all my sweat directly to Nebraska.

As the road switchbacks higher, the wind grows stronger—so strong that I have to lean left on my bike while turning right. My legs can't take much more of this. At 13,600 feet, I coast to a stop, and a surprise gale knocks me on my butt again. This time the bike falls on my lap too.

Squirming like an upside-down turtle, I struggle to untangle my handlebar from the chinstrap of my helmet when three more no-body-fat guys on road bikes spin by.

The first one asks: On a mountain bike?

The second: Think he'll make it?

The third: He looks pretty beat up. You OK?

Before I can answer, they cruise past at double my best speed of the day.

My manhood may be bruised, but it is not removed. I right myself and crank hard to catch those smug bastards, but nearly explode my heart after ten pedal turns. I rest again, this time bracing myself with both feet, and watch the road bikers glide up and around the next switchback.

I revert to my steady-as-an-ox mode, the method that seems to work for hiking. Slowly and surely, but painfully, I gain the parking lot at the top of the mountain. I struggle over to the three road bikers, but they click their cleated shoes into their pedals and set off back down the mountain.

What? No summit? The top of Mount Evans is still another 134 feet above the parking lot. I feel like heckling the road bikers. Oh, road bikers—too tired to try for the top today? But the wind is too loud to hear anything.

So I decide to summit by myself. I start pushing my bike up the hiking trail, but splat in the ankle-deep snow. My third fall of the day. I ditch my bike and scramble through snow until I finally stand atop Mount Evans. I try to take a picture of myself with one hand while using the other to hang on to a rock that, I'm hoping, will keep me from parachuting back to Denver.

I slip and slide back down to my bike in the parking lot, where my watch tells me four hours have elapsed since I first started pedaling this morning. In other words, I rode half the distance of my spin-class instructor, but needed an extra hour of time. He's no slacker.

In the parking lot a U.S. Forest Service ranger is warning drivers to exercise extreme caution before opening car doors in the wind.

He asks me: Was that you with that bike up on top?

Yep, I tell him.

He pulls a palm-size device out of his pocket.

Here, he says, take a look at this.

It's a wind meter. It reads 42 mph. My IQ feels lower.

Within easy eyesight of the summit of Mount Evans is its ridge-connected partner, Mount Bierstadt, which has the magic ingredients—quick road access from Denver, and a short, well-marked trail to the top—to make it one of the easiest and most popular Fourteeners. Every summer day a conga line of dozens, and sometimes hundreds, of hikers make for the summit. It is almost too much. Because of traffic jams, trail-rutting, and overflows at the vast trailhead parking lot, federal land managers have talked about restricting access on the busiest weekends.

Exhibit No. 1 in the debate whether Fourteeners are being loved to death, Mount Bierstadt and its neighbor were originally a testament to love.

Albert Bierstadt was the richest and most famous American painter of his day, creator of six-by-ten-foot western landscapes for the drawing rooms of eastern industrialists and European royalty in the 1860s and 1870s. Like his contemporary, Thomas Moran of Mount of the Holy Cross fame, Bierstadt liked to climb the peaks he depicted. After logging the first recorded ascent of the tallest peak visible from Denver, he decided to call it Rosalie, after his wife. The shorter Fourteener along the ridge to the west came to be known as Bierstadt.

A husband and wife, connected by solid rock—how romantic!

It was too perfect for the politicians to resist. Three decades after Bierstadt's first climb of Mount Rosalie, a nondescript Colorado legislature decided to rename the mountain after an unremarkable territorial governor, John Evans. Rosalie was shunted aside to a 13,575-foot peak three miles to the southeast.

Despite that unhappy ending, I remained impressed with the tale of devotion great enough for a man to name a mountain after the love of his life. I thought it would be fun to hike the peak with someone special. Alas, my wife had to work that day. Nobody else could swing a midweek day trip.

So with Merrill's permission, I hiked Mount Bierstadt with our dog, Otis. It was his first Fourteener. He seemed to enjoy being on a trail with a hundred or so other people and dogs. He led the whole way, and waited patiently for me. He showed no sign of exhaustion. He celebrated on the top by licking himself.

Chapter 11

The Elephant

MOUNT BELFORD 14,203'
MOUNT OXFORD 14,160'

Even after begging friends, and friends of friends, and acquaintances of friends, and acquaintances of acquaintances, I still had no hiking partners. No luck with man-dates on the Web either. It was June 16, and I still had thirty-five peaks to do. If I weren't telling time these days on a digital watch with an altimeter, I'd say the clock was ticking. I could feel the summer slipping away.

Merrill saw me shifting from frustration to desperation, which meant I was about to plead for relief from the no-solo rule, which meant she would say no, which meant I would roll my eyes and groan, which meant she would invoke the image of our children at a funeral because their father died of a sprained ankle, which meant I would admit once again that climbing was selfish and I was grateful that she was OK with me doing it, which meant she would remind me that she was still losing sleep over it, which meant I would thank her profusely and drop the subject of solo hiking altogether. Again.

Our back-and-forths over my abject failure to find hiking partners started to feel like an endless Ping-Pong rally, except that she never hit the net. Repeating the same debate so many times left both of us suffering from a kind of carpal tunnel syndrome of the brain. It hurt.

Because of either pity or sheer exhaustion, she cast out feelers for me to her own friends and acquaintances. One day, somebody bit.

Mike Brislin was the recent husband of one of Merrill's longtime friends. I knew him mostly as a road warrior—he flew somewhere four days a week for his job—who liked to ride a mountain bike at home on weekends. He had little experience with mountains in Colorado, but was game to try a Fourteener. I asked my wife: You think he could make it? Mike, she said, knew something about overcoming hardship.

Our two-and-a-half-hour drive to the mountains had all the feel of an arranged date. We were polite, curious, and a little bit anxious about how this was going to end up.

Mike's latest Sunday-through-Thursday night work gig was at sea level in Seattle, where he worked as a field manager for a giant business software company. He was nervous about his ability to handle a hike that started at 9,600 feet. His ability made me nervous too, though I didn't say so. My solution was to backpack two miles the evening before and camp at an elevation of 11,200; somebody somewhere once told me that sleeping at altitude helped lowlanders acclimate more quickly.

First we had to get there, though. I was dreading the pack in. The trailhead for Mount Belford and Mount Oxford was the same as for Missouri Mountain. The million switchbacks that had jellified my thighs with Shad and KirkT would jellify them again with Mike B., but this time with an extra twenty-five pounds of gear. Then I remembered my wife's heads-up: Mike had overcome hardship.

At 10,000 feet, with the sweat pouring down our foreheads and the afternoon sun dipping behind the ridgetops, I ask Mike about it. The story is harder than the switchbacks.

Mike was born and raised in South Africa as a white man who hated apartheid and whose family worked a kind of underground railroad for people fighting it. When the government turned over peacefully, he cheered for society but feared for his own prospects. It was the majority's turn. He understood the lust for retribution and didn't want to be part of it.

When he met his wife, Mary, in Johannesburg, they both knew they had to leave. Almost all their white friends were off on what they called their LSD trips—journeys overseas to Look, See, and Decide what country would make the best new home for them. Mike's wife was a travel agent who favored New Zealand. Mike's boss ginned up overseas job prospects for him, but the closest he could come was Australia. Other family had already immigrated to Canada, and lobbied for the newlyweds to join them there.

On June 26, 1999, they all gathered in Johannesburg for a half-Christmas. (It was winter in the Southern Hemisphere.) Mike and Mary had been married only five months, but there was hope for grandchildren and excitement over their impending move, which would be decided after a vacation in Paris and an extended stay near some of Mary's family in Ontario. On the day after exchanging gifts, they planned to ride bikes to watch a rugby game with Mary's brother. She was feeling sleepy, and urged Mike to go on without her.

When Mike returned, Mary suffered a seizure and collapsed. He revived her, then cried to her family in another room to call an ambulance.

Four minutes later, she was dead.

Mary was thirty-three. Mike was thirty-eight.

For days and nights and weeks after, Mike could think of nothing else. How did this happen? Could he have saved her? Why her? Why them? Why now? Family and friends gave him comfort and advice and counseling books, but nothing helped. He was in a bad spiral and he knew it. He had to get out.

Mike worked. He threw himself so wholeheartedly into his job that an eighty-hour workweek became an easy one. The more time he fixed software bugs, the less time he had for grief. When he finished his four-month project in South Africa, his boss offered him time off. Instead, Mike took on another three-week job in Australia, followed by three months in Singapore and six months in Ireland, which he extended to eight months. The work frenzy distracted his mind but exhausted his body. He accepted a six-month sabbatical, and bought an around-the-world plane ticket with fifteen stops. He was on his fifth stop when his mind started whirling again. He threw himself into another job, a two-month gig in western Massachusetts, but knew this was not a healthy way to live. He spent his fortieth birthday in Toronto with Mary's brother, then took off for a two-month trekking trip to South America.

Backpacking around the majestic peaks of Patagonia, he found the mix of immediate challenge—should my next boot step be here or there?—and longer challenge—how can I get my body to cover another eight miles today?—was keeping his brain fully occupied. Hiking became his new medicine for grief.

He returned to work in Massachusetts with new vigor and direction. The boss told Mike he couldn't offer him employment in Australia, but he could get him a pretty good job in the United States. It would still be a travel job, but he could live anywhere in America he wanted.

Anywhere? Anywhere.

Mike chose Denver because it was near the mountains and a more central base for travel than Portland or Seattle. He got an L-1 visa, which let him apply for permanent residency in the United States. His LSD trip was over, and, more importantly, his funk was ebbing.

As a road warrior, he struggled to meet people in his new hometown. He turned to the online dating service Match.com, where he met my wife's friend Tammy, who loved art, film, music, skiing, dogs, and hiking as much as Mike. When they married in 2004, Mike's best man was Mary's brother.

After a story like that, I feel like hugging him, but now it's pitch-dark and we've just cleared the last switchback and it would be awkward to lock in a heartfelt embrace just before we set up our tent. We pile inside—my head by his feet—and wait for exhaustion to overcome us.

I ask Mike what he's learned about grief and the way people react to it.

"Before this experience," he tells me, "if a friend had somebody who died, I used to feel awkward about saying something. I was afraid I'd trigger something for the people. But when I was the grieving party, people were just as afraid around me, and it was very awkward. I appreciated people who just came up to me directly. I learned that the right way to deal with it is just to deal with it. People worry about what they are saying, but it didn't matter what people were saying. It just mattered to me that they were saying it."

He rolled over and was quiet, which left me with my own thoughts. If I lost my wife, I don't know how, or if, I could recover. Having three children made the prospect even worse. When I think of hiking solo, I think of mountains. My wife thinks of grief. Her thoughts last longer.

The next morning we stand at the base of the first climb up Mount Belford. It's a big one—two thousand feet of gain in less than a mile, so steep that we can't see the top from the bottom. My heart's already in my throat just from the short approach to get here, and Mike can see the squeamishness in my face.

Mike points to the daunting pitch. "In Africa, we like to ask a question," he says. "How do you eat an elephant? One bite at a time."

I don't know why I ever doubted Mike's ability to do this hike. He may weigh more and have less experience at altitude, but his spirit is stronger. We summit Belford and see Oxford across the connecting ridge. It's a two-mile, 1,200-foot round-trip sufferfest, and my legs are balking. Mike will have none of that.

Several hours later we are back at my car with two summits in the bag and two bellies full of elephant. We have raw feet, sore knees, and jellified thighs. I ask Mike if his first Fourteeners hurt as much as he expected.

I've learned you can work through a lot, he says, if you take it one bite at a time.

Chapter 12

One Benjamin Franklin

CULEBRA PEAK 14,047'
SAN LUIS PEAK 14,014'

Compared to people in other sports, mountaineers don't complain
much. The refs are never screwing them. Groundskeepers don't make
their roughs too rough or their infields like outfields. Bad weather is
an expected part of the game.

But there is one surefire way in Colorado to turn a hiker into a
whiner. Just mention this place: Culebra Peak.

The only Fourteener encircled by private land, Culebra Peak has
been off-limits to climbers in varying degrees since 1960. That's when
a racist timber baron from North Carolina bought 121 square miles
of land, including the mountain, and set off the West's nastiest range
war in decades.

When Jack Taylor paid $500,000, or less than $7 per acre, for his
ranch in the Sangre de Cristo mountains, he knew there were legal
problems. The tract had been part of a vast nineteenth-century Mexican land grant that encouraged Hispanics to settle the area before it
was claimed by the United States as part of its Manifest Destiny. In
1864, the Mexican owners sold the land to William Gilpin, first territorial governor of Colorado, with this requirement: "All the inhabitants shall have the use of pasture, wood, water, and timber." For
nearly a century, the inhabitants of the town of San Luis, Colorado's

oldest, came to rely on the tract they called La Sierra for firewood for their stoves and irrigation water for their hay and vegetables.

By the time Taylor bought in, San Luis was overwhelmingly Hispanic and overwhelmingly poor. (The Peace Corps had briefly stationed volunteers there for a taste of rural poverty before sending them overseas to assignments in the Third World.)

Taylor had little sympathy for locals. Within months of buying the ranch, he filed lawsuits against local Hispanic sheepherders for supposed grazing damage and started fortifying the tract with new fences, gates, and NO TRESPASSING signs. In the prime of fall wood-gathering season, he sued another four hundred residents to extinguish all their legal claims on the ranch. Locals sued him back.

He carried a handgun everywhere, even while eating breakfast at the local café. It was white European private property vs. Spanish colonial sharing, with plenty of hot tempers to spare. It all boiled over on Thanksgiving Day.

Taylor and two ranch hands were cutting Christmas trees on the ranch when they found a trailer on fire and a tractor with bullet holes. Following horse tracks in the snow, Taylor and his men encountered three local men in their twenties, who said they knew nothing about any vandalism. The locals said they were looking for lost cattle.

Exactly what happened next was a matter of dispute. The result, however, was ugly: One local was knocked unconscious, another suffered a gouged eye, and the third a busted jaw. All three were tied up, pitched into the back of the ranch pickup, and driven to the courthouse in San Luis, where Taylor demanded their arrest.

Instead, the sheriff arrested Taylor and his ranch hands. The district attorney said the three locals had been "sadistically beaten."

That night, a hundred livid locals converged on the courthouse, kicked down a jail door, and shouted for Taylor and his men to be turned over for mob justice. Deputies waved them off with shotguns. The governor traveled to San Luis to calm emotions, but the anger remained raw.

Taylor and his hands were eventually convicted of misdemeanor assault.

The locals were all acquitted of property damage charges.

An uneasy truce resulted. Taylor shelved his major logging plans because few local Hispanics would work for him. San Luis residents started looking elsewhere for firewood and grazing pasture. The lawsuit to end local claims on ranch land bogged down in federal court.

By the early 1970s, however, a wave of Chicano power protests was sweeping the Southwest, and young San Luis men were returning home from the Vietnam War with a new dose of political activism. Four locals beat up Taylor's ranch foreman, but the sheriff backed off any arrest after the men said the foreman had threatened them with a gun.

One night not long after, Taylor was asleep at home when snipers with three rifles shot through the roof of his cabin and blasted apart his left ankle. Ranch employees asked for a police escort to the hospital, but the sheriff provided none. They sneaked Taylor to the emergency room after midnight with no headlights but two loaded guns.

State investigators converged upon the ranch, and a federal grand jury convened, but no one was ever charged in the shooting.

While trying to heal his ankle, Taylor shot himself in the political foot with a story in the *New Yorker* magazine that explained why he was so adamant about ending historic use of the ranch property: "I merely had the fortitude to do what's necessary. If I hadn't, this thing would linger on forever. It would have been a lot cheaper to pay someone off, but it kind of goes against the grain to do everything the Mexican way—with bribery." He went on to note that as a native of the South, he was no stranger to racial conflict. "I don't hate Nigras. I hate the people who are trying to shove them down our throats."

Taylor retreated home to North Carolina. When he died in 1988, the land-use lawsuit still churned in court. Locals hoped that his son, Zack, would be a less confrontational owner, but he opened the ranch to truly wide-scale logging.

With contracts to chainsaw up to 210 million board feet of lumber, enough to build 35,000 houses, the Taylor family was hoping to finally start making some significant money from its Colorado ranch.

Opposition was large, fierce, and immediate. Out-of-town environmentalists decried massive logging; neighboring farmers in San Luis feared it would clog creeks with silt and ruin their irrigation water supply. For two summers, protesters locked themselves to gates and blocked logging trucks with human chains. Loggers tried to clear the roads by flashing guns. Dozens were arrested. The sheriff, with only a nine-person jail, pleaded for reinforcements.

Zack Taylor tried to buy peace by offering to give away 2,500 acres for recreational use, but the deal was good only if locals would back out of the continuing land-use lawsuit. That offer went nowhere.

Ground down and exhausted, Taylor finally gave up. In a series of transactions that finished in 1999, the Taylor family sold the ranch for a reported $23 million.

Locals and climbers were thrilled. Would this finally mean free and open access to Culebra Peak? Sometimes over the years the Taylors had completely shut down the mountain; other times they would charge $25 or $40 for a hike. Shaking down dirtbag hikers for an access fee—the greed!

If anybody thought the new owner would be less interested in money, they were in for a rude surprise. The buyer was Lou Pai, the Enron executive who made more money than anyone—an estimated $270 million—from the crooked Houston energy trading company.

In Colorado, Pai introduced himself to his new neighbors by closing the ranch to absolutely all hiking. The Colorado Mountain Club sent begging letters: There were people who had spent years climbing fifty-three Fourteeners, and needed only Culebra to complete the list. The letters went unanswered. When somebody finally reached Pai's lawyer, he said Pai had no interest in opening his peak to outsiders.

Besides, Pai was more interested in mountains made of gyrating silicon. At one point, because of Pai's repeated escapades, Enron chief executive Ken Lay sent out a companywide memo banning employee reimbursements at strip clubs. (Pai and some other Enron executives were once reported to have dropped $800 on a single strip-club lunch.) After striking it rich at Enron, Pai dumped his wife for a peeler.

Though the stories of financial abuse at Enron were legion, Pai distinguished himself by repeatedly summoning the company jet forty miles from its hangar in Houston to another airport closer to his suburban home—and then flying him and his new stripper bride to the Culebra Peak ranch. Each flight was reported to have cost Enron $45,000.

Locals also noticed a big difference during the reign of Pai: He hired many more security guards than the Taylors. And Pai's guards couldn't be bribed to turn the other way during firewood gathering.

When the Enron financial scandal broke, journalists often depicted a ranch with a 14,000-foot mountain as an icon of Enron excess. One author said locals had even started calling the peak Mount Pai, but I found other locals more dubious. There was no need to rename a peak after a shifty, slimy, coldhearted executive when the mountain already carried such a fitting moniker. In Spanish, the word *culebra* means "snake."

Sometimes even a reptile cares what others think of him. After two years of pleading, Pai finally opened the mountain to a single hike of twenty-five people, at a cost of $25 each. Demand was so high the Colorado Mountain Club had to stage a raffle. Dozens were shut out.

In 2002, however, something truly remarkable happened. The Colorado Supreme Court granted the people of San Luis victory in their generations-old lawsuit over land access. For the first time since Eisenhower was president, La Sierra was to be open for use not just by the wealthy above the ranch gates, but also by people down in the valley.

Exactly how this would happen was still open to debate in the courts. While his attorneys battled with judges over logistics, Pai tried to build up some goodwill by opening the ranch to seventy-five hikers in the summer after the state supreme court decision, and seventy-five in the summer after that. He even let twenty-five people set foot upon the ranch's 13,908-foot Red Mountain, just down the ridge from Culebra.

By the summer of 2004, the courts made it clear that Pai's big mountain spread no longer belonged solely to him. Pai wanted no part of that, and he sold out to another pair of Texans, Bobby Hill and Richard Welch, who renamed the spread Cielo Vista, or Heavenly View. The reported purchase price: $40 million.

With the new owners came a new access policy. The good news was that just about anybody could climb. The bad news was the cost went up, really up—$100 per person in summer, $200 per person in winter, and $50 per dog. When climbers bellyached about the stiff hiking fee, Bobby Hill replied, "If folks don't like the fact that they have to pay a hundred dollars, I really don't mind that. They weren't around when it was time to write a check for the ranch." Hill himself had never stood on the summit of his own Fourteener. Maybe someday with a helicopter, he said.

In a state with more than four thousand free peaks, could one jaunt up one mountain really be worth as much as the cost of twenty six-packs of beer?

It is. The one big advantage of decades of no public access, it turns out, is decades of no public access. Culebra Peak is the only Colorado Fourteener—and one of the few prominent mountains anywhere— with no trails. The only footprint I saw all day during my hike belonged to an elk.

This is a pretty remarkable accomplishment, considering there were seventeen of us on the mountain that day. The group hike was set up on the 14ers.com Web site by a guy from Reno, Nevada, but I felt like I was the one gambling. What if I didn't fit in with these hardcore climbers? Could I keep up with anybody? If people saw me hiking like a turtle, would I be outed on the Web—and lose any chance of another man-date?

I confessed my fears over beers at a bar the night before with StevieTwoShoes, who was also joining the group hike. He assured me I'd do fine. If he weren't nearly a generation younger than me (seventeen years), I'd swear he was talking to me like a kind older uncle. I tried to repay his confidence by serving as his wingman to the young women—climbers, all—on the next barstools, but likely did more damage than good. I should have learned my lesson in the Mount Princeton hot springs, and remained naturally invisible, or at least silent.

The next morning a Cielo Vista ranch hand met us at the gate, where we signed away our lives on a legal waiver and forked over our Benjamin Franklins and Andrew Jacksons. The ranch hand stuffed the very fat wad of bills under the windshield wiper of his pickup truck. Good thing the wiper blade was supersized; the large cash transaction in the middle of nowhere had the feel of a sizable drug deal, except that the addiction for these junkies was altitude.

At the trailhead, the group sorts out according to nervous energy—taut people with no body fat who are nervous about their ability to be first up the mountain; huskier people like me who are nervous about their ability to survive the mountain; flatlanders who are nervous about their ability to breathe on the mountain; and single people under the age of thirty who are nervous about their ability to interest each other on and off the mountain.

I duck behind a tree to recycle some morning tea, and return to the trailhead to find the entire group missing. They've already started up the mountain. Alone on the caboose on the loneliest Fourteener isn't the best way to meet new climbing partners, so I speed up and try to catch the locomotive.

Fat chance. I hustle and struggle and finally catch Jeff Haas, fifty-three, a criminal defense lawyer from Tyler, Texas. He had driven eight hundred miles to climb this peak. Hiking Colorado mountains, he tells me, is a great change of pace from his hometown and his work. (After our hike he was assigned to represent a man accused of capital murder after police found his girlfriend dead and mutilated, an ear boiling in a pot on a kitchen stove, and a plate of human flesh with a fork on the kitchen table.)

Haas had hiked the previous day to San Luis's hilltop Stations of the Cross shrine, partly for inspiration and partly for perspiration. Last night in the Mexican restaurant he had been a fun but sometimes clumsy raconteur. When a straight female prison guard bemoaned the attention she gets from women in bars, the lawyer announced that if he were a lesbian, he would hit on her too.

Though he seemed to have a deep reservoir of stories last night over margaritas, he's all business this morning on the mountain. I try to keep the conversation rolling, but he seems consumed with watching the other hikers zoom up the peak. I'm used to being last; he isn't. He stops for a blow and urges me ahead. I go.

I hike alone for a good half-hour, and I do mean good. There's something magical about Culebra Peak. The quiet, the snow without footprints, the freedom to go wherever I choose because there is no trail—it's all invigorating. I want this feeling to go on and on and on.

Of course it doesn't, but I don't complain. From behind me approaches a young woman in black pants and black coat, with a blond ponytail and something peculiar strapped to her backpack: a purple velvet pimp hat with leopard trim. The woman is Caroline Moore, girlfriend of the Talus Monkey. It's her first major hike since David Worthington's awful accident, and she's carrying his hat to the summit of Culebra as a tribute.

I introduce myself, express my sympathies, and ask how she's doing.

She's been better.

Is it hard to hike again?

It is, but not hiking is even worse.

I ask how she got started on Fourteeners.

It was her father. He loved the mountains, and used to insist that the whole family join him on at least one Fourteener hike every summer. She started at age ten on Quandary Peak. She hated it—the predawn wake-up, the long drive in the dark to the trailhead, the incredibly hard work up the mountain, the whole idea of a full day away from her fourth-grade friends. She stopped hiking mountains as soon as her dad stopped making her hike mountains. Four summers ago, though, a college friend announced plans to try Tabeguache Peak. She tagged along, and got bitten by the Fourteeners bug. By the time she met the Talus Monkey, she had decided to climb them all. She wanted to hike enough to be able to finish with her father, who had kept climbing through the years and now had only a handful of peaks remaining. Caroline had brought David along on a hike up Mount Buckskin, elevation 13,865 feet, with her father. Her father liked the Monkey. This was the summer Caroline and her dad were going to finish together. David Worthington was going to help her do that.

The whole time she talks, I notice Caroline doing something odd. While I hike straight up the mountain, she walks in zigzags. Taking twice as many steps as I, and covering twice the distance, she is slowing her progress up the mountain to match my pace.

I thank her. I wish her well. She stops making her own switchbacks and beelines up the mountain at double my speed until she and the purple pimp hat disappear over a high ridge.

Somehow I catch other women up the mountain and we pass the time talking about dental X-rays, fly-fishing the Rockies, and living with teenagers. (Unfortunately, there was obvious advice for only the first two issues.) We're so busy blabbing that we hardly notice when all the up on the mountain is about to turn into down. We reach the summit, and win an ovation from the speed demons now lounging on top.

We wait for more finishers, then gather closely on the mountaintop. The correctional officer hands everyone a SpongeBob SquarePants paper cup filled with Mountain Dew, and KirkT, my acrobatic climbing partner from Missouri Mountain, leads us all in a summit toast to the Talus Monkey.

A small group continues another mile on a high ridge to summit Red Mountain, where StevieTwoShoes, who had greeted me on Mount Massive with the nastiest Ghostface Killah, tells the cute single women on this peak about his love for the movie *Titanic* and the saccharine belter Celine Dion. It's hard to tell which intoxicant is more powerful for men—altitude or pheromones.

As a happily married man, I have other priorities, the most important one being a requirement to find a hiking partner for some peak, any peak, on the next day. I try to ingratiate myself with several groups of people descending Culebra, but everyone is either returning home or claiming other plans. While unlacing my boots at the end of the hike, I hear a rumor that someone else is fishing for a partner.

His name is Prakash Manley. We agree to try to hash out a climbing plan in town at a restaurant, which presents an awkward situation for me, because after this long hike I am craving a juicy bacon cheeseburger and Prakash is an Indian national. I really, really, really don't want to offend the religious sensitivities of a potential hiking partner, so I order something bland with chicken. Prakash follows by ordering a rib-eye steak, medium-rare. He must have seen my eyebrows rocket past my hairline, because he quickly explains, "In India, I didn't eat beef or climb mountains, but I'm trying to make up for it here."

We have no problem agreeing on a hike—San Luis Peak.

If Culebra is the least-hiked Fourteener, then San Luis is the least-seen peak. The shortest and easiest way to reach the trailhead is by driving fifty miles of washboarded dirt roads. The county containing San Luis Peak is the size of Rhode Island and Delaware combined, but it lacks a single traffic light.

Prakash and I drive up in our separate cars to the San Luis trailhead and find another pair of hikers has claimed the only flat and shaded camping spot. Prakash pitches his tent so that his head is upslope. I park my truck, where I'll be sleeping, in the same direction. It's still an hour to sunset. On this day we have already climbed a 14,000-foot mountain and driven nearly four hours to reach this spot. We have not showered, not shaved, and not even changed our clothes. I am disgusted with myself, but remain absolutely irresistible to mosquitoes. I swat a fat one on my ear—blood in my palm!—and the two other guys in the primo campsite interpret this to be a wave howdy. They motion over Prakash and me.

Beneath the trees they have constructed a backcountry palace. There are coolers and a gas lantern and bag after bag after bag of junk food. They must see me salivating, because they offer me Doritos. Feeling guilty that I have nothing to offer in return, I say no. They offer cold beer. I cannot resist. Two gulps later and I'm elbow-deep in the bag of Doritos. They offer us fried chicken, which I decline, but a second cold and opened beer is placed in my hand before I can say no. Not that I would have said no.

So, one of the campers says, you guys are dirtbagging it?

My instinct is to say, no, I'm not a dirtbagger. I am forty-five years old and I have a wife and three kids and a dog and a mortgage. Given the circumstances, though, I am in no position to deny my dirtbaggery. I tell them my middle-aged bona fides, then seize another fistful of Doritos. Yeah, I'm a dirtbagger.

I also am a curiosity object to the two campers, who seem bemused that Prakash, who is a reedy and bearded twenty-six-year-old Indian, and I, who ain't, have traveled so far to hike a mountain together after having spent a grand total of about forty-five minutes with each other.

I ask the campers: Do you guys know each other pretty well?

One replies: Well, let me tell you a story.

Turns out both these guys are physicians from the suburbs of Denver. Not long ago, when one doc was turning forty, his wife decided to throw him a very dignified birthday party. Attendees wore fine cocktail apparel and nibbled on fine hors d'oeuvres and listened to fine background music. Just as all the fine conversation was about to reach a crescendo, the friend motioned the birthday boy into the center of the gathering and presented his gift.

It was a three-hundred-pound stripper.

The surprise peeler took the celebration in a direction that the wife hadn't anticipated—horror and humiliation had not been mentioned on the party invitations—and the buddy felt lucky to go home with his life.

So, the doctor tells me, to answer your question, I guess we do know each other pretty well.

When the guffaws around the campfire stop, there's an awkward silence. I strain my brain for a story of my own personal debauchery, but come up embarrassingly short. My only memory: a YouTube video, recently shown to me by our teenage son, that starred a young Texan firing a bottle rocket from his unprotected butt.

Everyone else had already seen the video. Was my life so safe and predictable that my best attempt at raunchy humor, which came via my teenage son, was already passé? Nobody seemed to care much, because I was soon to learn a more formidable lesson: Never try to go tit for tat on depravity stories with doctors who have worked in big-city emergency rooms.

At some point in San Francisco, a man entered a hospital complaining of pain in his backside. Physicians examined him and found a ball from a pool table embedded in an unusual spot. After considerable effort, they were able to remove the ball, but the man still complained of discomfort. Physicians examined the man again, and, after even more vigorous work, extracted a second pool ball.

Though some in the ER were tempted to ask the man if he had called his shot, discretion prevailed. Eventually, however, the patient volunteered to explain how this all had happened. The man told doctors, "I was just sitting there, minding my own business, when . . ."

When beer nearly snorted out my nose from laughter, I looked over at Prakash and realized that, under the stars and far from home, there was a learning process going on here. At lunch I was trying to figure out customs and culture in India, but at the campfire he was trying to figure out America. I fell asleep that night in the back of my truck wondering what he thought of a country where strangers in the deep backcountry break the ice with beer, Doritos, and talk of an eight-ball in a very dark corner pocket.

On the trail before dawn the next day, Prakash tells me that, while growing up in India, he had had four main sources of information about life in America: *Alf, Saved by the Bell, Seinfeld,* and *Friends.* The television sitcoms, he says, turned out to be fairly accurate.

For his first year in the United States, though, he didn't believe he was really seeing America. Almost all his friends were other Indian nationals, living here on H-1B work visas for foreign professionals, working technology jobs, and gathering on weekends to play cricket. Prakash was a pretty good fast-bowler, but a pretty lousy tourist. He wished he were taking better advantage of his new home.

When an American coworker invited him on a hike, Prakash jumped at the chance. Seven miles of trail and more than 5,000 feet of elevation gain later, he stood on the summit of Longs Peak in Rocky Mountain National Park. This, he decided, was even better than *Seinfeld.*

Since that day little more than a year ago, Prakash had been off on a climbing jag. He summited ten more Fourteeners on the summer and fall weekends after Longs, then felt empty when winter blasted the Rockies and his partners stopped hiking. So Prakash donned snowshoes and joined backcountry skiers on trips up a half-dozen more peaks. (Sometimes the skiers, who enjoy much faster downhills, waited for him for hours at the trailheads.) Now it was summer, and he was pushing even harder. For Prakash, San Luis would be Fourteener No. 31. With his U.S. work visa set to expire in a few years—Prakash was an engineer who designed cancer ablation devices—he was trying to cram in as much of the Colorado high country as fast as he could. He was as happy as a fully obsessed man can be.

In India, he tells me, people focus on getting food for their families. Hobbies are silly and trivial and a waste of time. To hometown friends in his southeast Indian port town of Thoothukudi, climbing mountains is beyond frivolous. It's crazy. So he just doesn't talk to them much about it. Sometimes he feels like he's living two lives—one with Indian friends who yearn for their homes, and one with American friends who yearn for the mountains.

I ask what he misses about India. I barely finish the sentence before he blurts out, "My family. My friends. The food." Though I can't cut the distance to his favorite people on the other side of the world, I do know something about Indian restaurants around Denver. He tells me they're just not the same. What he really, truly longs for is dosa for breakfast and goat biriyani for a main dish and the mangoes that are sweet and intense and the blowtorch curries of Andhra Pradesh and the dozens of different kinds of bananas that taste nothing like the tasteless wallpaper-paste ones in America and the—

Prakash stops himself in midsentence. There's a glassy look in his eyes. I had tried to make him feel better, but fear I've relit the wick on a long candle of homesickness. We've finished four miles of creek-side trail with more words than altitude, and find ourselves at the base of the first big climb.

He zooms up the slope with wiry legs that chew up trail with the cadence of a sewing machine needle. There's no way for me to keep up. I next see him hours later on the wide summit. He's flat on his back and sunning himself. I'm huffing and puffing, and lop off my pack for a snack. I've carried along two yellow bananas, but I'm too embarrassed to show them to Prakash. I down a Ding Dong in two bites.

Chapter 13

Gravity

LITTLE BEAR PEAK 14,037'
BLANCA PEAK 14,345'
ELLINGWOOD POINT 14,042'

When my boot slipped, and my hip hit the snow, and my legs began plunging down the avalanche runout, I didn't think to scream. My first instinct was to stop my fall by ramming my ice axe into the snow.

Then I lost my axe.

Shitttttt!

The slope is steep and the snow is slushy. Sliding feet first on my belly and accelerating, I jam my left fist into the snow. No brake. Right fist—same. Slush cements my nose and ears. Down five feet, then ten, then twenty, I gain even more speed. I push out my butt and thrust the toes of both boots into the slope.

I stop. And I scream again.

Shittt!

I'm thirty feet below my axe and two hundred above the unpleasant place where the snow ends in shark-tooth rock. I dig both hands into the snow to give myself two more solid points of contact and then kick each boot deeper. Whew. I'm stopped. I blow the slush from my nose. I'm still thirty feet from the side of the gully I was traversing. How do I get out of here?

"Are you OK?"

It's my climbing partner, Skip Perkins, a sixty-year-old Wisconsin schoolteacher, who has safely exited the snow gully and is watching all this from the rocks above me. His eyes are wide, his voice uncertain. I assure him I'm fine, but shout that I'm downhill from my axe. Probably not the safest thing for me to Spider-Man my way up to retrieve it.

Wait there, he tells me.

I'm trying my hardest, I tell him.

Splayed against the soft spring snow, I realize my skid made both perfect sense and no sense at all. It made perfect sense because we were at the end of a long and taxing day, and in my haste to get down the mountain, I had let down my guard. But my slip also made no sense because we had taken the worst this Fourteener could throw at us—and on this peak, that's saying a lot—and survived until this point in amazingly good cheer.

Little Bear Peak is a dark, hulking mess of a mountain, a fearsome mix of rotten rock and sinister slope that gives it the well-deserved reputation of having the nastiest, most dangerous standard climbing route of any Rocky Mountain Fourteener. When my wife asked last winter whether I really intended to climb them all, Little Bear was the one that made the little voice in the back of my brain scream, Hell, no! Its most infamous challenge is a stark, three-hundred-foot rock gash usually called the Hourglass, which describes its broad shape at top and bottom, with a ten-foot pinch in the middle.

When Skip and I climbed the gully early this morning, we learned why it also carried two other nicknames: the Bowling Alley and the Shooting Gallery. Five hundred vertical feet of jumbled boulders all balance precariously at the top of the gully, and the slightest nudge— a snowball's slip, a pebble's roll, a marmot's sneeze—can send an oven-size hunk of black rock tumbling directly down the climbing route. The slope in the tightest section of the Hourglass is about 50 degrees, which means it's more vertical than horizontal. The most direct path through the Hourglass is usually soaked with water from snowmelt and rainfall.

There is no escaping rockfall in the gully. There is only ducking.

It's like navigating the nastiest dark alley in the most dangerous part of town while bad guys stand on the rooftops and throw bricks at your head. Nobody conquers the Hourglass. They survive it.

Which is what Skip and I did on the way up, evading a dozen or so bouncing stones, some as large as a cantaloupe, all flying with the befuddling direction of a 70-mph knuckleball. The Hourglass is only three hundred feet long, but it's the longest football field I've ever crossed. We were wise to wear our helmets for it.

After successfully climbing the gully earlier that morning, we gave heartfelt thanks that no one else was on the mountain below us. Even the slightest foot drag sent more rocks tearing down the mountain and funneling into the gully.

When we finally scrambled to the summit, there was no telling who hugged each other harder. We whooped. We grinned. We high-fived. Skip was fifteen years older than I, but had the enthusiasm of a little boy. He was five foot eight and looked like he could bench-press a Volkswagen. I had relied on his cool experience—Skip was a rock climber who had already summited forty-eight Fourteeners, including a burly climb around crevasses on Mount Rainier in Washington—to talk me up the Hourglass. But when he veered later onto confusing cliffs that seemed steeper than the Hourglass, I found the right way out of the rock maze and pointed him on the correct path to the summit. Compared to most people who have stood atop Little Bear, Skip was older and I was greener, but no one could ever have been happier. We listened to each other and laughed with each other. Not bad for a first man-date.

On the summit, we agreed to be cautious and slow on the way down. Skip and I kept our end of the deal, but Little Bear did not. Loosened by snowmelt, or breeze, or perhaps a sudden outbreak of marmot asthma, rocks poured down the Bowling Alley. Skip descended first and I stopped counting when he had dodged his first ten stones. During my turn, I was too preoccupied to count, but distinctly remember one oblong boulder that could have picked up the 7–10 split. Several others bounced close enough for me to detect that very distinct smell of crushed rock. (Like iron striking flint.)

At the bottom of the Bowling Alley we said our whews and swapped our high-fives. The worst was over. We were grateful.

All that remained was an apron of snow at the base of the gully that we still had to traverse. This morning, while ascending in the cold, the snow was solid, and we had easily cramponed up the moderate slope, which was less steep than some of the runs I've skied at a resort. But while Skip and I were navigating the melted-out house of shards above the Bowling Alley, the snow was baking down low under several hours of Rocky Mountain sun. The result was two inches of slushy snow atop a hard base. The snow traverse was sixty feet wide, and steep enough for us to pull out our axes but not crampons.

Skip went first, planting his axe, kicking a step, planting his axe, and kicking another. I gave him about a forty-foot head start. I followed his steps without rekicking them. I was tired and eager to get back to camp.

Then I slipped. Though my axe was firmly planted, my hand on it was not, and the fall ripped the tool from my grip. Moving first on my side and then on my belly, I felt like I was stealing second base, except that this slide ran the length of a three-story building. Around the campfire on other trips, I had heard hikers debating the merits of attaching an axe to a climber's wrist with a strap. I decided against it after hearing of a climber whose tethered axe had slashed an artery during a fall.

Five body lengths below my axe on this slippery slope, I now realize I made a stupid choice. I wish I had my axe. I'm lucky I have Skip.

"Hold on," Skip shouts. "I'm coming."

He retraces his steps with crampons through the snow to retrieve my axe, then kicks new steps down to me. There's an odd, grim look on his face. I'm hoping it's more about relief than disgust, but I'm not quite sure. I made a boneheaded mistake, and we both know it.

"Nice job stopping yourself," Skip tells me.

We survey the rest of the snow run, especially the end at the rocks.

"Doesn't look like it's steep enough to kill me," I tell him in as much of a question as a statement.

"Sure hope not," Skip says.

I thank him again, but he waves me off. "Could have happened to anyone," he tells me. "Besides, you'd do the same for me." I appreciate his confidence. I'm glad I don't have to try to fulfill it. I kick my steps very, very carefully to finish the traverse.

We have nearly two miles to hike and descend until we reach our camp down at 11,800 feet at Como Lake. My feet want the miles to end, but my heart wants them to last forever. This has been one of my best days in the mountains, and I tell Skip so. We both marvel that two guys old enough to be the fathers of so many Fourteener hikers can live a thousand miles apart, meet on the Internet, and surprise ourselves by getting up—and down—a peak like Little Bear.

I ask if this has been his hardest mountain, because it's certainly mine. He says two other tough climbs come to mind.

Twenty years ago, he and his wife started scheduling regular vacations in Colorado to teach their midwestern sons about the glory of the Rocky Mountains. Unfortunately, the trips weren't always joyful. At one point, when the boys were eight and ten and struggling up a climb of Mount Sherman, the younger son decided he had had enough. The summit was only two hundred vertical feet away, but it might as well have been on the moon. The boy wasn't budging.

Skip gave the second-grader his best pep talk: It's gorgeous up there, it's so close, you've worked so hard to get to this point, people will be so proud to see you on the top.

Dad, the son said, the only person who will be proud of me is you.

No way that kid was moving.

OK, maybe he's right, Skip figured. While his wife stayed with the younger son below the summit, Skip joined his older son for the remaining half-mile of trail. He and his ten-year-old were celebrating on top when Skip spotted the younger, stubborn boy, suddenly moving strongly up the mountain. Skip ran down to accompany and congratulate him.

The father was thrilled, but had to ask: What made you change your mind? Was it my talk? Was it the beauty of the mountain? Was it the pride?

No, Dad, the boy said. Mom promised me twenty dollars at Toys "R" Us if I summited.

On the top of the mountain, Skip wondered about the sanctity of summiting a mountain via bribery, but ultimately concluded he could be happy and proud that his family included one climber who was an undisputed professional.

The other tough mountain Skip remembers is Capitol Peak, near Aspen, which climbers routinely place on the list of the nastiest Fourteeners. Skip climbed it with his older son, who was sixteen at the time. On the approach he scrambled off-route and accidentally put the two of them, unroped, on a technical Class 5 face with a six-hundred-foot drop-off. One thing worse than putting yourself in danger, Skip says, is leading your child to danger.

When they both survived, the son told Skip, "Dad, I've never heard you say the f-word before, much less that many times."

There was one advantage to their misadventure, though. When they reached the gnarliest stretch of the Capitol Peak climb, called the Knife Edge, which looks like it sounds and juts through a thousand feet of sky, it was no big deal. In fact, Skip's son even hammed it up on the Knife Edge with a tightrope pose, which seemed cool at the time but turned dicey when Mom saw the pictures at home. Skip felt fortunate to be without any photographic evidence of their wrong turn on the nastier rock before the Knife Edge.

Skip realizes both stories involve his boys, but there's a reason for that: When it's not terrifying, working with kids can be a real blast. For twenty years, Skip threw everything he had into a sporting goods store in central Wisconsin, but realized that it just wasn't fun anymore. At age fifty-two he went back to college—it had changed since

he had last attended in the late 1960s—and earned a teaching certificate. For the past six years he has worked as an elementary school
teacher in a town of two hundred in northern Wisconsin, where he's
thrilled to take lowland kids up the Colorado high country. So far
he's guided about twenty midwestern fourth- and fifth-graders to the
tops of Fourteeners.

Of course, those are all peaks Skip has already summited. Skip
worries about the ones he hasn't. He has only six more Fourteeners
to go, but they are all either hard physically, or hard technically, or
simply hard both ways. Now that silver has completed its hostile
takeover of his scalp, he wonders how many more hard peaks his legs
can withstand. The clock ticks against him.

Or does it? When Skip and I return to Como Lake, we find two
tents pitched only thirty feet from ours. Vast mountain—crowded
camp. It makes no sense. From one tent emerges a man who is tall,
spindly, and most assuredly not young.

His name is Malcolm Watts. He is seventy years old. He has two
artificial hips. He intends to climb Little Bear tomorrow.

My first instinct is to say, "Whoa, cowboy!" I don't, though,
mainly because I'm trying to fit in with the political creed of the
mountains, which holds that at home, there are Democrats and Republicans, but in the mountains there are only libertarians. When we
tell the seventy-year-old about the rockfall and snow on Little Bear,
he seems to consider our cautions as serious disrespect to his climbing
ability. Malcolm is an accomplished climber, and he wants us to know
it, which he does by rattling off a series of impressive walls and peaks
he has scaled in Europe and the United States.

He is such a showboater that I wonder if he's for real. His fifty-
nine-year-old climbing partner, Greg Evans, a Colorado farmer who
met Malcolm on the summit of Snowmass Mountain the prior summer, assures me that the seventy-year-old is one tough hombre. According to one of the most-repeated sayings in mountaineering, there
are old climbers, and there are bold climbers, but there are no old,
bold climbers. Malcolm seems intent on proving himself the excep-

tion to the rule. He plans to take on Little Bear without crampons. I have done my best to dissuade him; I have failed. I retreat to my tent partly to duck responsibility, and partly for a nap. *Qué será, será.*

When I wake, it is pitch-black. My nap has turned into an eight-hour slumber, and I realize I am totally, utterly hosed. I had planned to go tent-to-tent at dinnertime around Como Lake—dozens are camped here—with hopes of finding hiking partners for the next day's climb of the easier, neighboring mountains, Blanca Peak and Elling-wood Point. (Skip had already climbed both years before and had no interest in repeating them.) Right now, however, no one is awake at 1 a.m. By turning into Sleeping Beastie, I have lost any chance of keep-ing my no-solo promise to my wife. In my down sleeping bag, I wring my hands and gnash my teeth. Then I fall back asleep.

Just before dawn I wake and set out on the trail all by my lone-some. There are so many people camping here, I figure I'm bound to meet somebody on the trail to hike up with. Alas, I don't. For the first mile, I don't even see a soul. At a steep climb that skirts a waterfall, I hear voices behind me, and see a group of three jogging up the trail. No way for me to join them. I trudge on and realize how much yes-terday's climb took out of me. The knots in my calves are the size of hard-boiled eggs; my thighs are as mushy as cottage cheese; my shoul-ders have been pounded by a meat-tenderizer mallet. Did I mention food? After two days of dehydrated backpacking fare, I'm obsessed with it. I dream of a breakfast burrito with scrambled eggs, potatoes, bacon, and green chile—lots and lots of green chile.

Blanca Peak is one of those mountains that look too foreboding to be scaled by any mere mortal. As black and jagged as a rotten hound's tooth, Blanca is the hub that connects via sharp ridgelines to three other Fourteeners, Little Bear, Ellingwood, and Lindsey. There's sup-posed to be a straightforward trail up it, but the key word here is "up." Blanca towers six thousand feet above the flat floor of the San Luis Valley. I'm facing the steepest stretch.

For the Navajos, the peak is the easternmost of the four sacred mountains. They call it Tsisnaasjini, or Dawn Mountain, and right now it's living up to its name. The sunrise is breathtaking. The sky is orange and sunbeams shoot brilliantly around the triangular summit. If there truly is a higher being watching over this peak, I'm hoping it will bless my legs with some power.

Above the falls and past a lake the summer trail disappears into a long snow gully. Learning my lesson from Little Bear, I take no chances and strap on crampons. Ahead of me several climbers navigate the same hardpack. The ones who don't have crampons move very, very slowly. I offer help, but they don't want it. They debate whether to turn back. I pass them.

A confusing series of ledges and cliffs follows. After my third icy nose-high ledge—I thought this peak was supposed to be easier!—I want to quit. I'm tired and there's 1,500 vertical feet of talus to the summit. Who needs this?

I plop on my butt and choke down yet another PowerBar. Chocolate, oatmeal, peanut butter—they all taste like hard chalk, but stick in my teeth too. The only way I can jam it down is to chew it up, suspend the particles in a mouthful of water, and swallow hard.

Downhill I see more people struggling up the hardpack snow. If I quit now, I'd have to descend that. My choice: an hour-and-a-half of pain uphill, or thirty seconds of terror down. After my lesson on Little Bear yesterday, I opt for up. My legs won't soon forgive me.

If there's a trail somewhere in the dishwasher-size talus, I can't find it. So I opt for the most direct route—straight up. In my dreams I bunny-hop from boulder to boulder, but in reality I'm using my hands to push and pull my way upward. I am sore. I am tired.

And finally, I am on the summit. There's another solo hiker already on the top. He's about my age. I say hi. He says hi. Then he opens his pack and offers me a treasure trove of cheese, sausage, crackers, Fig Newtons, M&M's, and full-bore chocolate. The Navajos are right: This is a sacred mountain.

His name is Jeff Cruzan, and he's visiting here from Sharon, Massachusetts. He asks if I'd seen him fall on the snow earlier. I say no, but am taken aback by his honesty. I haven't met too many people on the mountains who introduce themselves by admitting mistakes. I tell him about my misadventure yesterday on Little Bear. Over mouths full of junk food, we swap stories of our backcountry stupidity.

What's amazing is that he had any tales of doofusness to offer. Jeff is a biologist who has spent most of his career doing postdoctoral work at Harvard University. He has had three articles published in the premier professional journal *Science*. I asked what he's doing two thousand miles from home.

"I like the mountains because they make me feel small," Jeff says. "They help me sort out what's important in life."

His biggest sort-out came last year, when he wearied of the cutthroat politics in postdoc life. So he ditched academia and hired on as a high school science teacher. It was his best work year yet.

We both eye the half-mile connecting ridge to Ellingwood. I'm spent and he is tired. I'm nervous that so much of the ridge is plastered with snow, and so is he. I tell him about the time Gottlieb and I stood atop Mount Shavano, and doubted our ability to traverse to Tabeguache Peak until we met Bulldog, the sixty-two-year-old Kansan, wearing shorts in the snow. There is no such man on Blanca today. We decide to try the traverse anyway.

Thanks to either chocolate or unexpectedly refined conversation— we talked about the highlights of quantifying hydrogen bond cooperativity in water through VRT spectroscopy of the water tetramer, as well as the lowlights of hand-to-hand combat in the ivory towers to decide whose name is listed first as an author on an academic paper— the scramble passes quickly.

At the top of Ellingwood Point, we are greeted by an unusual smell. Scott Estabrooks, thirty-eight, is taking deep drags on the summit from a Marlboro Red. It's the first time I've seen anyone in such an oxygen-deprived sport filling lungs and the summit with tobacco smoke. Scott, who works as a surveyor, says the cigarettes help to calm his nerves. I look around the top and notice for the first time that, hey, there's about a thousand-foot drop-off on the other side of the summit block. This Marlboro is his fourth today.

We decide to join Scott and his three buddies for the descent, which is straightforward and uneventful until we reach our first steep snowfield. Jeff and I pull out our ice axes; Scott pulls out his Marlboros. I hop on my butt and find that, once again, everyone glissades in my very wide wake. Scott finishes with another smoke.

After two more glissades by me, and even more cigarettes by Scott, we're off the mountain and back in the trees at Como Lake. Coincidentally, at the same time I return to camp, so does Malcolm Watts, the seventy-year-old with two artificial hips. He has successfully summited Little Bear. I ask him about it, and he proclaims the mountain to be easier than expected. I raise an eyebrow to his climbing partner, who says some of the most difficult parts of the day were cajoling Malcolm to give up the harder, more exposed Class 5 scrambles for the easier Class 4 reaches.

It ain't bragging, he says, if you can back it up.

Chapter 14

Guts

WETTERHORN PEAK 14,015'
UNCOMPAHGRE PEAK 14,321'
REDCLOUD PEAK 14,034'
SUNSHINE PEAK 14,001'

The long winters of Gunnison, Colorado, have always been bitter enough to give a man heartburn. But for an anxious group of prospectors, the cold blast of January 1874 was especially hard to stomach.

The six men were stuck the entire month in a Ute camp while news swirled of a spectacular gold find just seventy-five miles to the south. Weeks passed. Snow piled up. Temperatures dropped. The whole idea of spectacular riches not far away continued to gnaw at them.

Though the Utes warned against winter travel, the prospectors' hunger for gold got the best of them. They gathered enough food for a ten-day trip and set out into the wild on February 9, 1874.

Two months later, one prospector, Alfred Packer, emerged alone from the ice and snow. He had several wallets full of money. He was not thin. He walked into the Los Pinos Indian Agency with just one thing on his shopping list: whiskey.

The curious wondered what happened to the group's other five prospectors. The whiskey-drinking prospector explained that he'd hurt his leg on the expedition, fell behind the group, and figured he'd be trailing the other five men into this camp. Days passed at Los Pinos, but there was still no sign of the other miners. Around the Indian agency many asked: What exactly happened to the five prospectors? Were they lost, or just swallowed up by the winter wilderness?

Soon after, an Indian guide on the same trail reported finding sliced strips of an unusual type of meat.

Alfred Packer was a cannibal.

In a confession given at the Indian agency, Packer—his birth certificate name was Alfred, but "Alferd" was mistakenly tattooed on his arm, and he apparently used both names at different times in his life—said winter in the Rockies soon overtook the prospectors, and they died of starvation and exposure, one by one, on their failed expedition to the goldfields. He claimed the oldest prospector, sixty-five-year-old Israel Swan, died ten days into the trip and was eaten by all five surviving miners. The next, James Humphrey, went from man to meal four or five days later. Not long after, Packer said, he returned from a wood-gathering expedition to find two surviving prospectors dining on Frank Miller, who had died in some unspecified accident. Packer was too famished to resist.

Hunger pangs soon returned, and Shannon Bell supposedly offed eighteen-year-old George "Calfornia" Noon with someone else's gun, and then came after Packer himself.

Acting in self-defense, Packer claimed he "killed Bell; shot him—covered up the remains, and took a large piece along."

The authorities had had their fill of this story. They arrested and jailed Packer on suspicion of murder.

With Packer awaiting trial behind bars, a reporter in the field for *Harper's Weekly* magazine stumbled across a grisly scene: the bodies of the five dead prospectors, piled together in one spot near the banks of the Lake Fork of the Gunnison River. One body had no head, a second was missing a slice of thigh, and a third had lost a breast cutlet. The discovery of five bodies in one place, all in various states of mutilation, directly contradicted Packer's claim of deaths spread over the course of a long journey.

When authorities rushed to confront the cannibal as a liar, they found Packer's jail cell empty. The man-eater was on the lam.

Outside the mine camp that came to be known as Lake City, the legend of Packer grew. Some believed he was a cold-blooded criminal who had killed for money and dined for pleasure. Others believed he was a victim of circumstance who, faced with life or death in the backcountry, decided to survive by doing something extremely distasteful.

In the end, it was Packer's laugh that gave him away. Nine years after his jailbreak in Colorado, Packer was heard guffawing in a saloon in Wyoming by someone who had originally planned to join his ill-fated expedition. Packer was shipped back to Denver, where he signed a second confession.

This time, Packer coughed up an entirely different story. Confronted by storms and deep snow, Packer said, the expedition had run out of food on its fourth day, leaving prospectors to survive on rose hips and pine gum. About eleven days in, Packer said, he returned from an unsuccessful hunting trip to find Shannon Bell feasting on Frank Miller's leg. The three other prospectors, Packer said, had been smacked in the head by a hatchet and laid out next to a campfire. When Bell saw that Packer was the last surviving prospector, he attacked with a hatchet, but Packer said he shot and killed him with his hunting rifle. With snow too soft and deep for him to escape, Packer claimed to have waited for spring melt. He lived off the flesh of his traveling companions for sixty days.

A jury in Lake City rejected Packer's self-defense argument and convicted him of the premeditated murder of Israel Swan. According to the local newspaper, the judge sentenced Packer to death with these famous words:

Stand up yah voracious man-eatin' son of a bitch and receive yir sintince. When yah came to Hinsdale County, there was siven Dimmycrats. But you, yah et five of 'em, goddam yah. I sintince yah t' be hanged by th' neck ontil yer dead, dead, dead,

as a warnin' ag'in reducin' th' Dimmycratic populayshun of
this county. Packer, you Republican cannibal, I would sintince
ya ta hell but the statutes forbid it.

(Though the newspaper's version of the sentencing statement has
been regurgitated millions of times over the years by Colorado political operatives—mainly Dimmycrats—the official court record indi-
cates the judge actually used much less colorful and more official
language.)

Amazingly, Packer's conviction was overturned by a legal techni-
cality. He had committed the crime when Colorado was a territory,
but prosecuted under law enacted after Colorado's 1876 statehood.

So Packer was tried again and convicted again. This time he was
found guilty of manslaughter, and sentenced to forty years. He served
fifteen years before newspapers took up Packer as a circulation-build-
ing cause and built sympathy for his case. In 1901, Governor Charles
Thomas, noting the inmate's advancing kidney disease, released
Packer from prison on parole. The man-eater was promptly hired as
a security guard by my former employer, the *Denver Post*.

Though it was widely rumored that Packer died a vegetarian, his
memory lives on at the University of Colorado in Boulder, where students dine at the Alferd G. Packer Memorial Grill. The motto: Have
a Friend for Lunch!

We're in Lake City having a late lunch at the Cannibal Grill, which is
only appropriate, because my latest hiking partner has a problem
that's really been eating him.

His challenge: What to do now that he's a success.

For as long as he can remember, David Wallace wanted to score
big in business. He blasted through the University of Texas School of
Business with one eye on the books and the other on buy-out targets.
He met a former ARCO oil worker who held a patent to make an
obscure safety part for oil rigs that only ARCO seemed interested in

buying. David and his brother, a banker who specialized in turning around bad loans, knew hardly anything about the oil business, but together they thought they could make something bigger of the invention. They spent months hitting up friends and not-so-friends for money to buy the patent. When they finally succeeded, they wondered if it was worth it.

David traveled 180 days a year to thirty-five countries, most frequently to Saudi Arabia, Venezuela, and Indonesia. To help seal business deals in Pacific Rim restaurants, he ate bat, snake, fried beetles, and flying bamboo squirrel. The Middle East was even tougher. Though rich oilmen in conservative Muslim countries almost never drank, they almost always had a secret stash of liquor for infidel guests, and expected them to imbibe heavily before their inevitable descent to hell. Let's get Yankee boy drunk—cheap entertainment for sheiks, or shrewd business negotiating tactic? David just wanted to make the sale.

Pouring his time, money, and energy into selling one piece of high-pressure plumbing to the world's most impenetrable oil companies, David lived hand-to-mouth. Because of work, he put off dating, marriage, and children, the trappings of the normal life that he really wanted, until somehow, some way, the business could stand on its own feet.

One day, it did. The oil giant that had seemed most resistant to change, the Saudis, placed an order. And if it was good enough for the Saudis, then the Venezuelans were interested. And the big American companies too. David married. A few years later came the big buyout deal.

Suddenly David and his brother had enough to pay their $10-an-hour floor workers a bonus of $5,000. Machinists got $50,000, the production manager $300,000.

After fifteen years of struggles, David and his brother had struck it rich.

Which should have been the happy ending, except it wasn't. With the money pressures off, David wasn't quite sure what to do with himself. He moved his wife and their two young children to the

French Alps for three months to ski. He hunted elk. He drove three hours each way for the best one-day mountain bike trips.

And he fished. He had once run into someone who was trying to catch every game fish in the world on a fly rod, which David thought was interesting, so he started chasing fish too. He caught permit in Mexico, bonefish in the Bahamas, peacock bass in Venezuela, steelhead and salmon in Alaska, and sea-run brown trout in Argentina. For months his nemesis was tarpon, because he kept catching fish of less than fifty pounds. It took five trips to the Florida Keys, but he finally landed his big one.

Though he's between fishing trips now, David sounds like he's wearying of the World Pro Fun Tour. What he really wants is to be working. The sale of his company finally completed six months ago, and he'd like to get cracking on something new. It's just not as easy as it sounds. As he wrote me in our first get-acquainted e-mail:

> I have found that having some money and the chance to pretty much do what you want is more daunting than one might think—a sort of be careful what you wish for, because Working For The Man, so to speak, is an easy excuse for not living out your dreams. When faced with the midlife realities of what are my dreams and do I have the guts to go after them with no financial excuses—well, that is a lot more pressure than one would think.

I met David because his wife was in my wife's book club. Before he started working like a fiend, he had summited twenty-seven Fourteeners, mostly by climbing the hardest ones first. I was thrilled to have him on this trip, but I wasn't quite sure what he wanted out of three days in the backcountry with a total stranger. A time to think? A time to forget?

Early this morning we had summited Wetterhorn Peak, a spectacularly jagged mountain atop a gorgeous, lush plateau. David, a rock climber, had seemed happy with the climb—awesome beauty, no crowds, short approach hike, and then an attention-grabbing scramble to the top. Back in town, though, I think the reality of this trip had started to sink in. My other man-dates had just been day hikes or short overnights. This trip, however, was a full-on three days in mountains five hours from home. He seemed sullen and distracted. Did he have second thoughts? Was the problem that I was a much slower hiker? Or that I had been a little creeped out during the down-climb of a steep Class 3 gully with several hundred feet of exposure? Or that my instinct was to scoot down the worst parts while crab-walking on my butt like a rookie instead of facing toward the mountain like a true rock climber?

Did he think I was in over my head? Did he want to go home?

Actually, he tells me in the Cannibal Grill, he was just wondering if I wanted another cold beer. Some questions are easy to answer.

Our beers are just about drained when the skies open above the bar patio. There had been some thunder and lightning earlier in the day, but nothing like this—a full-on Noah-hurry-up-with-that-carpentry-project rainstorm. As the gullies wash, I watch the color drain from David's face. Last night we had slept at the Wetterhorn trailhead, I in the back of my truck, and David under a tarp on the ground. Tonight we're supposed to do the same. Unfortunately, I've forgotten to bring the life preservers.

I don't want to seem like a sissy here, but I'm in no mood for a backcountry water bed. Nervously I eye David, swallow my pride, and pop the humiliating question: What would you think if we got a motel room tonight?

David's mood swing is instant and dramatic, a change neatly summed up by the statement I overhear him making to his wife on a cell phone conversation as I emerge clean and unstinking from a very long, hot shower in the last available motel room in the entire town of Lake City. "It's going pretty well," he tells her. "We're about to have sex."

Not really, but the Great Indoors has made us both exceedingly happy.

The next morning we're back on the trail before dawn, and see that the weather gods have spun mischief on Uncompahgre Peak. The top five hundred feet are plastered with an inch or two of fresh snow. July 12 in the Rockies—we could be sledding. Our sense of awe and wonder is equaled only by our determination to make every footstep a solid one. The trail guides claim that the north face of Uncompahgre is a sheer seven-hundred-foot cliff, but the clouds and fog remain so dense that we can't see more than a hundred feet around us. Somewhere in the gloom is an abyss. It's eerie and exhilarating.

By early afternoon we're back in town for another decadent restaurant lunch. Real hydrated food with silverware—I could get used to this. The two peaks we plan to scale the next day have a full-fledged campground at the trailhead. Who needs that? David and I shack up again in the same motel, and in the parking lot run into the father of Caroline Moore, aka USA Keller from 14ers.com. He's here to hike too. I tell him about meeting his daughter on the group climb of Culebra Peak twenty days earlier, and he tells me about the shock he felt with the death of the Talus Monkey. "I always felt Caroline was very safe with him," Fred Moore tells me. "He seemed very careful, very responsible." By contrast, Moore tells me he has his doubts about another one of his daughter's hiking partners, Jordan White. "Now that guy—my gosh, he skis down Little Bear!"

I neglect to tell Caroline Moore's dad that I've set up a hike with that very same Jordan White, another 14ers.com regular, later this summer. Sometimes the world of the Fourteeners-obsessed can be uncomfortably small.

David and I start our dawn hike up Redcloud Peak and Sunshine Peak in silence. After two peaks, two bars, two restaurants, and two motel rooms in two days, he knows my jokes, my life story, and, worst of all, my slow hiking pace. He takes off up the trail for the first time this trip at his own comfortable speed, which quickly puts him beyond my eyesight. The only thing that hurts more than Fourteeners on three consecutive days is trying to catch up with someone on Fourteeners on three consecutive days.

I catch him about two-and-a-half miles and 2,000 vertical feet later, where he sits on a saddle and spies a herd of fifty elk in the next drainage. I show up; the elk disappear, and so does David. He consumes the final mile of trail and nearly 2,000 feet of elevation gain in less than a half-hour. This is about triple my best speed ever. I've been hiking with a superhuman and didn't even know it.

At 8:30 a.m. my caboose finally catches up with David's locomotive on the summit of Redcloud Peak, which is indeed made of reddish rock, though at this point we're not discussing aesthetics, because our next goal is a mile-and-a-half atop an S-shaped ridge across the sky to our next Fourteener. The sky is azure, but the first white puffball clouds of the day are gathering in the distance. The down-and-up traverse to Sunshine, which requires 1,200 feet of climbing round-trip, has been a magnet for bad weather for as long as anyone can remember, or at least since its first recorded ascent in 1874, when Franklin Rhoda, a twenty-year-old engineer on a mapmaking expedition, first described a "tickling sensation" on the roots of his hair. That feeling was

> accompanied by a peculiar sound almost exactly like frying bacon . . . The effect on our hair became more and more marked, till, ten or fifteen minutes after its first appearance, there was sudden and instantaneous relief, as if all electricity had been suddenly drawn from us. After the lapse of a few seconds the cause became apparent, as a peal of thunder reached our ears. The lightning had struck a neighboring peak, and the electricity in the air had been discharged.

The storm, however, was not done, and his hair soon was standing on end again. Rhoda reported:

> At this time, it was producing a terrible humming, which, with the noises emitted by the thousands of angular blocks of stone, and the sounds produced by our hair, made such a din that we

could scarcely think. The fast-increasing electricity was suddenly discharged, as we had anticipated, by another stroke of lightning.

Rhoda's partner, mapmaker A. D. Wilson, grabbed his surveying tool from the summit and ran for his life. Lightning blasted his footsteps; Wilson dodged the electrical bomb by only thirty feet. (Good thing Wilson survived: Two Fourteeners near Telluride were later named for him.)

Despite the literally hair-raising experience, the mountain came to be known as Sunshine Peak. David tells me that he does not enjoy stories about lightning; he has a fearsome one of his own.

Several years back he and his wife were hiking Mount Sneffels, near Telluride, when a storm swept in just as they approached timberline. The first lightning bolt made them duck and cover; the second made David scream. The third had David telling his wife how much he loved her. When a bolt exploded a nearby tree, David went berserk. His wife, however, remained serene. He believes she was resigned to death. He was convinced of it, too, but he certainly wasn't calm about it. He figures they were surrounded by nearly three dozen lightning strikes before it all ended. Ever since that time, he has gotten jittery about thunderstorms above timberline.

When we summit Sunshine, it ain't. We are smack-dab in the middle of one of the strangest weather phenomena I ever have seen: The summit is a meeting place for every cloud for miles around. The only place we can see a dark cloud is directly above our heads, but it is growing taller, wider, and blacker. The sky has gone from blue to menacing in less than an hour, and I see the look in David's eyes.

Let's get the hell out of here, I tell him, and don't wait for me.

It's hard to say what's more staggering: the sheer speed of David unleashed, or the sheer numbers of oblivious hikers still advancing along the traverse directly into a towering dark cloud. When someone in the first group of college-age kids tells me, "You're moving pretty fast," I turn and point to the gathering storm. "We're keeping an eye on it," she responds. I'm tempted to say: Of course you are—you're walking right into it, but I'm trying hard to stay a libertarian in the mountains.

At the bottom of the traverse saddle, as I start reclimbing Redcloud Peak, I see a dad with two middle-school-age kids in jeans and hoodie sweatshirts. I'm running away; they're walking into it. I'm breathless and a little scared. The dad looks at me like I'm insane; the kids look like they'd rather be somewhere else. When kids are involved, my libertarian days are over.

"Pretty nasty cloud up there," I tell them. "I'm getting out of here."

The dad responds with words aimed more at his kids than me: "We're watching it. Not far to the next summit."

They keep hiking up and into it. I can't stand the idea of kids in peril because of a dad's dumb decision, so I call to them, "Did you see the other guy running ahead of me? He got caught in a lightning storm once. He didn't want to be caught again."

The dad pauses midstride, but never turns around. He leads his kids toward Sunshine.

I struggle the last five hundred feet up Redcloud and am too scared to join the dozen hikers resting and snacking on the top. It's 10:30 a.m. I point to the expanding cloud, which appears ready to have God start blasting the Ten Commandments into stone for Charlton Heston. The hikers hear my cautions, but no one moves. They're all consenting adults, so I hightail it downhill. I'm guessing there are forty hikers on one of the summits or the traverse between them. They must think I'm crazy running. Maybe I am, but I still prefer cardiac arrest over electrocution.

At 12,600 feet, near a big bend in the trail, I see a truly wild sight: a lone man wandering the willow scrub with a metal shaft five feet above his head. Is he Ben Franklin on another lightning experiment? The sky is black around him. Maybe it's a GPS antenna. I don't stick around to find out.

About a hundred yards from timberline I finally hear it: *crack*

BOOM, *crack BOOM, crack BOOM*—three horrific snaps of thunder, striking up high and echoing down the valley. In the trees I feel safe, but the sky above flashes again: *crack BOOM*. The lightning is on the ridgetops. I feel awful for the people up high, but probably not as awful as they feel themselves.

There are two more snaps of thunder, and I hear fast footsteps behind me. It's the guy with the metal rod.

Thanks for trying to draw all the lightning away from me, I tell him.

No problem, he says, though that wasn't the main goal. The long metal staff is to do field population counts on a federally protected endangered species of butterfly. This should be good, I think, so I cinch down my pack and walk down the trail being entertained by tales of an insect.

Less than an inch-and-a-half wide and with wings speckled a dull brown and rusty-orange, the Uncompahgre fritillary has a lackluster appearance, but a life story rooted in coolness.

Biologists believe this creature is a remnant of the last Ice Age. Ten thousand years ago, the fritillary favored the wet edges of the vast glaciers that covered much of North America. As the climate warmed, the butterfly found fewer places to survive. It followed the cold, snow, and a particularly tasty type of willow to higher and higher elevations.

Today Uncompahgre fritillaries are found only above 12,500 feet. They remain confined to a handful of sky island habitats in the southern Sawatch and San Juan ranges of the Rocky Mountains in Colorado. (The largest colony is on the flanks of Redcloud Peak.) It has the smallest total range of any North American butterfly. Fewer than five thousand are believed to survive. The bugs are already struggling to stay cool at 12,500 feet, which, on these peaks, leaves them with just 1,500 feet to retreat. Scientists view them as a possible first casualty of global warming.

The guy with the big metal pole is a student who won't give me his name, because he's afraid he'll screw up a fact and anger the professor directing his work. He does tell me that before the storm, he spotted thirty Uncompahgre fritillaries—a pretty good day.

About a half-mile up from the trailhead, with thunder still crashing occasionally above us, we're jarred from our talk about butterflies by a woman on the edge of panic. She has a two-way radio. Still up on the mountain, buffeted by lightning, are several members of her family. Radio reception comes and goes and she's very worried. So far everyone is safe, but not all are well, she says. One terrified person caught up high during the lightning storm has pooped himself.

I wish her well, and continue down the trail. At the parking lot, David waits. Our legs are sore, but our pants are clean. Our throats are dry, too, so with the thunder clapping safely away above us, we pop open two cold ones from the truck. This makes us minor celebrities. Though we certainly are not the first ones to ever swill beer at 1 p.m. at this trailhead, we are most certainly the first ones to do it in this particular crowd.

My truck is parked directly next to an informal aid station for the Hardrock 100, the baddest-assed footrace in the Rockies and possibly the hemisphere. Founded by deranged runners who thought that 26-mile marathons were too easy, and that 50-milers were barely enough to break a sweat, the Hardrock 100 was supposed to be a true test of character: 100 miles of trails with 33,000 feet of climbing through snow, over cliffs, and away from the occasional bear. The racecourse punishes lungs with an average elevation of 11,186 feet. It continues through the night and must be finished in less than 48 hours. The record winning time is 23 hours and 23 minutes.

David and I had been feeling good about our 12 miles and 4,800 feet of vertical gain this morning until we watch the front-runners of the fifteenth annual Hardrock 100 cross in front of us. They are in mile 30 and have already climbed more than 10,000 feet. They all look considerably fresher than us. They do gaze wistfully at our beers, though. We raise our cans in salute to them as they begin their ascents of Handies Peak, elevation 14,058 feet. Kind of makes the Boston Marathon's infamous Heartbreak Hill, which towers a grand total of

88 vertical feet, seem like little more than a tight-jawed New England whine.

Watching the Hardrockers climb at triple my speed, even after running more than the length of a marathon, reinforces an old rule someone once told me around a campfire: In the mountains, no matter how tough you think you are, there's always someone tougher. That's certainly the case with Fourteeners.

The first men to summit all Rocky Mountain Fourteeners were two climbing buddies, Carl Blaurock and William Ervin. They did it in twelve years, finishing in 1923. They completed the peaks with knickers, the sketchiest of maps, and few paved roads for approaches. Blaurock celebrated some summits by smoking a cigarette.

The first female finisher, and fourth finisher overall, was Mary Cronin. She needed one more year than the men, but faced obstacles the men never worried about: Hardly any mountaineering equipment at that time was made for women, which forced her to customize clothes and adapt oversized gear. Because few women were mountaineering, she had to plead for inclusion on male trips in an era that, for Cronin, started just one year after the United States allowed women to vote. Cronin finally did find a dependable female climbing partner, but that friend, Agnes Vaille, was killed during a 1925 winter climb of Longs Peak. Cronin finished her Fourteeners quest in 1934.

For decades only a few hardy souls per year reported finishing the Fourteeners. Almost all were more interested in survival than speed. In 1937, though, a Breckenridge schoolteacher, Carl Melzer, lugged along his nine-year-old son, Bob, and together they completed the whole circuit in a single year. Still, this impressive feat seemed to have as much to do with filling up a summer vacation on a schoolteacher's salary as it did with setting any speed record.

Construction and expansion of major highways after World War II vastly eased access to the backcountry, and the pace of Fourteeners climbing picked up. In 1959, a twenty-eight-year-old dental student, Cleve McCarty, survived wet army surplus clothes, a balking 1947 Willys Jeep—and a lightning storm that turned rocks blue atop Mount

Princeton—to finish fifty-four Fourteeners in fifty-four days. Though he did set the speed record, McCarty said he wasn't trying. He only wanted to finish up before his school started again in St. Louis. His July 4–August 26 adventure was exceedingly lonely: On all but nine peaks, McCarty reached the top, and bottom, without seeing another soul.

Others weren't far behind his footsteps. In the summer of 1974, suburban Denver real estate agent George Smith scored a big house sale that, he thought, would carry his household financially for a few months. So he packed up his four sons in a blue Econoline van and borrowed jeep and mounted a family assault on the Fourteeners speed record. They were an unlikely group: The father had a crippled arm and wrist from a childhood car accident, and none of his sons was a particularly talented high school runner or athlete. All five, however, were Eagle Scouts who knew how to survive in the backcountry. And all five had previously summited all the Fourteeners, including the youngest son, Tyle, who had completed his fifty-fourth peak at age eight.

The biggest challenge was apparent to anyone who ever has been the parent of teenagers: The sons—ages fifteen, seventeen, eighteen, and twenty-one—simply wouldn't get out of bed early for alpine starts. As a result, the Climbing Smiths rarely began hiking before 10:30 in the morning. They faced many thunderstorms and spent several nights bivouacking in precarious places such as the ridge from Humboldt Peak to Kit Carson Peak. Still, no one was ever hurt, and, perhaps most amazingly, no one brother ever socked another in the nose. The only truly scary moments came when the father and four unwashed sons had to squeeze together inside the jeep to descend kidney-rattling four-wheel-drive roads without a low gear. They finished the Colorado Fourteeners in thirty-three days. They then went on immediately to climb thirteen more Fourteeners in California and one more in Washington, giving them a total of sixty-eight Fourteeners in the continental United States in forty-eight days. (Tyle Smith didn't even stop after that; by the time I was struggling with my first peaks, he had already gone on to summit Fourteeners 646 times.)

With the boom in backpacking in the 1960s and 1970s, and the explosion of marathons and 10K races in the decades after that, the hills were soon filled with tens of thousands of people who could go a long way without stopping. Peaks that had been climbed by dozens a year were now being summited by thousands who enjoyed the stark beauty of the mountains, the physical challenge of ascending them, and, for obsessives, the tidiness of a neat to-do list requiring fifty-four specific checkmarks. A whole nonprofit group, the Colorado Fourteeners Initiative, sprang up in 1994 to build trails, erect signs, fortify trailheads, and generally try to keep the Fourteeners from being loved to death.

Some decried the trail improvements, which had been going on informally for years, because they made it even easier to hike Fourteeners—and attract more crowds. Others saw the work as a necessary evil to prevent trail ruts, shortcutting, and other ecological damage on the mountains. There was, however, no dispute about one consequence of trail improvements: They let fast people race up Fourteeners even faster.

After winning a 150-mile race across the Brooks Range of Alaska, a 505-mile race across the Lewis and Clark Trail in Washington State—and running 2,040 miles through the Himalayas in 101 days—California software programmer Adrian Crane was looking for a new endurance challenge. In 1992, he trained his sights on the Fourteeners, and finished them in an astounding 15 days, 17 hours, and 19 minutes. Though he was proud of his new record, Crane was most exhilarated at the feeling of spending two weeks above timberline. "You start to feel invincible," Crane said. "It feels wonderful."

Ultrarunners across America were shocked and awed. Some Coloradans, however, took Crane's record as a serious dis. A record for Rocky Mountains set by somebody from the California Sierras? The longer Crane's record stood, the more it grated.

In 1995, the Hardrock 100 ultramarathon was canceled in Colorado because of a monstrous snowpack left over from winter. The decision left hundreds of hardmen and hardwomen with impressively trained legs, but no race to run them. Instead of the Hardrock, two Colorado locals and Hardrock 100 veterans, Rick Trujillo and Ricky Denesik, decided to try to run down some Crane.

The two Ricks were accomplished runners. Trujillo was an international mining geologist from Ouray, Colorado, who had won the Pikes Peak Marathon six of seven years in the 1970s; Denesik, a finish carpenter from Telluride, was an All-American at 1,500 meters in college who had just placed sixty-fourth overall in the Boston Marathon with a time of 2 hours, 24 minutes.

Neither knew much about the Fourteeners—Denesik had previously summited only eight, and Trujillo had climbed twenty-one— but they figured that their combination of Trujillo's stamina and Denesik's speed would be enough to reclaim the record from the Californian. Their lack of Fourteeners experience became quickly apparent. On their first day, August 6, during the approach to Mount Eolus, Denesik looked down and saw the biggest drop-off of his life—hundreds of feet of air below his heels. "What the hell are you taking me through?" one Rick asked the other. The exposure only got worse. So did the route finding. With no prior experience on so many peaks, the two wasted much time wandering the wilderness. They lost the trail on the approach to Capitol Peak, and spent hours shivering in the dark at 12,700 feet and waiting for dawn. They were lost on a relatively easy traverse from Mount Harvard to Mount Columbia, and they even got lost on perhaps the easiest, least confusing peak, Mount Bross, while trying to descend it at night.

What they lacked in know-how, however, they made up for with muscle and stubbornness. On August 22, 1995, they ran down Longs Peak with a new Fourteeners speed record: 15 days, 10 hours, and 55 minutes.

Though they had vanquished the Californian, the two Ricks, or Rick Squared, as they came to be known, were gnawed by the knowledge that they had blown so much time on a record attempt being lost in the backcountry. They knew, they just *knew*, they could lop hours, if not days, off their record if they had another go at it.

Two years later, on July 29, 1997, they set out to break their own record. This time, they knew the routes, and they had enough experience to know they needed logistical help. They rented an RV and lined up four volunteers to drive them around and cook for them.

They thought they could finish the Fourteeners in twelve days. Mother Nature disagreed.

During their first four days they were forced to climb through, respectively, rain, more rain, dense fog, and lightning. On the fifth day, during their push into a driving rain and lightning storm on Crestone Needle, three retreating climbers asked the two Ricks if they were scared. "If it's our time, it's our time," Trujillo replied. Lightning missed them fifty feet from the summit.

On days six, seven, and eight, they climbed through rain again. On day nine they were greeted with four inches of snow, stiff winds, and visibility of less than fifty feet. Trujillo had already vomited and battled diarrhea. On the summit of Grays Peak, with the snow blowing sideways, he decided he had had enough. He retreated to the warmth of the RV; Denesik continued his traverse to his thirty-second mountain of his record run, Torreys Peak. Just because Trujillo stopped didn't mean he quit, though. He joined Denesik on a climb later that day of Quandary Peak.

Day ten was their first cloudless day. Trujillo commemorated it by dislocating his shoulder during a dodge of a tumbling table-size boulder on the traverse from Snowmass Mountain to Capitol Peak. Though Trujillo took the rest of the day off, Denesik soldiered on. Over the next three days, the wounded Trujillo managed to accompany Denesik on nine of thirteen summits.

The last day was the most disheartening. Denesik was hours ahead of his old record pace on his last peak, Longs Peak, when, at 13,100 feet, he was nearly blasted off his feet by a fearsome rain-and-wind storm. Just 1,100 feet from his final summit, he was forced to quit. Denesik retreated to a Mexican restaurant in Estes Park and waited for the storm to pass. Four-and-a-half hours after his retreat from Longs, he set out again to climb it, guided by the light of a quarter moon, and, more importantly, by Gerry Roach, author of the premier guidebook on the Colorado Fourteeners. At 3:45 a.m., Denesik finished his run with a new Fourteeners speed record of 14 days, 16 minutes. "What I learned," Denesik told me later, "is that the mountains are very powerful and they don't care how fast I want to climb them."

Nursing his raw shoulder and stomach, Trujillo was also humbled by the stiff demands of the mountains. He emerged with one other truism that guided record-seekers in the years hence: "Time is gained not by moving faster, but rather by avoiding mistakes and linking key peaks with traverses."

That direction was taken to heart by Andrew Hamilton, who knew as much about mountaineering as the two Ricks knew about running. As a teen growing up in Colorado, Hamilton had trailed his stepfather up some of the state's most difficult peaks. He was not exceedingly fast, but he did have experience with Fourteeners routes and traverses—especially the shortcuts—that did not appear in guidebooks.

His August 1999 start made it clear Hamilton, twenty-two, a computer programmer with a ponytail, also had extraordinary stamina. In just his first 41.5 hours, he had finished off all ten peaks of the Sangre de Cristos, a range that includes three of the most difficult Fourteeners. On day three, while racing up a snowfield at 13,400 feet on Mount Eolus, Hamilton was confronted by an awful sight: a fallen climber, face smashed in and legs akimbo, motionless on the rocks below. Hamilton called out. No answer. He stumbled down the scree and prepared to offer CPR, but when he checked the fallen climber for a pulse, the arm was stiff with rigor mortis. It was the first time he had ever seen death. A lifetime of adventure above timberline had taught him much about brawn and courage, but little about mortality. What should he do? He had sweated and worked and sacrificed for months—he had trained by running barefoot up a 1,200-foot climb, Mount Sanitas in Boulder, in less than forty-five minutes—just to toughen up for his shot at breaking the speed record. He was already ahead of the record pace, but time was now his enemy. Every second spent waiting with this body above the clouds was a minute that counted against Hamilton's dream. Should he tick away more time calling for help and waiting for Flight for Life to send a helicopter for the body? Or should he press on to the summit? He rearranged the body into a more dignified position. He covered the face with a red bandanna. He choked back tears. His mind raced. What should he do?

Hamilton punched 911 into his cell phone and waited. After a long, long pause, an emergency dispatcher answered, took the details, and told him to wait until a search-and-rescue crew called back. Hamilton waited and waited and waited. He scrambled to a high ridgeline with hopes of finding a stronger cell phone signal. After another twenty minutes of waiting, search-and-rescue called back and asked him to wait another twenty minutes to coordinate a helicopter for body recovery. In that time Hamilton climbed to the top of Mount Eolus and saw that the fallen climber, a judge from Amarillo, Texas, had signed the summit register and scrawled one final word: "SLEET."

After Hamilton waited more than an hour for search-and-rescue, a helicopter flew in. Crews spotted the body, thanked Hamilton, and told him he was free to go. But should he? This was still a race against the clock, and precious hours had just slipped away. Sunset loomed. He decided to press on anyway.

At 13,400 feet, while descending his next mountain, Windom Peak, Hamilton was engulfed in sleet, rain, and wind. The sun was long gone. He huddled beneath his poncho and drifted to sleep, but was awakened by a nightmare of the dead climber's face. He was cold and wet and unable to fall back asleep. He climbed on to Sunlight Peak, one of the most difficult Fourteeners, and summited at 1:30 a.m. He summited eighteen other peaks at night.

The following days were a blur of foot blisters, ice, trailers stuck in mud, lightning, and hemorrhoids that reduced him to tears. His knee hurt so badly that he descended some peaks backward. He was so exhausted on Huron Peak that he swore that elves were riding on his shoulder. His dirt bike was impounded by a jerk at a Buena Vista gas station. He gagged on La Plata Peak after being forced to navigate around a group of hikers on the summit who were wafting one of the world's highest clouds of pot smoke.

He had shed twenty pounds from his body—starting at 160, ending at 140—but, most importantly, he had shaved 1 hour and 28 minutes from Ricky Denesik's record.

Or had he?

Hamilton was no master of logistics. On one of his last mountains, Pikes Peak, his mother was driving him up the road to the summit when he realized she had reached 13,000 feet. This was a big problem. In 1974, the Climbing Smiths had set an important but unwritten speed-record standard, which held that there was no official summit unless the climber had gained at least 3,000 vertical feet of the mountain or mountain traverse by unassisted foot power. The drive up to 13,000 feet on Pikes Peak meant that Hamilton was 2,000 feet short of the 3,000-foot rule. So he found a fifty-foot hill on Pikes and did forty laps on it in an hour.

When Hamilton publicly disclosed his laps afterward, a furor resulted. Sure, he had let hours slip away as a Good Samaritan while working with search-and-rescue to recover the dead climber from Mount Eolus. But many believed that substituting laps for real hiking on Pikes Peak just wasn't cool. In yet another proof of the maxim that the smaller the stakes, the more bitter the fighting—there were no trophies or cash prizes for setting a Fourteeners speed record—a feud erupted. Hamilton believed he had set the record. Others insisted he had not. Egos and tempers stewed over the long Rocky Mountain winter.

When the snow finally melted, the fight was finally settled in the best way possible—on the mountain. The summer of 2000 was one for the Fourteeners record books.

Ricky Denesik, haunted for five years by the what-might-have-beens of his storm-marred 1995 record, was motivated into action by

Hamilton's 1999 record. He blasted off early in the summer of 2000 and, for once, enjoyed weather that was not always miserable. He ended with the first undisputed Fourteeners speed mark in less than fourteen days—12 days, 15 hours, and 35 minutes.

Coincidentally, at about the same time, Danelle Ballengee decided that this wasn't just a man's game. A professional endurance athlete who had won women's marathons at 17,000 feet in Mexico, 14,000 feet in Tibet, plus four consecutive Pikes Peak marathons, Ballengee returned to her home state of Colorado for her next backcountry challenge.

For six days of the same days in July, Denesik and Ballengee ran Fourteeners, though never together. Denesik ended on July 26 with dry skies. Ballengee, who was just six days into her quest, continued on. Her skies turned brutal. On Mount Lindsey, she was stuck in a lightning storm that made her hair stand on end, created buzzing in her ears, and produced thunder so loud that it knocked rocks off cliffs. Scared and wet, she dropped back to her crew at the trailhead and promptly quit. No speed record, she told her helpers, was worth death by electrocution. She cried as they drove away.

Soon, however, the storm broke, and the crew helped Ballengee rally. Though she had lost hours turning around on Lindsey, and more hours crisscrossing the state to dodge other storms, Ballengee resumed her record hunt. She was stranded for hours by an ice storm on Castle Peak, and battled hallucinations on Handies Peak. She lost hours pleading with Lou Pai's ranch hand for permission to climb Culebra Peak. Her mother cried.

On August 4, Ballengee finished on Longs Peak with a time of 14 days, 14 hours, and 49 minutes. She had the first women's speed record.

One month later came the most driven and quirky ultraman of them all, Teddy Keizer.

A student body president at Brown University, Keizer hired on after college as an environmental staffer for Congressman Patrick Kennedy and started preparing for his own political career. After a few months, Keizer realized he knew a lot about the Ivy League and high-level Washington, but little about everyday America. The best way to learn about workaday voters, he figured, was to actually work with them. For the next five years Keizer took on as many different jobs in as many different places as possible. He worked as a pizza deliveryman in Louisiana, hot air balloon pilot in Arizona, sea kayaking guide in Maine, Dungeness crab gutter in Oregon, high school teacher in Massachusetts, and, most memorably, ski hotel worker in Colorado. To save rent, Keizer lived a full winter in a cavern just up the road from his job in the pricey resort town of Crested Butte. From this cold, dark, and dank winter came his nickname—the Cave Dog.

Few dogs were ever so thoroughly prepared. For two-and-a-half years beforehand, the Cave Dog readied himself by running four marathons, poring over maps, and picking the brains of experts like guidebook author Gerry Roach for the best Fourteener routes. After reviewing the day-by-day climbing logs of prior record holders, the Cave Dog concluded that the biggest preventable waste of time came from being lost in the mountains. His solution: Climb each peak at least three times before even attempting a record run. He was also surprised to learn that the other speed climbers usually insisted on a solid night of sleep. A man who had spent a winter living in a cave saw sleep as an unnecessary luxury, and decided to climb as much as possible through the night. His goal was to live nearly two weeks on two-and-a-half-hour power naps.

He tried planning for every contingency. For his Fourteeners record attempt, the Cave Dog assembled a support crew of family and friends, called the Dog Team, that included an executive sous-chef from a restaurant near Aspen, a doctor, a backcountry guide, a Web page designer for live updates, and a postdoctoral student in math who handled press calls and navigation between trailheads. The Cave Dog knew that Andrew Hamilton had lost considerable amounts of time with balky trucks and a dirt bike that would fire up only when rolling downhill in gear. So he assembled his own vehicle fleet with plenty of backup: an RV for sleeping and eating; a jeep and backup four-wheel-drive vehicle for bumpy approaches; two ATVs to reach the especially nasty trailheads; and a Subaru for shuttling around crew members. The idea was for the Cave Dog to waste no time in the field on logistics. At the end of a climb, he would simply show up at the trailhead, be whisked by his crew into the RV for a hot meal, and then nap during the drive to the next trailhead. He contacted twenty-two people ahead of time to make sure he could get up Lou Pai's Culebra Peak without incident, and finally won permission only with the help of local congressman Scott McInnis and a bouquet of flowers sent to a ranch secretary. He weighed and reweighed his gear, trying to shave precious ounces, and ended up with as little as six pounds of shoes and clothes on his body, three pounds of gear in his pack, two-and-a-half liters of water, and one PowerBar to munch on every peak. He planned his days literally to the minute. After researching decades of weather data, he decided to start his quest on September 4 because that two-week stretch offered the lowest chance of thunderstorms. He may have been the Cave Dog, but he was also the Logistical King, an ultrarunner who was also an ultraplanner.

The benefits quickly became apparent. Compared to other record runs, the Cave Dog suffered relatively few surprises. Sure, the RV had backed into a fire hydrant in Canon City, and lightning had stiffened his hair on El Diente, and there was that slip on ice that left him swinging by one arm eight hundred feet above the valley floor during the traverse from North Maroon Peak to Maroon Peak. None of that had eaten up much time, though. The one mistake that really grated on him came on the top of Kit Carson Peak, when the Cave Dog reached into the pocket of his running shorts and found a dime. Oh, the horror! How much energy had been wasted lugging an extra 2.2 grams up the prior twenty-one mountains? (He actually calculated it—2,133 pounds of lift.) The Cave Dog unloaded the dime as soon as he reached the RV.

In the end, he had scaled 138,558 vertical feet and hoofed across 315 miles. He averaged five Fourteeners a day, and completed sixteen at night. He lost fifteen pounds.

And he finished in 10 days, 20 hours, and 26 minutes. The Cave Dog hadn't just broken a record. He annihilated it. And he had so few mishaps en route that many wonder if his record could ever be broken. In the eight years since, no one has even come close.

Others tried different ways. Andrew Hamilton was so bothered by the sniping over his laps on Pikes Peak that he decided to mount another try for the speed record. This time, though, he wanted to do it his way. On June 24, 2003, Hamilton saddled up his bicycle at his home in the foothills above Boulder, pedaled 125 miles south, ditched his bike in the woods near a campground—and climbed Pikes Peak. It was the first day of his attempt to set a human-powered speed record. Though a crew would haul his gear, Hamilton would rely solely on his feet, either in shoes or on pedals, to go up peaks and between trailheads. Because of continuing access problems, he was forced to skip Culebra Peak. He ended up riding 862 miles on a road bike and 380 miles on a mountain bike while hiking 249 miles and gaining 130,000 feet of elevation. He finished in 19 days, 10 hours, and 40 minutes. In the years since, everyone has been either too amazed, or too intimidated, to try beating his human-powered record.

Of course, some thought any kind of speed record was just too easy in the summer. Some set out to climb all the Fourteeners in the calendar winter, December 21 to March 20, when avalanche danger is worst. So far a handful have succeeded. The best-known was Aron Ralston, the adventurer who gained fame by cutting off his arm with a pocketknife to escape a Utah desert slot canyon. Ralston one-upped the other winter climbers by scaling all his peaks solo. It took him seven years; fourteen of his winter Fourteeners were climbed after the self-amputation.

Others thought that walking through neck-deep snowdrifts to reach ice-encrusted summits in the dead of winter was too pedestrian. They increased the Fourteeners ante by strapping on skis. Lou Dawson, a carpenter who built homes for the rich and famous in Aspen, skied his first Fourteener, Castle Peak, in November 1978 with two buddies and ended on May 9, 1991, on Kit Carson Peak as the first person to have skied all the Fourteeners. Though the skiing was often hairy, the toughest part of finishing off the peaks was finding partners to do it with him. Many expert skiers had the ability to descend steep faces; few had the desire to camp on exposed peaks in the dead of winter while also possessing the strength and skill to climb them without a lift ticket.

Fifteen years later, Chris Davenport realized his glory days on the professional extreme-skiing and ski movie circuit were over at age thirty-five. He and his wife had two young sons to support, and one more was on the way. With hopes of extending his career, he searched with his businessman's eye for a new ski project that would be exciting, win gobs of attention, and keep his sponsors happy. His decision: Try skiing all the Fourteeners in a calendar year. Since Lou Dawson's big run, mountaineering ski equipment had improved dramatically, and so had skiers. Davenport had an easier time finding ski partners, but tipped his helmet to Dawson's pioneering work by trying to ski more difficult runs down each peak. By the end of his Fourteeners run, Davenport had racked up more than 500,000 hits on his promotional Web site, had stories and pictures published about him in dozens of magazines and newspapers, and thrilled his publicity-craving sponsors. He did not fall a single time (though one partner did two accidental double backflips off a cliff above the Bowling Alley on Little Bear Peak and finally stopped himself three hundred feet below with a gashed hand). Davenport beat his one-year deadline by three days. "Ski mountaineering is all about being in control," Davenport said. "I feel like my job is being a risk manager." What was good for his goose, however, wasn't necessarily good for his young ganders. There's no way, Davenport told me, that he would ever want any of his sons to recarve Dad's S-turns by skiing the Fourteeners too.

Others were in the field trying to be the first to snowboard all peaks, and to play bagpipes, and to have a dog summit without human assistance. The single coolest record attempt, however, came from Christina Graham, a clinical psychology professor from Seattle.

At last count, she had been photographed naked on top of thirty-three peaks, making her trip reports on 14ers.com the overwhelming audience favorite. Her naughtiest mountain experience: having a light plane repeatedly buzz the summit and tip its wings as she stood in only her climbing boots atop Capitol Peak.

Chapter 15

Scruples

MOUNT DEMOCRAT 14,155'
MOUNT LINCOLN 14,293'
MOUNT BROSS 14,172'

After I survived the climb—and, more importantly, the descent—of Little Bear Peak, the talk back at camp turned inevitably to other difficult mountains.

"So when are you going to climb the Maroon Bells?" one climber asked me, referring to the towering red peaks near Aspen with the reputation of being spectacularly great to view and spectacularly awful to climb.

"Maybe never," I replied. "Those peaks scare me. A lot of people have died there."

Somebody else piped up: "If you've done Little Bear, why don't you think you could do the Bells?"

Then someone else: "A lot more people have gone up the Bells than Little Bear."

And another: "If you can do Little Bear, you can do them all."

Really? This last thought was novel to me. I had started this summer thinking that I could try them all, but not do them all. What if Little Bear truly was as bad as it got? Sure, on that mountain I had made a dumb mistake, and I had slipped, and my stop may have been lucky, but I was not going to let anything like that happen again.

No way. Not in a million years. No chance.

Besides, what good is a lesson learned if it's not put to use?

As my head spun with other delusions and possibilities of mountains to climb, yet another person interjected: What about the Decalibron?

It was as if the little boy in one of our sons' favorite bedtime stories, *Mike Mulligan and His Steam Shovel*, had finally asked how Mike was ever going to get his beloved digger out of that very deep hole. Around camp the question reverberated: What about the Decalibron? Yeah, what about it? What are you going to do about the Decalibron?

Few questions have ever made my shoulders slump faster. The Decalibron was a circuit of four peaks—*Democrat, Cameron, Lincoln,* and *Bross*—that had been closed to all legal hiking for the past three years. Though the vast majority of Fourteeners are public peaks surrounded by public land managed by the federal government, there are exceptions. The hundred-dollar peak, Culebra, is the only mountain that's entirely on private land. Several other mountains, however, are a mix of public and private land. On most mountains with private in-holdings, such as Little Bear, owners simply don't seem to care if anyone scrambles across their property.

For decades, the Decalibron had been open for unrestricted climbing too. With four summits in a seven-mile loop that required only 3,700 feet of elevation gain, the hike was the easiest way in America to accumulate so much real estate above 14,000 feet in a few hours. Tens of thousands completed the circuit. No one protested.

One day, though, a lawyer was trekking the Decalibron when he noticed some century-old mining ruins on the flanks of the peaks. He was so alarmed by the sight of open adits and ramshackle props that he found a mine owner working his claim and asked: Do you know what kind of a legal catastrophe you'd face if some hiker got hurt on one of your collapsed mine workings? The owner, Maury Reiber, age seventy-seven, actually had contemplated that nightmare, but he was letting it slide. As he told me, "The view from the top is fantastic, and

I wouldn't want to deny people a chance to see that." Still, he had been getting increasingly frustrated with the amount of vandalism and outright destruction on his property.

There were unseen dangers too. The Decalibron was honeycombed with miles of mishmash tunnels that, Reiber feared, could collapse under the weight of some unknowing family of hikers. When the U.S. Forest Service started posting Internet advice on the best way to hike the Decalibron—without mentioning that the summits were on private land with ongoing industrial operations—Reiber and the other miners came unglued. Enough is enough, they declared, and shut down all public access. I knew the miners on Mount Antero were packing heat to protect aquamarine crystals worth hundreds of thousands of dollars. How would the miners of the Decalibron protect gold and silver reserves worth tens of millions? (One engineering report pegged the value of unrecovered silver in the century-old dumps outside mines on one peak, Mount Lincoln, at $80 million.) Around mines with Rottweilers I'd seen enough signs that promised "Trespassers Will Be Eaten." If junkyard dogs could turn so tough and mean while living at sea level, I could only guess the level of orneriness that would come from a guard dog's life above timberline.

When I had decided to try climbing all the Fourteeners, I worried about my own age, nerves, and inexperience—not attorneys, trespassing, and the liability insurance crisis. Why risk my neck on the hairiest Fourteeners if the walk-ups of the Decalibron were off-limits? I could just quit now and never wake up before 3 a.m. on a lazy summer day again.

Whoa, there—not all hope is lost, said Rob Witwer when I explained my problem to him. Though he was used to dealing with desperate people who wanted something outrageous out of him, Witwer seemed to genuinely feel my pain.

Let me make a few calls, he told me, and I'll see what I can do.

What exactly he did, I didn't know, but I was grateful for the results. Rob Witwer won me permission from Reiber and other landowners to hike their peaks. Better yet, I'd be able to hike them with

Rob, who, as a Republican member of the Colorado House of Representatives, had worked his tail off to win passage of a law to restore access to the Decalibron and other trails. (I had gotten the idea to call Rob from the Cave Dog, who during his Fourteeners speed record had relied on the help of a congressman to get him access to Culebra Peak.)

Like me, Rob is the father of three, but he's ten years younger. He has just announced plans to retire from the state legislature after only three years in office. The reason: His wife was pregnant again, which would give them their fourth child under the age of seven. "I have this great family and I have this great career, and they both wanted and needed more time," he tells me. "I felt like the guy with one foot on the dock and one foot on the boat, and I knew that story never ended well. I didn't want to be the dad who paid the bills but didn't really get to know his kids before sending them off to college." A politician who quits office to spend more time with his family, and then actually spends more time with his family? That seemed as rare as a summer afternoon without thunderstorms in the Colorado high country. Was this guy for real?

Not only real, but fast, too, as I learn right out of the trailhead. Politicians can talk like fish can swim, but talking while climbing 1,200 feet per hour requires a special gift. Rob has it. Local politics is hard, he says, but addictive. To win election he had to persuade more than three hundred people to give him more than $65,000—he started by calling everybody he could remember since kindergarten—to be able to send out 90,000 pieces of campaign mail and put up four hundred yard signs. That was the bad part. The good part was the walking. He did it three or four days a week for months, and ended up knocking on the doors of 7,200 houses. There's something about politics, he says, that leads strangers to have instant heart-to-heart talks. He remembers the single mom struggling to raise two autistic boys; the financial bigwig who had lost his job six months earlier and was about to lose his new McMansion; and the grieving widow whose recently deceased husband had always told her how to vote. One time he walked in on a couple arguing in their garage. "Excuse us," the wife said, "we're deciding to get a divorce." Rob thought she was joking. She wasn't. When another voter found out Rob was a Republican, he started screaming, "Screw President Bush!" Rob explained that he worked in state government in Denver, not national government in Washington, but added that if he ever met the president he could certainly pass along the voter's concerns. To which the voter replied, "Screw President Bush!" For this job Rob was paid $30,000 a year.

In Rob's district, which ran from the conservative Denver suburbs to the more conservative mountain foothills, winning the Republican Party primary was tantamount to winning the general election; the only Democratic opposition was token. But that didn't mean the Republicans were happy campers. On his walks throughout the district Rob heard grumbles, then outright anger, over a party leadership that viewed environmental regulation mainly as an impediment to business.

As Rob and I top out on our first peak of the day, Mount Democrat, I figure there's no better place for me to ask: What's up with Republicans and the environment?

"I think a core value of conservatism is conservation," he tells me. "Conservatism and conservation mean being frugal and careful and protective of what you have, to guarantee the special things we have for future generations to enjoy. That's what Teddy Roosevelt, who was a Republican, was all about when he created the first national wildlife refuge. Barry Goldwater was a conservationist. But some in my party have been getting away from this core value. There are a lot of very strong conservatives in my district—people who are pro-life, anti-tax, pro-gun—who like to remind me that you can always build another city, but you can't build another Rocky Mountains. These mountains are here because God put them here, and it's our duty and responsibility to make sure that beauty is not destroyed for short-term interests."

I am in awe. Here on a summit at 14,155 feet, I can hardly breathe, but Rob is delivering a political manifesto faster than I can scribble notes.

We take one victory photo and begin the long and gentle traverse to Mount Cameron. It's a non-Fourteener Fourteener, which means it's named on an official government map as a peak higher than 14,000 feet, but isn't distinguishable enough from its neighbors to be included on the Colorado Mountain Club's list of Fourteeners. Cameron's misfortune is to have shoulders that fail to drop at least three hundred feet. Some mathematically oriented climbers have expended thousands of beers arguing over when a bump on a ridge over 14,000 feet makes for a mountain. Most people assume Cameron isn't. I'm not about to argue, because it's easy enough to walk across, which Rob and I do together.

On the way to our next peak, Mount Lincoln, Rob explains his new law, which absolves landowners of legal liability from hiking accidents on private land if there's a marked trail around mine workings and signs warning of dangers. It was his first bill in the Colorado legislature, and he was unsure how his older colleagues would treat him. So he personally contacted every member of a key committee and lobbied the hell out of it, even though the bill had no public foes. When it came time for a vote, however, some old-line legislators decided that the rookie needed some hazing. With straight faces, the senior politicians voted unanimously to kill Rob's bill, then waited for all the blood to drain from his face. Only after he expressed a sufficient amount of shock did the good old boys revive the bill with an obscure parliamentary procedure and pass it unanimously.

Pimped by the Agriculture Committee! Oh, those madcap legislative high jinks!

The legislature, Rob says, is like a high mountain: There's always something to surprise you. One of his favorite stories involves another conservative Republican colleague, Senator Shawn Mitchell. What most people know about Mitchell is that he's a Mormon from Brigham Young University with seven children and a true-believer political pedigree from places like the Federalist Society and the Independence Institute. What they don't know about Mitchell is that he's a fanatical rock climber who has free-soloed—climbed without ropes—a complete circumnavigation of the exterior of the Colorado State Capitol. Never infer somebody's personal interests, Rob says, by knowing only their political labels.

We hit the top of Mount Lincoln, and Rob shouts with glee. A thousand feet above us a peregrine falcon, the fastest animal in North America, swoops down to terrify some brown-capped rosy-finches. A dozen other hikers on the summit, trespassers all, see the spectacular dive and collectively sigh: Ho-hum. Rob, however, is as excited as a schoolboy on Christmas Eve. The environment isn't just a political issue for him. It's a source of wonder and beauty.

On Lincoln we feast on Ho Hos and Fig Newtons, then plan our retreat. Mount Bross is the next and final leg of the Decalibron. On every other peak we have specific permission from landowners to climb, but the legal property rights on Bross are murkier and more complex.

I ask Rob: What do you think about Bross? What Rob thinks about Bross is that he won't climb it without specific permission. I survey the summit just a mile and three hundred vertical feet away and tell Rob that I see no signs or rifle-toting miners with rabid guard dogs warding me away. It's not even 10 a.m., and there's barely a cloud in the sky. Bross beckons.

Rob says: I can't do it. And he hikes away toward the car.

I look at Rob, and I look at the Fourteener.

Of all the things I learned today about life and the legislature, the most painful was the realization that I have fewer scruples than a politician.

Chapter 16

Gnawed

MOUNT LINDSEY 14,042'

For seven full days at home in Denver, I thanked Merrill for letting me hike this summer; took the kids to the pool; helped them build a potato cannon; cut the grass; blew raspberries on our youngest boy's belly; launched model rockets at the park; paid bills; pedaled bikes to the hot dog stand; did laundry; made frozen chocolate-dipped bananas with the kids because they sounded delicious; threw out frozen chocolate-dipped bananas because they tasted disgusting; sorted out tears between brothers; argued with the phone company about our sketchy Internet connection; ate at two different restaurants with my wife; swore at the EZ toilet repair kit that wasn't; turned the lawn sprinkler on the kids on the block during the hottest day of the summer; helped our middle son memorize lines for a play in his summer day camp; gave the dog a bath; and shoveled his crap out of his corner of the yard.

It was great because it felt like old times. It was awful because the phone never rang with a hiking partner. The summer climbing season was marching on without me.

A buddy from Los Angeles had swung through Colorado on vacation, and before I said hi, I pleaded with him to hike with me. He just laughed. Then he thought for a minute, and remembered that he had a buddy from Houston via New York City who had moved to Colorado Springs and professed interest in mountains. I nearly jumped across the lunch table to seize the cell phone that had his buddy's phone number. I called right away and repeated my awkward windup:

Hi, you don't know me but your friend gave me your number even though he says he still likes you. I'm writing a book on being fat and old and still trying to find people who will climb the Fourteeners with me anyway. I have one summer to do this. In September my hiking boots vanish like Cinderella's slippers. If I beg hard enough, will you hike a peak with me?

There was a pause on the other line.

Who gave you my number?

Craig Matsuda. Please don't hold that against him.

Another pause.

Have you climbed Mount Lindsey yet?

My yelp of joy nearly blew out the cell phone network. No, I had not climbed Lindsey. It had been at the top of my to-do list for weeks, but I couldn't find anyone to try it with me. It was supposed to be pretty, but it was a long way from Denver for a day trip, and it was notorious for having crumbly rock.

Well, he told me, if you're interested, a buddy and I are planning to do Lindsey tomorrow. We could meet in Colorado Springs and carpool down the rest of the way.

When I returned home, our sons were having a who-can-make-the-loudest-fart-sound-on-the-arm contest, but I was too thrilled to even try pretending that I was offended. Hiking again after a week's layoff—could I keep pace? How early would I have to wake up at home in Denver to be in Colorado Springs by 3 a.m.? Just who were my latest man-dates?

Their names were David Just and Dean Toda, two buddies who had met during a field class at the Colorado Mountain Club. Both were such good guys that they waited an extra half-hour for me after I took the wrong interstate exit to meet them. They waited for me again after I got carsick on the two-hour drive from Colorado Springs to the trailhead. They even waited for me when I fought nausea, unsuccessfully, during the first two hours of the hike.

What a pair of princes. I was embarrassed but grateful and told them so. Why were they sticking with me?

In the case of David Just, he was unusually experienced with outdoor mishaps far worse than mine. Chief executive of the Colorado Springs office of the Red Cross, he knew all about tornadoes and flash floods. Before the Red Cross he had run the Wilderness Medical Society, which taught him about lightning strikes, snakebites, and heart attacks for fat guys at altitude. After toiling more than twenty-five years for nonprofits across America, he passed along his save-the-world bug to his two children, who now worked as schoolteachers in Thailand and Syria. David was the first climber I'd ever met who, after telling me to take my time on a climb, actually waited around for me to follow his advice.

If David Just was all about patience and recovery, then Dean Toda was a pro at fresh starts. After twenty years as an editor at the *New York Times,* Dean loved the adrenaline surge that came with life at the center of the news. Then his marriage, which was two years older than his job, went kaput. The day-to-day routines that he once loved only deepened his sadness. He had to get out of New York. Dean ended up as a deputy managing editor for the *Gazette,* the daily paper in Colorado Springs. Half his *New York Times* colleagues thought he'd gone nuts. Though his star reporters no longer covered the collapse of Communism, genocide, or war in the Persian Gulf, Dean got a kick out of smaller but competitive hometown stories, such as the gay-sex-and-drugs scandal of a local evangelizing preacher.

Better yet, moving two thousand miles west of the Hudson River gave him a fresh eye for the familiar. Shortly after moving to Colorado, he found his old high school girlfriend, who turned out to be single and living in Houston. He called. They talked. They laughed. She took a new job in Colorado Springs, and they moved in with each other. Thirty-five years later, he was together again with his schoolboy crush. Dean had faith in things working out.

His quiet patience was a good thing, because the weather on the mountain was starting to turn on us. At the base of a stiff climb we stashed our hiking poles along the trail and scrambled quickly with hopes of beating the storm to the summit. At 11:30 a.m., we did. David dove into his backpack for what I assumed was going to be a trail snack, but the mellow, bearded do-gooder whipped out an orange University of Illinois war flag and had me take a victory photo for his alumni magazine. Testosterone at 14,000 feet!

Not that I was complaining, because we needed some kind of extra energy to get our butts moving back down the mountain. The clouds had turned from wispy to wicked, and they were headed our way fast. We scooted down a steep and loose gully while dodging the occasional rock from late hikers above. A few minutes later we found that rocks were the least of our problems.

At the base of the gully where we had stashed our hiking poles, we had visitors. They were hungry.

Three yellow-bellied marmots—woodchucks that usually spent their days lazing around and sunning themselves above timberline— had turned our hiking poles into a late lunch. The main course was my handgrips, laden with salt from sweaty hiking palms. The dessert was the wrist straps and powder baskets and anything else flexible enough to be chewed. There were few leftovers.

My first instinct was to punt the fat, hairy bastards into the next county. They were, after all, about the same size and color as a football. Later, though, I checked in with Dr. Marmot, aka Dan Blumstein, a UCLA biologist working on a forty-seven-year study of a single marmot population in the Rockies near Crested Butte, Colorado. He managed to make me feel sorry for a rodent that had ruined my $80 piece of equipment. According to the good doctor, the life of a mountain pole gnawer is brutal and short.

About half of all yellow-bellied marmots die before their first birthday. Some fall victim to the wind, snow, and arctic blasts that come from a life above timberline, but many become lunches for coyotes, golden eagles, badgers, foxes, and other bloodthirsty predators.

Though most rodents are nocturnal, marmots have adapted to their cold environs by spending most waking hours in summer under the warm sun. To survive the punishing winters, they have become one of nature's most efficient hibernators, with a body temperature dropping to within a few degrees of their burrow air temperatures. High-altitude marmots stay huddled underground from October through May, though during that time they must usually wake up at least once every two weeks to pee. (Older marmots, like older men, wake more often for nature's call.)

When you spend more of the year underground than above, there's a big incentive to make up for lost time. Marmots celebrate the end of hibernation by immediately having sex. They follow that with five months of gorging on food, doubling their body weight to about fourteen pounds. It's still not clear why some marmot colonies thrive while others struggle, though Blumstein is researching his own theory. "It seems that the way to be a successful male marmot is to have a lot of daughters and sleep with them," he told me.

If I'd known that marmot was a perv, I would have punted him after all.

It's even tougher to be the marmot's diminutive high-country neighbor, the American pika. A fist-size creature that looks like a guinea pig but is related to a rabbit, the pika has a dangerous flaw: It is not a sound sleeper. Unlike the marmot, which simply snores through the nastiest winter blizzards, the pika must grit it out. Pikas don't hibernate.

Biologists say the pika's sensitivity to cold makes it a leading indicator of climate change. The irony is that pikas freeze to death because of global warming.

The cycle works like this: Because winters in the Rockies have turned warmer, there's less snow. For pikas, snow is the great insulator that guards against fast temperature swings in their winter homes deep below the mountain talus. With less insulation, underground temperatures plummet. And pikas die.

In the High Sierras of California, researchers found that six of twenty-five pika populations that had existed for at least a century have been wiped out in recent years. And nine of twenty-five populations have been extirpated over a similar time frame in mountain ranges of the Great Basin in Nevada.

For more than a hundred years, pika populations had been moving to higher elevations, following the greater depths of snowfall, at the rate of one meter per year. For the last decade, however, uphill migration by pikas has accelerated to ten meters per year, according to Chris Ray, a pika researcher at the University of Colorado.

While I was hiking Fourteeners, Ray, a new mother, was hopping talus all summer with her nine-month-old son in a backpack. Her work with pikas was taking her higher and higher. She couldn't help but wonder how high her son might have to scramble to see pikas on his own someday.

Chapter 17

Day at the Office

PYRAMID PEAK 14,025'

If it wasn't an inquisition, it was at least an interrogation. The hard-man on the other side of the table looked me in the eye, judged my handshake—was it rock climber tough or city boy soft?—and fired away:

How many mountains had I climbed? What's my pace up the hill? Any Class 4 peaks? Rope experience? What's the most exposure I've faced? Comfortable or scary? Ever scrambled on loose rock? Was making the summit important to me?

For the privilege of answering all these questions, I was paying $495. After striking out a million times to find a weekday hiking partner for difficult peaks, I had turned to a guide service in Aspen for help up Pyramid Peak. My wife was thrilled—if she had her way, I'd have a guide, parachute, and jet-powered backpack on every peak—but I was nervous. Everyone else I had hiked with was, like me, a weekend warrior. A guide, however, did this for a living. My insecurities bubbled. It's one thing to fail miserably on a mountain with a fellow workaday schlub. But failing in front of someone who knew exactly what I was doing wrong, and then telling all his buddies around the campfire about it? Not my idea of fun. If I wanted to be publicly humiliated, I had three children at home perfectly willing to do it for free. I shuddered to think what they could do to me for $495.

Luckily, Jeff Fassett, the guide at Aspen Expeditions, persuaded me to see things from his side of the table. For starters, killing a customer was not good for business, especially one that relied so heavily on word-of-mouth referrals. Besides, it wasn't just my own neck on the line on the mountain; his mattered too. He always put safety above summits, though he believed both could be achieved with enough care and work.

Then it was my turn to ask questions: Had he ever climbed Pyramid before?

More times than he could remember. Between Pyramid and the other difficult peaks around Aspen, he had done about fifteen Fourteeners a summer for the past fifteen years.

Did he think I could make it up a notoriously dangerous peak like Pyramid? After all, this same mountain had already killed another writer, the acclaimed physicist Heinz Pagels, during his seventh climb of it. If there was anyone who fully understood the risks of gravity on a mountain, it was a physicist.

The guide's answer: It was his job to give me the best and safest possible shot at the mountain.

He shook my hand again—tough or soft?—and we agreed to meet at the trailhead early the next morning.

In the dark at 5 a.m., Jeff Fassett and I meet in a parking lot and learn we have at least two things in common. We are both about the same age, and we both slept in our vehicles last night. "I'm a white-collar dirtbag," he says. At least he was in a van. I sacked out in the back of LaKisha. Ah, the joys of housing in Aspen.

For most people in the West, Aspen is to Colorado what Disney World is to Florida—a reliable source of entertainment connected only occasionally to reality. In Aspen last year the average home price was $5 million. A 60-by-100-foot rectangle of dirt sold for $3.5 million. Overlooking town was Aspen's own idea of the Magic Kingdom, a comfy getaway owned by Saudi prince Bandar. Named Hala

(Welcome in Arabic) Bandar's spread was larger than the White House, with party space for 450, fifteen bedrooms, and sixteen bathrooms. It was on the market for $135 million. No tour was allowed unless your name appeared on the Forbes list of billionaires.

Problem was, the wealthier the man in Aspen, the more desperate he grows for help. Somebody there had to help out all those poor rich people by cutting their grass, shoveling their snow, washing their dishes, hauling the trash, changing their sheets, pressing their dresses, and polishing all the children's silver spoons. Proper operation of Bandar's part-time home required a staff of twelve. Hotels and restaurants required thousands more. All those worker bees have to live somewhere.

In Aspen, the most popular gambling game in town is not Powerball or the Colorado Lotto. It's the annual lottery for public housing. Some had waited eight years for a chance to buy or rent one of the city's 2,700 government-regulated affordable homes. Of course, the definition of who could afford what was a little skewed. To be impoverished enough to qualify for life in the projects in Aspen, a married couple could make $193,000 a year, with net assets of $900,000.

Jeff Fassett saw all the hassle and posturing and paperwork and concluded, to hell with all that. He started living out the back of his carpeted van, where aluminum carabiners and steel crampons clinked together every time he turned a corner. Sometimes a friend let him park in the driveway and use the bathroom inside. Other times Fassett relied on a health club and the local Starbucks. A portable DVD player in the back of the van added a homey touch. For most of the cold months he and his wife lived in a house in Tucson, but summers in Aspen were just too nice for him to resist. His wife didn't want to live in a van—imagine that!—so he ventured to Aspen alone and hoped to find a local room to rent for $600 per month when she joined him later this summer.

Though I really, really wanted to dislike Aspen, I understood its allure for Jeff and the other unrich and unfamous. It was a seductively friendly place with free rock and classical music concerts, free public transportation, free dance festivals, free hiking and biking trails, free art shows, free outdoor theater, and some of the grandest free scenery anywhere. Aspen had an impressive public pool, indoor ice-skating rink, and public library. There were great playgrounds for kids, rapids for kayakers, nature preserves for bird-watchers, and riffles for fishermen. The only missing cultural amenity was a zoo, but the Hyman Avenue street mall featured plenty of wild creatures in leopard, crocodile, and cashmere. Plus, the bars brimmed at night with voracious cougars. (So I was told.)

Sure, it was a bummer that Aspen had become a rarefied suburb of New York and Los Angeles, but the rich people were no fools. If I had my own Gulfstream, I'd park it with a hundred others at the Aspen/Pitkin County Airport too. For now, though, my eight-year-old pickup and Jeff's van were good enough.

And so at an early-morning hour when the hungover one-night-standers of the nightclubs of Aspen are heading back home in their Walks of Shame, Jeff and I are heading up Pyramid Peak for our Walks of Pain. After a relatively flat half-mile approach through the woods, we face a half-mile of steep switchbacks, a half-mile of boulder-hopping across a talus amphitheater, and, finally, a half-mile grunt up an even steeper gully coated with ball-bearing pebbles. When we gain a high saddle, my legs are half-spent, but we see that we aren't even half-done.

Hiking with a guide makes some things easier and some things harder. Easier because I can turn off the part of my brain that worries endlessly about route finding. Harder because I am constantly being judged. At the outset of the hike Jeff tells me we'll climb only as long as he feels both of us are safe. Some of his previous customers hadn't even made it this far. We stop for a snack on the saddle and, expecting to get a lecture on the dangers of afternoon thunderstorms, I ask what he's looking for. He says he's looking at me: How fast am I moving? Am I leaning into the mountain like I'm tired? Are my feet shaky or steady? How hard is my breathing?

There's a pause, and I ask him: Well?

So far, so good, he says. We are at least an hour and a thousand vertical feet from the summit. The hiking is over, he tells me. Let the climbing begin.

By now the sun is high enough to fully review the task at hand. It is awesome for a postcard but fearsome for a hiker. A towering jumble of red sandstone blocks, Pyramid Peak is shaped like its name. If it had been built like this in Egypt, though, Pharaoh would have demanded the heads of his construction crews, because much of Pyramid Peak crumbles upon touch. To protect our noggins, Jeff and I strap on our climbing helmets. To protect the rest of us, he straps me into something I have never worn before—a climbing harness.

There's little room for error on this peak, Jeff explains, so all clients must move through dicey sections while protected by him with a short rope. On some scrambling sections with long drop-offs, he'll climb up first, set up behind a rock, and be ready to pull like mad if I start to slip or fall. The number of times he'll short-rope me depends on how well I move up the rock. And that is yet to be determined.

Shortly after the saddle we are confronted by the infamous Pyramid ledges, a series of flat traverses about as wide as half a sidewalk, but with an abyss below. I move as fast as Jeff in this section, which makes him happy. Then he stops. Directly in front of me, a massive rockfall has knocked out a three-foot gap in the ledge. Beneath the gap is a thirty-foot drop onto another ledge, with a three-hundred-foot drop after that. If the three-foot gap were a puddle on the street back home, I'd skip over it without a second thought. The consequences of twisting an ankle here, however, are profound. Jeff hops over first, then braces himself on the flanking wall with the rope. I feel like a dog on a leash. I jump over the gap and never feel the rope.

A few feet beyond, the ledge really narrows, so that my toes touch the rock wall while my heels dangle over several hundred feet of thin air. For whatever reason, the heights don't bother me. Maybe I got used to them this winter while hanging Christmas lights from overhangs on our roof. Maybe my mind just doesn't comprehend drop-offs so vast. Or, as my wife has often noticed, maybe I am very good at denial and simply refuse to acknowledge anything frightening or distasteful.

We clear through the spot and Jeff dishes out a compliment. Another test passed.

A massive thousand-foot face reaches before us, and one thought dominates: We're going to get up *that*? Jeff shifts from skeptic to confidence-builder. You're moving well, he tells me, and you got through that exposure back there just fine. We've got plenty of time.

I ask if he's ever had a customer nervous about heights, and he laughs. Only about a thousand, he says. His standard advice: The bigger the exposure, the smaller you make your world. Instead of dwelling on the drop, focus on your next immediate move. If you concentrate hard on testing every handhold and foothold before committing, you won't have time to freak out about freefalling thousands of feet onto meat-grinding rocks.

Actually, I made up that last part. On hairy sections of mountains I have heard climbers talking about falls about as many times as I have seen *Alive* as an in-flight movie. It just isn't done. Bad mojo.

We traverse for several hundred yards of easy terrain—easy, meaning that I can walk it, but tripping over a shoelace would still turn me into talus panini—and then the terrain turns dramatically more difficult. Jeff stops and looks around. Oops—wrong turn. We double back and try a new direction. It's strangely satisfying to see even a guide screwing up a route on a confusing mountain.

There are several more steep sections to scramble, all with loose rock but nothing with the barrage of Little Bear. After a few twists and turns over blocks, through chimneys, and across scree, we hit the top. Or at least, I do. Jeff is a little funny about it. He insists on remaining below the actual apex. I ask why.

It's all about friends and friends of friends, he says. Though there are gobs of very physically fit people in Aspen, many don't have much mountaineering know-how. Acquaintances often ask Jeff to give them for free what he is supposed to do for a living—guide people up Pyramid Peak. So even on paid trips, he forgoes the last few feet of Pyramid on principle. "This way," he says, "I can tell people in town, 'You know, I've never actually summited Pyramid,' and I'm being completely honest."

Jeff tells me his true love is rock climbing. He has scaled the famously difficult El Capitan in Yosemite and the Fisher Towers near Moab, Utah, while pioneering routes up the rugged granite domes of the Cochise Stronghold near his home in Tucson. Jeff used to be able to scale rock rated at 5.12—highly technical faces with overhangs and tiny, fragile holds—the realm of elite climbers. Now, however, he says years of taking less proficient customers up easier rock has dramatically eroded his own climbing abilities. "Guiding ruins you," he says, "because you work well below your ability level." Still, he'd much rather be on rock than Fourteeners, mainly because it's a lot easier on his body. In fact, as we start our way down Pyramid, he grunts and tells me that if he doesn't lose at least three pounds today, he'll never do a Fourteener again. "This just beats me up too much," he says.

I wonder whether I should be rooting for or against his weight loss. On one hand, Jeff has been a safe guide and an excellent teacher, and I'd recommend him to anyone. At the same time, he hikes like the old BB King song—the thrill is gone, baby. When we—or at least, I—summited Pyramid, there was none of the celebratory backslapping that I had enjoyed with Skip Perkins, fellow amateur, on top of Little Bear Peak. To me, summiting Pyramid, one of the hardest Fourteeners, feels like a really beautiful day at the office. I know many people who dream of living in one of the nation's most beautiful places and climbing mountains for money. Jeff is living their dream, but up close to me it seems more like just another job—and a joyless, grueling job, at that. Jeff had turned to mountain guiding after years of work as a mortgage banker had taken a toll on his peace of mind. Now years of climbing were taking a toll on his body too. On our descent of Pyramid Peak, he tells me his new dream, at age forty-nine, is to take up a more sustainable career.

His plan: golf. In between his days on rock and in the mountains,

Jeff has gotten his golf handicap down to an impressive four. Next summer he hopes to pass the test to become a golf pro. "Golf is going to be easy," he tells me. "All you do at a golf lesson is stand there for an hour and boss somebody around. That's pretty easy on your body." Jeff and I scramble our way back down to the narrow and exposed section of ledge that requires the three-foot leap of faith. He senses my uneasiness, and assures me it's easier to jump the gap than try to climb the unstable rock around it. Of course he's right, but that still doesn't mean I like it. Jeff has one other piece of advice. "You know the thing about golf?" he says. "It's really not that dangerous."

Chapter 18

Limits

MAROON PEAK 14,163'
CASTLE PEAK 14,279'

The sky was gray, but that might not be bad. Jordan White and his father, Kip, had enough experience with snow climbs to know that a cloudy day could steady the temperature of the mountain. That meant less avalanche danger. And if there was one thing they needed on this day, it was less danger.

Their goal was the top of one of Colorado's diciest mountains, Maroon Peak, followed by a traverse to its temperamental twin, North Maroon. Even in perfect summer conditions, the Maroon Bells, near Aspen, were among the most unforgiving Fourteeners, having killed more climbers than all but one other Rocky Mountain. This father-and-son team was scaling the Bells in May, with both peaks still buried under several feet of snow. Hard peaks made even harder.

Of course, if it were easy, they wouldn't be interested. Just last weekend, while attempting Longs Peak, they were confronted by a shell-shocked mountaineer in retreat who warned that the route was so treacherous and icy that he cheated death five separate times. Jordan and Kip thanked the man for his advice, then continued on up. They were so unfazed by the conditions that they took a half-hour nap on the summit. No big deal.

They had climbed together so many times that each man always seemed to know what the other was thinking. They had started together when Kip took Jordan up his first Fourteener, San Luis Peak, at age five. When Jordan was in sixth grade, his father led him through chest-deep snow on a three-night, thirty-mile winter odyssey up the Mount of the Holy Cross. While his classmates parked for entire weekends in front of their PlayStations and Nintendos, Jordan worried about frostbite and whether he was living up to the expectations of his father, who never did anything halfway. Some men played tennis; Kip worked hard enough to make his university team. Some played guitar; Kip wrote and produced seven albums of his own Christian-themed songs. Some worked as engineers; Kip founded his own consulting firm and had engineers working for him. There were times in middle school and high school when Jordan hated all the pain and hardship that came from climbing mountains in winter with his father, but the last few years he had come around to love the trips. They were a formidable team: both six foot four and two hundred pounds, with blond hair and blue eyes. Kip was forty-nine. Jordan was nineteen and home from his first year at Colorado State University. Together they moved fast up a mountain.

Their route for Maroon Peak was the Bell Cord, a 45-degree gash up the mountain that narrowed to as little as fifteen feet. In late May, the snow in the Bell Cord was higher than a man's head. At night the snow froze hard enough to let a climber walk atop it. By day, however, the warm spring sun softened it all into a mass of goo that, at best, had climbers sinking with every step up to their crotches and, at worst, posed a serious avalanche and rockfall hazard. The idea was to be done with the Bell Cord before the Bell Cord was done with you.

To reach the snow at the magic temperature—pliant enough to kick steps, sturdy enough to prevent postholes—they had set off well before dawn. They settled into a strong rhythm. It was 1,800 feet of unrelenting up.

About halfway up, the clouds started spitting. Just below the top of the Bell Cord, at 13,800 feet, the snow fell a little more frequently, but remained wispy and gentle. Kip and Jordan stood less than a half-mile from the summit of North Maroon Peak. In the best of conditions, the traverse from Maroon Peak to North Maroon is one of Colorado's nastiest scrambles, a ferocious mix of rotten rock, boot-width ledges, and crumbly cliffs with sheer, 1,200-foot drop-offs. It might take two hours on a bluebird day.

The father and son decided to go for it. The snow was more of a nuisance than a threat. Besides, the Whites had ropes and other climbing protection, as well as the confidence built up from years of successful climbs on other burly peaks.

About an hour into the traverse, though, the light flakes turned wet. Skies darkened. As Kip and Jordan prepared to cross from the east to the west side of the connecting ridge, the snow fell like one of those shaken winter wonderland snow globes.

At the very top of the ridge the snow globe turned mean.

Suddenly they were blasted by 30-mph winds laden with heavy snow. On their scramble up the Bell Cord, the massive east face of Maroon Peak had sheltered them from weather advancing from the west. No more. On the exposed saddle ridge they were fully exposed to the elements, and suffering because of it.

Visibility plunged to twenty feet. The cold sapped their strength. Every step was a struggle. Over the wind Jordan yelled to his father, "This is ridiculous." Kip agreed. They decided to retreat.

They tried to work their way back along the high ledges, but handholds were slippery and the gales threatened to pitch them down the mountain. Kip remembered a couloir feeding back into the Bell Cord that offered a shortcut. It was snowy and very steep at the top—perhaps as sheer as 65 degrees—but it offered shelter from the west winds and an escape from the icy tightwire of the Bells' connecting ridge.

Kip set up a belay at the top of the gully and protected Jordan with rope as the son downclimbed 250 feet. Kip followed with sure feet, but no safely secured rope.

The two huddled together and debated what to do next. Below them the slope eased into a rock band that dropped fifty vertical feet over a hundred-foot run. Kip didn't want his son to risk an unprotected downclimb in such snowy conditions, so he set up another anchor for the rope. Jordan clipped in, and his father lowered him through the cliffs until his feet dangled twenty feet above the rocks.

Then the rope went slack.

Jordan landed on his feet, but the force of a two-story fall buckled his knees. He somersaulted once and tried to stop himself and somersaulted again. He reached out in desperation, but his hands went empty. He ragdolled and rolled and hit a rock and the world went black.

He woke up under nine inches of snow, which was mostly red. His climbing helmet was split at the forehead. His left eye hurt. His left shoulder screamed. His left leg didn't want to move. His right knee felt numb. He wore only one glove. He sat up and the pain shot everywhere. He wondered: Where am I? What happened? Where's my dad? Jordan needed a drink, but his only water bottle was cracked and empty. With his one good arm, he threw the bottle in disgust. It cascaded out of sight down the mountain.

His head throbbed with the pain and fog of a severe concussion. His understanding slowly returned. He was back down in the Bell Cord. He'd been unconscious several hours. He'd tumbled at least four hundred feet. His shoulder was dislocated. His leg was broken. His face, chest, and back were covered with scrapes that oozed blood every time he moved. His nose was a gusher.

Where was his dad? Stuck on top of that cliff? Hurrying down to get help?

Jordan stood carefully. He was on a 45-degree snow slope and his ice axe was lost. He brushed snow off his shredded clothes. His climbing harness had survived. He was still clipped into the rope. He tugged and saw it was buried in the snow and running downhill. He followed it. He tugged the rope again and saw something move from under the snow.

It was his father's leg.

Jordan rushed over and swept off the snow. Kip's foot was pointed uphill. His helmet was split in half and coated in blood. His face was purple. Jordan's father was dead.

Jordan fell back to the snow and sat for a long time. All that moved were the questions in his head: What just happened? Is this for real? Is this a nightmare? When am I going to wake up from this?

Snow was still falling, and dusk approached. Jordan knew he couldn't do anything to save his father, but he still had a chance to save himself. He was 3,700 feet above the valley floor, with a long, steep, slippery gully to negotiate by himself.

With so many broken bones, every bootstep hurt. The more he tried walking, the more the pain ratcheted up. He could hardly bear it. He had no axe, but decided that glissading was his only way off the mountain. He sat on his butt and slid, hoping that he'd never have to use his fractured tibia as a brake. He skidded a few yards and stopped, then repeated. The new snow that was so disastrous up high was proving to be his savior down low in the Bell Cord, because it helped control his sliding speed. He had no watch, so couldn't guess how long the descent was taking, but it felt like forever, and he swelled with relief when it was over.

Then the realization set in: He was still three miles from his car. The sun had set and Jordan's headlamp was lost in the fall. He lost the trail, and kept bashing into logs and rocks with his broken leg. He fell as much as he walked. He couldn't take it anymore. He gave up. He collapsed next to a big boulder in the pines. His mind put the accident on an endless loop. His dad was still on the mountain above him. He tried to sleep but couldn't. He shivered all night.

At dawn he wrested himself from the ground and stumbled back to the car. He drove eight miles through the canyon before reaching a cell phone signal. Jordan tried calling 911, but a rush of increasingly frantic voice-mail messages overwhelmed both his phone and his father's phone. He was finally able to dial out by the time he reached the highway, three miles later.

When a sheriff's deputy met him on the side of the road, he looked at Jordan's face and winced. Jordan hadn't seen himself yet. He peered in the rearview mirror and understood the cop's reaction.

The deputy offered to drive Jordan to the hospital, but Jordan figured switching cars wasn't worth the hassle. He parked outside the emergency room and called his mother, who was the source of most of the voice-mail messages.

"Papa's dead," he told her. "We had a climbing fall and Papa's dead."

They had been married twenty-five years. Her tears dissolved him.

Jordan spent the next eight weeks in casts and slings. On the tenth week, he climbed Mount Belford and Mount Oxford in a day. With his left leg weak from two months of immobilization, he face-planted several times on the trail, but he felt proud of himself for making it. He thought his father would have wanted him to keep climbing, and so Jordan did. He summited fourteen more Fourteeners before the snow flew again that fall.

Two years later, I made the mistake of doubting the tenacity of Jordan White.

We had arranged to meet at 5 a.m. Saturday on the flanks of Maroon Peak. He was coming from his summer internship apartment near Aspen; I had backpacked in 3.5 miles the night before to camp at 10,500 feet near a landmark along the trail known as Bent Tree. The ascent up Maroon Peak was supposed to be physically challenging, and I knocked off as much distance as possible the night before the main event. I wanted my legs to be fresh in the morning.

But at 3 a.m. it started raining. Not hard, but enough to penetrate the canopy of pines and soak my tent. At 4 a.m. my wake-up alarm rang, and I discovered fog so thick that my headlamp could see no more than ten feet into the gloom. At 5 a.m., our planned meeting time, Jordan was nowhere to be seen. At 5:15 a.m., I wondered if he was still coming. At 5:25 a.m. I unlaced my boots and snuggled back in my sleeping bag, convinced he had decided to stay home and dry. At 5:35 a.m. I heard sticks cracking in the woods. I poked my head out of the tent. "Hey," Jordan said. "Sorry I'm late."

On the hike in to meet me, Jordan had jumped a deer in the dark, which proved more startling to man than beast, because Bambi could hear him coming, while Jordan had his two ears pounding with Collective Soul from his iPod. Hiking alone through thick predawn fog after scaring up a big wild animal was not the most relaxing way to start a weekend. Jordan seemed glad to see me.

And I, him, though I wasn't sure we would do anything with our backcountry meeting. The fog was so thick it dripped off trees. Was hiking blind really the best way to take on a confusing, treacherous peak like Maroon?

Jordan's answer: Let's give it a try and see how it goes.

Since the 2005 tragedy with his father, Jordan had summited this peak twice. With steep slopes, route-finding challenges, rock scrambling, and spectacular views, Maroon had just about everything he liked in a mountain, except for the memories. At this point in the summer, the Bell Cord route up Maroon Peak has long since melted out. Our plan is to take the easiest way up, though the easiest path for this mountain is harder than for all but a handful of other Fourteeners.

With sunrise the fog thins, but still prevents us from seeing much more than thirty feet ahead. This may be a good thing. From Bent Tree rises the most punishing, unrelenting gully of any standard route on a Fourteener—2,800 feet of gain in less than a mile. Though the gully is not technical, it is brutal.

Jordan is such a physical specimen that he can usually climb a phenomenal 2,500 vertical feet per hour. I've warned him that my own physical limit is about two-and-a-half times slower than that. To make sure the message sinks in, I tell him to imagine that he's hiking with his mom. I intend it as a joke, until he tells me that his mother is only five years older than I, and that she has climbed a bunch of Fourteeners. Hmmm. Just imagine, I tell him, that tapioca is my favorite food, *The Golden Girls* my favorite show, and that the waist of my Sansabelt rides just below my armpits. I'm not sure he understands the *Golden Girls* part, but he does get the overall message. He slows to a pace that grants me enough oxygen to both climb and speak.

I ask if he ever considered giving up climbing. A little, he said, but then he realized he loved it too much. He has replayed his father's death about a million times in his mind, and still isn't sure exactly how or why it happened.

They both thought they had enough snow experience to try a climb like that. They both made the decision to turn back when they did. They both thought their rope was securely anchored. They both thought the shortcut was the fastest and, given the conditions, the safest way down the mountain.

I ask what he learned from the tragedy.

The main lesson, he says, is that the human body is capable of being pushed through incredible pain, fatigue, and fear. Few people ever have an inkling of what it's truly like. The people who do know, however, find it both shocking and humbling. Jordan says he understands why people try hundred-mile footraces up and down the mountains. To reach your physical and emotional limit and push beyond it—way beyond it—is about as life-affirming as it gets.

I ask what he learned about grief.

Mostly, he says, that everyone does it differently. For Jordan, grief was awful but eventually bearable. He says his younger sister has had a harder time. He thinks the difference is the closure he received from being with his father on the mountain, but he's still not sure. The key, he says, is to back off and let people grieve the way that best fits them.

Then he asks me about tapioca. I apologize again about my pace, but he tells me I'm doing surprisingly well. What he wants is a change of subject. I tell him I feel bad about bringing it up in the first place, and he waves me off. He wants to climb.

About two thousand feet up the gully we stop and revel in a thrilling sight: The clouds are far below us. The fog is gone. The weather is clearing. Sometimes you just don't know, he says, unless you give it a try.

He asks me about my climb of Pyramid two days earlier, and I tell him about the leap of faith, the befuddling route-finding, and the gorgeous weather up top. Oh yeah, I add, I did it with a guide.

This stops Jordan in his tracks.

He asks: A guide? Why would you want a guide? His face looks like he has just sniffed something that is particularly rancid.

I tell him about my difficulty finding hiking partners, especially on weekdays, and my no-solo pledge to my wife, and my desire to learn about climbing from people far more skilled than I. He shoots me a noncommittal uh-huh and keeps pushing up the slope. I feel like I've let him down.

From the top of the gully, the summit appears depressingly far in the distance, with a perplexing maze of sofa-size blocks to navigate along the way. Jordan, however, knows the route by heart. With no route-finding decisions to debate, my nervous energy plummets, and I'm able to put everything I've got into the climb. I need it.

On the top he high-fives me.

"I've got something to tell you," he says. "You don't need a guide."

I don't even think before the words blurt out of my mouth.

"And I've got something to tell you," I say. "You might be only twenty-one years old, but you're more of a man than a lot of the adults I know."

As soon as I say it, I feel stupid and condescending. Jordan, however, smiles. "There's something about being up here," he says. "I like being up here. I really do."

That afternoon, back in the comfy confines of downtown Aspen, I'm in my biggest trouble of the day: My man-date for tomorrow is AWOL. We had swapped e-mails, picked a mountain, and agreed on a day to climb it. Except that, for the past two days, he has refused to answer any of my phone messages, of which there have been many. I try again for good measure but get the same four-rings-and-a-voice-mail. I shoot him an e-mail from the public computers at the Aspen library, but that goes unanswered too.

Weeks ago, when I first started scrounging for man-dates on the Internet, I had admitted that I was desperate. But putting my faith in a man-date and then coming up empty—what did *that* make me? I knew the answer—pathetic—but I didn't particularly relish the thought of admitting it to my wife. I was too embarrassed to speak to her in anything but hushed tones.

I got dumped, I told her over the phone. Stood up. Stiffed. Abandoned. Left alone at the trailhead altar.

Merrill and I both knew what was coming next, but neither of us would outright say it. So I told her I had called a couple of friends who live an hour down the road, and begged them to hike with me tomorrow, but they were busy, as was another friend two hours away, as were another three, etc., etc., etc.

She asked: Was there still a chance that guy might show up?

There's always a chance, I said.

Well, maybe that other guy will show up. Or maybe there will be some other people at the trailhead to hike with.

Maybe.

Would I promise to be careful?

I promised to be careful.

Would I call her with my cell phone from the mountain?

I promised.

The truth was, Castle Peak was not supposed to be a difficult mountain, and it probably wouldn't have been, if only I had followed the correct trail, avoided that loose refrigerator-size rock, and not mistaken that pile of crappy sandstone for a cairn marking an easier shortcut to the top. No matter. I still survived my solo scramble, and it was probably better for my ego that no one else had seen how easily and routinely I could gunk up a straightforward climb.

On the summit before me is a lone woman, older than me but looking significantly less frazzled. Her name is Kathie Lamm. She couldn't find a hiking partner, so she backpacked up last night and camped by herself at 12,000 feet. She is sixty-two years old and she lives near Aspen. Unlike me, she took the right path up the mountain. Judging by the grin on her face, she's taking the right route through life too. We talk about descending together—I'd like to be able to tell Merrill I hadn't hiked completely solo—but she's headed back to her tent. I feel the pull of nearby Conundrum Peak, another non-Fourteener Fourteener less than a half-mile away along an uncomplicated ridge. Though it is fun to stand atop a second summit, the real attraction of the traverse for me is at the bottom of the saddle, where I see a very long snowfield pointed toward my truck and think: Glissade!

Which is exactly what I do, until I realize that it's getting late in the summer for a glissade, and the snow is hard and bumpy and—oof!—flecked with fist-size rocks. The seat of my pants rips from the crotch to the waist. I'm grateful that the only thing damaged is my trousers.

The big tear does make for an interesting hike out, though, especially when I meet up again with Kathie Lamm, who is either too tired, or too polite, to say anything about the fashion sense of a man walking down a mountain with a long tail of blue boxer shorts hanging out a strange and very large ventilation flap in the back of his pants.

Chapter 19

Man Maker

MISSOURI MOUNTAIN 14,074'

Our oldest son returned home from summer camp two inches taller and one octave lower. He didn't need a shave, but a haircut was non-negotiable. So was some serious time together for the two of us.

After he sent out a trillion text messages, ate a billion burritos, saw a million movies, swapped a thousand new iPod songs with a hundred best friends at a dozen parties, it was finally down to just the two of us. I had a hike in mind that he didn't seem to mind. Better yet, we decided to make a camping trip out of it.

Missouri Mountain, we're coming to get you.

It would be my third time up the very same trail—the first was during my unsuccessful summit attempt with Shad Mika and Kirk Tubbs, and the second was with Mike Brislin en route to Mount Belford and Mount Oxford—but I didn't care. Two days in the backcountry with my son and no TV, PC, or PS2; I hoped for LOLs but feared the :-(

I want to set the right tone for the long grind uphill, so I start in on a story from the first part of his life. Cass was five months old and I was on my first paternity leave when I decided that we both needed some socks. I walk over to the local department store with him in a backpack. Fresh from a big score on closeouts in the baby section, I was angling over to the men's racks when our son decided he'd had

207

enough. He bawled. I took him out of the pack and tried to comfort him with a pacifier, bottle, and even my best lullaby, but the baby would have none of it. He wailed more. As I gathered up all our stuff for a quick exit, a fiftyish man approached with an armful of stacked twentyish eye candy. His chest was out and his smile was smug.

Over the baby's bawls, the guy summoned his best Ted Baxter voice. "Sounds like somebody needs his mommy," he told me.

"Wrong," I replied. "He's actually a jerk detector, and you just set him off."

Thirteen years later, Cass is hearing the story for the first time, and he enjoys it. I seize the moment.

You're still a pretty good jerk detector, I tell him, even if you don't cry as loud about it anymore. And then I launch into my regular fatherly reminder about peer pressure and teen sex that begins, "You know, it's all about love and respect, for yourself and for others . . ." He knows where this is going, and he cuts me off, which is fine, because I'd much rather have a dialogue than a monologue, especially since he told me earlier this year that two girls in his seventh-grade class were already on birth control.

"Hey, Dad," he says. "At camp we had these dances every Saturday night."

"And there were girls?"

He's ahead of me in the woods on the trail, but I can feel his eyes rolling from here.

"Yes, there were girls. There were a few from Sweden."

What my male mind wonders: From Sweden? Wow! What did they look like?

What my parental mouth says: "Were they nice?"

"Dad! Anyway, we had these dances and a lot of guys wanted to dance with the Swedish girls," he said, providing the unsolicited answer to my male mind question. "But no one was having much luck. There was one guy who really, really wanted to make a big impression. He thought if he could speak some Swedish to them, it might really help. There were some Norwegian guys at camp who knew a little bit of Swedish, so he asked them for help—how to say, 'I really want to dance with you,' but in Swedish. So the Norwegian guys taught him what to say, and made him practice it a few times until it sounded right. The guy walked over to the girls with a big smile on his face and said the whole thing to the girls in Swedish. And in front of everybody, one girl slapped him."

"So when the guy thought he was asking the girl for a dance in Swedish, what was he really saying?"

"Can I show you my penis?"

Holy crap! My son's first raunchy joke! Should a good parent be horrified, disgusted, or aghast? This takes too long to consider. I do what comes naturally and laugh hard enough to make water spurt out my nose. Cass may never look at me the same way again.

We reach our campsite well above timberline in less than two hours. It's my fastest time up this trail this summer, despite our thirty-pound overnight packs. I tell Cass that he hiked a hard grunt at a man's pace, and he just shrugs. At camp, he says, we did a thirty-mile backpacking trip.

This means he knows what it's like to lop off a sweaty pack at the end of a long hike. Joy, pride, relief—we feel more than we say. Outside our tent at 12,200 feet, we eat dinner by headlamp and watch Jupiter rise to the south just above the Milky Way. I throw my arm around his shoulder and he doesn't flinch.

We reach the ridge on Missouri at about the same time as the morning sun, and the view amazes me. Gone without a trace are the cold, foreboding ice, and snows of my May hike with Shad and KirkT; in their place are grassy knolls and wildflowers pink and purple scratching out a living from dirt around the talus. It's not quite the green vista from the last scenes of *The Sound of Music,* but it ain't the slip-and-slide of winter either.

Just below the top we pause at the same traverse that stopped me in my tracks two months earlier. Cass asks: What's so bad about this?

In the snow, I tell him, it's an entirely different mountain.

He just shrugs his shoulders. I guess some things you have to see—and be terrified by—to fully appreciate.

On the summit I tell him how proud I am of him, and he flashes a big grin. He finds a cell signal. "Hi, Mom," he says. "We made it."

It's a gorgeous day, sunny, blue, and windless, and there should be no better time for a massive summit lunchtime feast. Problem is, it's not even 8 a.m. This may be the first and only time my thirteen-year-old son has turned down junk food.

I remind him of the time we stopped short of summiting Torreys Peak. That was only last summer, but it seems like a lifetime ago. There are no crazy feet on this trip, just feet that have grown enough to require size 10 1/2 boots. That's the same size as mine. On the way down off the ridge he urges me—me!—to be careful.

There's a trail switchback about five hundred feet above the valley floor that turns just above a rock gully. Though the trail zigs and zags many more times, the gully goes straight down. Cass wants to go straight down. I protest by showing him that the gully ends on the wrong side of a rock rib that we'd have to climb. I am categorically opposed to any more climbing when we are supposed to be descending, even if it's a shortcut. He says the gully skirts the rib and avoids any up.

I tell him I'm right and he's wrong. He tells me I'm wrong and he's right.

The best way to learn, I figure, is to make your own mistakes and solve them. So I agree to go his way, even if it is the wrong way. We talus-hop down the gully with me reminding him all the way that we're doing this only because he insisted, and that he can't blame me for having to ascend an extra two hundred vertical feet because of his wrongheaded shortcut.

Whatever, Dad.

And then we reach the bottom and discover that, sure enough, the shortcut works. He's right and I'm wrong. I apologize and tell him I feel bad for being so bullheaded and stupid. He tells me that if it will make me feel better, I can still go climb the extra two hundred vertical feet.

I'd give him a stiff kick in the pants, if only I could catch him. I started this hike thinking my son was a boy. I'm ending it watching him turn into a man.

Chapter 20

The Needles

MOUNT EOLUS 14,083'

SUNLIGHT PEAK 14,059'

WINDOM PEAK 14,082'

In college we called him the Prince of Inertia. He woke up late, lived in shorts, and spent much of his time tanning on a deck. No one ever saw him go to class. When he floated a Frisbee, physics students stopped to gape. He had more jazz records than the campus radio station. He dated three women at the same time. He seemed physically incapable of breaking a sweat.

Twenty-four years after college graduation, when I put out my all-points-bulletin e-mail for hiking partners this summer, the Prince was the only one who responded. He had never climbed a mountain in his life. He lived in the flatlands of New York. He volunteered to hike a week with me in Colorado in August.

I thanked him profusely, but reminded him that inertia wouldn't get him up a mountain. Less tanning and more training might be in order.

His response: Well, in the past five months I've only run four marathons, but if you think it will help me get used to altitude I'll start running with duct tape over my nose and mouth.

Now I was the one who needed duct tape—to prop up my dropping jaw. From schoolboy physics I remembered Sir Isaac Newton's law of inertia, which holds that an object in motion will remain in motion unless acted upon by an external force. I could not fathom the external force necessary to start the Prince of Inertia on a single jog, much less four marathons in five months. Now that he was moving, my goal was to be the force that moved the Prince up a mountain.

First I had to find out what the hell had happened. We had a seven-hour drive from the Denver airport to the start of the hike in Durango, so he clued me in.

Turned out that on college graduation day, when some friends fretted whether they'd be called up onstage for a diploma, the Prince graduated with a 3.7 grade point average, a degree in economics, and a 99th-percentile score on a graduate school admissions test. (He had always been able to finish the crossword puzzles I could only start.) He enrolled at a top-five business school, the University of Chicago, and left two years later with an MBA and a plum job offer from the corporate giant AT&T. He bought a condo. For six years he supervised a battalion of telemarketers. He was making good money. He wore suits. He was completely miserable.

On the most frightening day of his life, he went golfing with his father, who was running the same bank that had given him his first job thirty-five years earlier. His father had put him through college and business school. The Prince knew what he wanted to tell his dad, but was so worried he'd chicken out that he gave himself a deadline of the thirteenth hole to say it. When the thirteenth hole arrived, he bucked up and told him: Dad, I hate my job and I want out. He waited for the parental wave of disappointment to wash over him.

It did not come. His father's advice was simple and direct: If you don't like your job, then get out. Do the things you want when you're still young enough to enjoy them. Don't be trapped. Follow your muse.

The Prince didn't wait for a second opinion. He ditched corporate life and spent the next two years driving America in a two-seat convertible with golf clubs in the passenger seat, a suitcase in the trunk, and no regrets in the rearview mirror. He hit forty-two states. He sliced his golf handicap in half. He spent more nights sleeping on the sofas of friends than on any permanent bed. He had no one to boss, and no one bossing him. He smiled—a lot.

And then the money ran out. Though his road trip had come while on leave from AT&T, he couldn't imagine going back. After spending two of the best years of his life working for nobody, he had no appetite to work for somebody.

So he decided to scale back. He gave up the condo and moved into a family cabin with no roads, no television, no cell phone signal, and no winter insulation. The only access was a half-mile boat ride across a deep, clear lake. To pay the bills, he patched together writing work for Web sites.

Without an office or travels to fill his days, though, his mind went restless. He missed mental and physical exhaustion. While on sabbatical, out of boredom and frustration he started running—slowly at first, then 10K jogs just to see if he could finish, and finally bumping up to a marathon. By the time he volunteered to try his feet on a Colorado peak, the Prince—his real name was Steve Mott—had finished twenty-two marathons. His times in his two most recent marathons, in Houston and Cincinnati, had earned him a qualifier's spot in the Boston Marathon.

Once again, I braced myself to be smoked up a trail by someone in much better shape. This time, though, there was a hitch: All my remaining peaks were rough ones—rough for exposure, or spicy scrambling, or long backpacks, or all of the above. The Prince didn't seem to mind, though. His only request was a trip to remember. Interestingly, he never specified whether the memories should be good or bad.

Nevertheless, I had my mission, and I accepted it with glee. If the only person who had agreed in advance to hike with me this summer wanted a memorable trip, then I was going to make sure he got one. But how could I make the West stand out to a native New Yorker? For the first time all summer, I had a new obsession.

For his introduction to the Rockies I fell back on my old standby—

a bar. The saloon in the 120-year-old Strater Hotel of Durango in southwest Colorado was dark, scruffy, and layered with more red velvet wallpaper than a Victorian bordello. It was also directly beneath the hotel room where Louis L'Amour wrote many of his Sackett series Westerns. The barmaids were all done up in vintage outfits—fishnet stockings up to here, cleavage down to there—and the piano player pounded out an impressive array of ragtime and other old honky-tonk songs. But what most impressed the Prince was the friendly lug on the next barstool, a big-game outfitter, who had had enough bourbon by the time we met him to give us detailed instructions on the best way to field-gut a moose. (His main advice: Don't accidentally puncture the intestine.)

We excused ourselves before completely losing our appetites, but for some reason still heeded the guide's advice to dine at his friend's steakhouse, where the slabs of red meat came as thick as a saddle, with whiskey, pumpkin-size potato, bucket of butter, and defibrillator on the side.

The Prince's eyes glazed, but I pushed him on. I knew my only chance at slowing a twenty-two-time marathoner to my hiking pace was to clog his arteries and poison his liver. I'd seen him withstand worse in college. With Advil, much is possible.

It makes a fine breakfast, too, which is a good thing, because the next day was a big one. Our goal was so formidable that we needed a steam-powered locomotive to reach it.

There were three Fourteeners so deep inside the Weminuche Wilderness area, Colorado's largest, that the most practical way to reach them was by train. The Durango & Silverton Narrow Gauge Railroad is a smoke-belching relic of the nineteenth century that now exists mainly to transport old men obsessed with trains and young boys obsessed with trains from the tchotchke shops of Durango to the fudge, funnel cake, and jerky shops of Silverton. For 200,000 tourists a year, it is a ninety-mile-round-trip ride through a sheer river canyon behind a 143-ton steam locomotive that had once moved $300 million of gold and silver to market. The same Wild West train had transported John Wayne, Jimmy Stewart, Marilyn Monroe, Robert Redford, Paul Newman, and Marlon Brando in films like *How the West Was Won, Ticket to Tomahawk, Butch Cassidy and the Sundance Kid,* and *Around the World in 80 Days.*

My hope was that the Prince would be impressed by the Hollywood ride, but his eyebrows raised mainly over the two women just across the aisle from us. Neither wore a wedding ring. One was an assistant district attorney who had just won a conviction of a serial arsonist; the other was the admissions officer for a hospice. Though they were sipping their morning Bloody Marys like party girls on holiday, they were both headed to the same backpacking destination as the Prince and I. Mindful of the Prince's history of dating multiple women at the same time, I reminded him that if he tried something questionable with these two, they could easily make sure he rotted in prison before suffering a very slow death.

Two-and-a-half hours after whistling out of Durango, the train halted deep in the canyon at a suspension bridge over the river. It was our stop. The Prince and I joined about twenty others to extract our backpacks from a pile in the cargo car. As the train pulled away, I struggled to tell whose eyes were wider—the people on the train, who were just realizing that we were being left in the middle of nowhere, or the Prince, who was just realizing that we still had a seven-mile backpack until camp.

Though the two women were fun, they quickly figured out that backpacking 35-pound loads wasn't the easiest after Bloody Marys on the train. The Prince and I plowed ahead. Destination: the Chicago Basin of the Needles Range, home to three amazing Fourteeners.

One great thing about hiking the Rockies with a flatlander: watching the awe in his face. Every bend on our pack up the Needle Creek trail revealed one sight more stunning than the next—a towering cliff, an avalanche chute strewn with aspen trunks, a footbridge that spanned a waterfall. With views like this, nobody cared about hiking pace.

We set up camp at the base of a high cathedral of rock. Towering pink spires lorded over a valley lush with wildflowers, willows, and spruce. Fritillaries flitted between violets, and black swifts darted high over the tumbling creek. We were too slack-jawed to talk.

After the two-and-a-half-hour backpack in, however, our bladders were too full to rest. Just as the Prince started to relieve himself, something strange happened. He was charged by a mountain goat.

In hindsight, "charged" was too strong a word. "Approached very swiftly" was probably more accurate, though the speed of the wild animal's approach was nothing compared to the haste that the Prince employed to zip up his fly and flee. That's when something even stranger happened. The mountain goat had no interest in goring anyone. What it wanted was pee.

Starved for salt, the goat dug into the dirt and grass and started feasting on the Prince's urine. While we stood in wonder just fifty feet away, three other goats hightailed in through the trees and bluffed and nudged and pushed until finally the biggest goat asserted dominion over the Prince's precious pay dirt.

This was wrong on so many different levels. The mountain goat was supposed to be the very symbol of high-country wilderness, a creature tough enough to scramble with ease up sheer rock walls and through a brutal Rocky Mountain winter. But here they were, down in the trees, racing each other through campsites laden with Vibram and Gore-Tex to wrest control of the freshest puddle of man piss.

Problem was, I had to go too. I sneaked away a few hundred yards, checked to make sure I was alone, unzipped—and had another goat emerge from the trees like Pavlov's dog. Gee whiz!

All the goats—we counted two dozen, sauntering around with no fear of humans, anxiously eyeing our zippers—made us view our breathtaking camp with new eyes. Like tinsel on a Christmas tree, goat fur was draped from every low-lying tree branch; in August the goats were still molting their winter coats. We considered moving, but every surrounding campsite was laced with fur too. Besides, the goats didn't seem to pose any danger. So we just waited and watched them come and go as they watched and waited for us to go.

After an hour or so of this we started viewing the mountain goats a little like Labrador retrievers, friendly and lumbering, but with a weight of two hundred pounds and eight-inch pointy horns. Another icon of Wild America strutting just forty feet from the rock where I was reading a book? Ho-hum.

Suddenly behind us erupted a crashing sound that seemed to come from a dramatically bigger goat. We turned and saw, emerging from the thicket of trees, a creature that did not have hooves.

It was a man with a backpack. The crotch and rear of his hiking shorts were covered with white goat fur.

We laughed. His face flushed red.

"It's not what you think," he said. "Honest."

The Prince and I could not resist.

"Here comes a baaaaad man."

"He's been on the lam."

"Looks like he got his goat."

"Somebody pulled the wool over his eyes."

"Poor billy."

"Seems kind of gruff."

"Can't make a U-turn, but he can sure make her eyes roll back."

A normal person might have punched us in our noses. This hiker was not normal. He asked to camp next to us. We set two conditions: (1) He had to take off all that goat hair; (2) he couldn't make us feel cheap for sleeping so easily with a stranger.

We had a new camp partner.

His name was Walt Johnson, and he was an adrenaline junkie. He had scuba dived at night with sharks and no cage, jumped off rock ledges on a mountain bike, and run two marathons. Most of all, though, he climbed. His rock résumé was a Who's Who of Big Walls across America—the thousand-foot Diamond on Longs Peak, the 1,800-foot Washington Column at Yosemite, the Direct Exum route up the Grand Teton, and six trips up the Devil's Tower in Wyoming from *Close Encounters of the Third Kind*. It took him four days to scale the Lurking Fear route on El Capitan in Yosemite, but what he remembered most was sleeping 2,200 feet off the valley floor in a cot roped to the sheer wall. In his prime, he could do a hundred pull-ups with only two rest stops, and if he was feeling especially strong, three pull-ups with just his right arm.

Like us, he was here to climb the three peaks of the Chicago Basin. I practically begged him to join us. These mountains were supposed to be difficult, and I'd be grateful to hike them with someone with so much experience.

Walt said he'd love to, but there were a few catches: For starters, all of his biggest climbing accomplishments came years ago. Now he was fifty-three. His days of hundred-pull-up workouts were over.

No problem, I told him. I can't do pull-ups either.

And another thing? He wasn't an early-morning person. He couldn't promise he'd make our planned predawn wake-up call.

I told him I was willing to take a chance. We'd still love to have him along.

And one other thing? Walt had been out of work for the past four years because of a major injury to his back—three ruptured disks— that had resulted in a long and complicated legal case with his employer. The attorneys back home in Los Angeles were working out some settlement now, but Walt wasn't sure how, or whether, his back could withstand one Fourteener, much less three hard ones.

In other words, on the mountain he'd rely on us as much as we relied on him. Fair deal, I told him, though I wondered secretly how the hell he could score a lawyer-size settlement while backpacking fourteen miles round-trip with plans to climb these three Rocky Mountains.

And so we sat around on our rocks at camp and swapped stories, some of them true, and dug into our freeze-dried dinners with spoons and told more stories and watched as the two women from the train suffered past us with heavy backpacks muttering how long hikes and Bloody Marys were a really, really lousy mix.

As dusk approached we thought the clouds were billowing up for a sublime sunset, but instead they pounded us with a drenching downpour. The Prince and I jumped into our sleeping bags, but the rain drummed so loudly on the roof of our tent that talk was tough. When lightning flashed, again and again and again, I could see his eyes. They were wide. I told him he'd do fine on the climb in the morning. I hoped I was right.

The rain stopped about an hour before our 4 a.m. alarm. I knew because I was already awake. In fact, I was awake most of the night wondering if the storm would pass, or if I was crazy to bring the Prince up here, or whether he was having fun, or if I had the skill and endurance to get up these three peaks, or how I would get help if we ran into trouble when town was a long backpack and train ride away. I also wondered if I did so many brainless things during the day because my mind spent so much time spinning through the night.

I poked my headlamp out the tent and saw puddles on the ground but stars in the sky. Excellent news; the storm had passed. I woke up the Prince and started my automaton morning rituals—get dressed, cram down a chewy bar for breakfast, pop in contact lenses, triple-check daypack for all hiking supplies, and go. Luckily the goats weren't awake, but Walt was, and waiting to join us.

The first thousand vertical feet are muddy and steep, with traverses across sixty-foot rock boilerplates that are difficult to track in the dark and difficult to grip with the moisture. All the horsing around from last night is gone. Our goals for the day are Sunlight Peak and Windom Peak, and I'm hoping the upper rock dries off by the time we reach it.

As I suspected, the Prince is an animal of a climber, but he lags back to our pace, partly from courtesy and partly from fear. It's his first time hiking by headlamp, and it's his first time waking up at 4 a.m. on a vacation day. I can't say he's enjoying either new experience, but my goal is still for him to remember them.

We cross a stream at a waterfall and Walt stops to filter water for his bottle. I ask if he wants to use some of my water—after all, it's pretty early in a hike for anyone to be refilling their supply—but he tells me it's an old rock climber's habit. Walt is so attuned to extra weight on his body that he can actually feel the difference when his water bottle is only half-full. In fact, he started this hike with a half-full twenty-ounce bottle. I'm too embarrassed to tell him that I always carry at least a gallon on every climb, and I'm too fat to ever tell when I'm running low.

Above the falls we reach a pink rock bench with two lakes just as the first rays of dawn clear the horizon. The Prince is smiling. I am too. It is glorious.

We grind up a steep, loose gully of Sunlight Peak for another thousand vertical feet. The Prince doesn't even have to breathe through his mouth; Walt doesn't even have to mess with his back. What's messing with me, however, is the damp rock. The sun has cleared Windom Peak to our east, but clouds have returned and block any warming sun. The mountain still holds enough moisture to clog the bottom of my boots with slippery mud and grit. This makes me nervous.

At 13,800 feet, we top out on the shoulder of Sunlight Peak. The wind kicks up. The temperature drops down. We pause for water and a snack and scan the remaining route. It is a hodgepodge mess of rounded boulders the size of Volkswagens, balanced precariously against each other, with four-hundred-foot plunges all around.

The hiking is over. The climbing is to begin.

We hands-and-feet it up some well-placed boulders and traverse along the base of an impressive cliff. No big exposure yet, but I stop to ask the Prince how he's doing. He's not so sure. Walt and I stop and explain that the climbing is supposed to get trickier and airier after this. How does he feel about that? He wants to wait and see. We take our time moving up.

At the base of a steep rock shoulder I stop and freeze. There's a long, angled crack up a smooth, forty-foot pitch that has no room for error. Walt scampers up it without even pausing to consider his moves. I turn to the Prince.

No way, he says. I'm pretty sure I can get up this, but coming down scares the crap out of me.

I'm awash in guilt. What in the world was I thinking? What kind of person would take his buddy up Sunlight Peak for his first mountain? This Fourteener is giving me the creeps. I can't imagine what it's doing to him.

Let's get out of here, I tell him.

Don't be stupid, he tells me. Look at all the work it took to get here. Don't turn around for my sake. Go ahead and finish. I'll wait here.

Waiting at 13,900 feet in the wind and temperatures in the thirties? I'm not going to do that to a friend.

Go, he says. If it were me, I'd do the same. I'll be fine. Just go.

And so I do.

Walt waits for me at the top of the shoulder, and helps talk me up it. As is the case with many Fourteener routes, it's not as bad as it looks. I remember Mike Brislin's old advice about eating elephants, and I consume Sunlight one bite at a time.

There are more difficult moves, accompanied with more advice from Walt, and then we're up. Or at least we're up to the U.S. Geological Survey summit marker. Problem is, the actual summit is still about thirty feet above us.

The very top of Sunlight is so tiny, and so exposed, that even the U.S. government chickened out of affixing the summit marker there. The summit block is an assemblage of seven leaning boulders that looks like a Jenga game for Stone Age giants.

I point to the block and ask Walt what he thinks.

He says: I'm fine right here. He tells me the worst accidents he knows about all happened on Class 3 and Class 4 approaches that everyone said were too easy to rope up for protection. We have no ropes. The rock is wet, and the treads of our boots are filled with damp gravel from the loose gully up. The last move to the actual summit, I've heard, requires a hop across a thousand feet of air.

If the guy who did El Capitan isn't going to do it, should I still do it?

I scramble along the first few slabs of granite. Everything I've read says the rock is grippy, but on the morning after a nighttime thunderstorm, it's not. Neither are my damp boots. I look at the top block. Do I really want to hop across a thousand feet of air with wet rock and wet boots?

Hell no.

Walt and I drop down and meet up again with the Prince, who has grown cold on the ridge from wind and inactivity. I apologize again. He rejects it again. I ask if he wants to return to camp with me, and he rejects that idea too. He wants to stand atop a Fourteener. We have a target. We launch a boulder-hopping traverse to Windom Peak.

Reports say Windom is much easier than Sunlight, but from down low the upper ridge looks pretty jagged to me. In fact, the whole peak is a jumble of blocks. The Prince's legs remain strong, and his face is all business. As for Walt, I can only hope I move as well as he, bad back or not, at age fifty-three.

From Sunlight to the valley floor we lose nearly a thousand feet, which we must regain on our grunt up the flanks of Windom. I still feel like a jerk for trying to start out the Prince on a difficult peak like Sunlight. I'm watching his every step and hoping I can redeem myself with a push up Windom.

Along the broad shoulder we find there's no real trail, just a mass of herky-jerky rock. We pick our way up and around and over and across until we reach a notch at 13,800 feet. Just beyond it is a small saddle. I look down and feel 800 feet of vertigo. I do not show it to the Prince.

There's some fun hands-and-feet scrambling with little exposure. We reach the summit block, and I have to wonder: What is it with the peaks around here? While the Sunlight block was smooth and slippery, Windom's is sharp and blocky. It looks impassable, but cairns lead us around the back, through a notch, and—wow!—what an airy and spectacular summit.

The Prince beams. Now this, he says, is something to remember.

For the first time all day, I beam, too, and feel the cloak of jerkdom slip a little lower on my back.

The biggest thrill, however, comes from Walt, who suddenly seems a little choked up. He says he's grateful to be in the mountains again, and especially grateful to be there with people he likes.

"I just love all this," Walt says. "The sights, the smells, making the effort and pushing yourself and getting something that's really hard to get. I'll fly on a plane and people will look out the window at thirty thousand feet and say, 'Isn't this view good enough for you?' And I say no, it's not good enough. I didn't earn it. In the mountains, I earn it."

Such total emotional sincerity startles me. I check my altimeter, and, sure enough, we're still in the true confessions zone over 12,000 feet. The gates are open.

Walt has had an awful five years. First his best friend—an accomplished climbing partner who joined Walt on difficult summits of Bear Creek Spire, Ice Mountain, and Vestal Peak via Wham Ridge—died at age forty-four after mistakenly taking the wrong heart medicine.

Then Walt lifted a 170-pound file cabinet and suffered his debilitating back injury, which left him hospitalized for a week. Even worse than the injury was the recovery.

Walt was deathly afraid of needles. At the age of five, while in the hospital for a tonsillectomy, Walt was told by a nurse that she'd send his mother away unless he stopped crying about getting a shot. He tried to run away. She overpowered him and jabbed him with the needle anyway. For years after, he had to be forcibly restrained for vaccinations, which only deepened his fears. Even after adulthood, he did whatever he could to avoid medical care. When he ruptured his disks, he had not been examined by a doctor for eleven years.

Because of his excruciating back pain, Walt was told by doctors he needed regular epidurals and rhizotomy, a surgery to slice and destroy pain-detecting nerves in his back. "I can't be around needles," Walt warned the doctors. "You don't understand."

They didn't understand. When the first nurse pulled out a needle, Walt bolted out of the hospital. They found him weeping in the parking lot. They guided him back inside, locked the door, and put him on his belly so he couldn't see the needle coming. He lay frozen with fright until he smelled the sterilizing alcohol. That's when he learned one big thing that had changed since he was five years old: Now he could overpower the nurses. He punched them in their faces, kicked them in their groins, and screamed loud enough to make the blood run cold in the hospital waiting room. Or at least that's what they told him later. A needle to Walt was like a full moon to a werewolf. It made him do bad things he couldn't even remember.

To make his back heal, he had to do this once a month.

He was too ashamed to let his wife help, but he doubted she could do much, anyway. He has tried hypnosis, meditation, and therapy. No help there either, though the psychiatrist offered an explanation: At age five, Walt had been raped by a needle.

Walt acknowledges it. He understands it. He talks about it. He can't solve it.

After months of awful panic and dangerous violence, Walt and the nurses finally found a routine that eased the trauma. They would dope him up with a horse-size cocktail of sedatives and anxiety relievers—200 milligrams of Demerol, 125 milligram of Vistraril, and 2 milligrams of Ativan—and then call in five nurses. One would grab each arm and leg, and one would stick it to him. After several months, Walt and the nurses finally reached a grudging truce.

Just as his back healed enough to scale back his painkilling shots, Walt developed another problem. He needed a hemorrhoidectomy. He researched the procedure on his own and discovered two terrible truths: (1) the surgery required needles, and (2) women who had had hemorrhoidectomies reported that the pain hurt more than natural childbirth.

Weeping in the medical waiting room, Walt went through the whole humiliating panic again, but this time with new doctors and new nurses who doubted his fears of needles. Though the day of surgery was brutal, the aftermath hurt even more. He spent weeks lying on his stomach and sitting in the bath and praying. "I'd be saying, 'Please, God, don't make me hungry, because if I eat I know where it's going,'" Walt tells us. The surgery didn't work as well as intended, and Walt needed extra stretching-out sessions. He can laugh about it now. At the time, not so much.

And then Walt stops in midtrail. He is grinning. He is joyful. He says he can't believe he's hiking again, and that he's having so much fun doing it. He starts talking about his dead best friend and how grateful he is to be on a mountain again without debilitating pain, and better yet, with good partners. He's put me on the verge of blubbering when, from the spruces in front of us, a mountain goat crosses our trail.

"Waaaaaaalt," the Prince neighs. "Welllllllcome baaaaack."

The next morning, or, more accurately, premorning, the Prince was not budging from his sleeping bag. That was a good thing. Today's peak, Mount Eolus, was supposed to be another difficult one. Walt and I hiked through the dark, but there was no tension, no nervousness. The true confessions from the day before had given way to easy familiarity today. The father of two grown children, he ladled out advice on surviving the teenage years. We swapped war stories about mountains, and even though his peaks were tougher and far more numerous, there was no one-upmanship. We climbed. We cursed. We cackled.

Like Pyramid Peak a hundred miles away, Mount Eolus was sheer, blocky, and cut by a confusing maze of narrow ledges. At one point, while scrambling around a freezer-size chunk of granite, Walt muttered, "Don't look now, but there's about six hundred feet of air below your ass." I thanked him for the update, and asked why he was checking out this particular part of my body. A few hundred more feet of banter and we were backslapping on the summit.

We ran from an approaching storm but got soaked anyway. By the time we reached camp, the storm had broken, and the Prince was splayed on a rock beneath the high ridge and deep into his book. He'd had his peak. He'd had his view. And better yet, he said he'd had a trip to remember.

Chapter 21

The Bald Leading
the Blind

WILSON PEAK 14,017'

I was getting close. I could feel it. Forty-one peaks down, thirteen to go. I had lost ten pounds, gained five hundred feet per hour of climbing speed, and won the confidence to stop throwing up the morning of every hike. I could pack for a trip in ten minutes. I woke up every day at 4 a.m. without an alarm. The back of LaKisha looked and smelled like a dorm room, but I slept better every night in the back of that truck than any night in my four years of college. I was in the last lap of my mountain run. I was committed.

My kids were even doing fine without me. This was the one change that hurt. Though I had tried hard to keep from being gone more than two nights in a row, I sometimes returned home and found I was clogging the gears of everyone's routine. *Dad, I don't need a bath because I took one yesterday. Dad, it's not my turn to pick up the dog poop in the backyard. Dad, I like chocolate ice cream now, not vanilla.* As for Merrill, she was edging closer and closer to sainthood, though I occasionally wondered how often saints asked their spouses: When are you going to be done?

The answer: Soon, I hope. (Followed by immediately offering to do all the laundry, shuttle the kids to summer day camp, and take her

228

out to dinner.) For each of my remaining peaks I had hiking partners or guides lined up. Or so I thought. While in the field for peaks in the San Juan range of southwest Colorado I learned that one mountain I had been counting on, Wilson Peak, had been shut down to public access.

This one hurt. Wilson Peak, in southwest Colorado, was an icon of the Rockies—so triangular and classically majestic that it has been pictured more often than any mountain in the world. (It's the star of Coors beer cans and bottles.) For decades it had been opened to climbers with no restrictions whatsoever. Then a private landowner along the main access route sensed a moneymaking opportunity, and, à la Culebra, started charging $100 per hike. Soon, however, $100 a pop wasn't enough. The landowner, Texas real estate developer Rusty Nichols, began pressuring the U.S. Forest Service to swap his 300 acres up a four-wheel-drive road for another 2,200 acres much closer to the top-dollar ski resort town of Telluride. According to a Forest Service appraisal, Nichols wanted to swap his $2 million of property for public land worth $33 million. When the Forest Service told him to go jump, Nichols shut down access to Wilson Peak—no climbing for $100, no way, no how.

Unlike the Decalibron closure, the shutdown on Wilson Peak was actually enforced. Climbers reported being shagged off the route by a man on an ATV with a gun in a scabbard.

And so my worries mounted. What I hoped this summer was to try all the peaks, not all the peaks minus one. Unfortunately, I knew no politician who could pluck me out of this pickle. I climbed on and tried to put my Wilson Peak problem out of my head. Like my wife said, I was good at denial.

The closer I got to the end of the summer, the more it began to bug me. I was running out of time with no apparent path up Wilson Peak. What I needed was a fixer, a climber's consigliere, somebody with the mojo to turn a no-go into a yo-go. But who had the know-how to stop a Texas real estate developer from his taxpayer shakedown scheme?

The answer: a guy who knew how to work with snakes.

In an amazing and unbelievably fortunate coincidence, a neighbor the next block over—renowned on our street for posting a "Lost" sign on the corner light pole for his five-foot python—had secured one day of climbing access to Wilson Peak. Tim Wohlgenant was the new Colorado director for the Trust for Public Land, which was cutting a deal with Rusty Nichols to buy his property and restore public access. The price: $3.25 million for two hundred acres. The snake had been charmed.

First, however, the Trust for Public Land needed money to do it. To build publicity for a fund-raising drive, the trust was sponsoring a special one-time group climb up Wilson Peak. For star power, the climb was being led by Erik Weihenmayer, the first blind climber to scale Mount Everest and the highest peak on each of the seven continents. I begged my neighbor hard enough, and he let me latch on to the Wilson Peak climb too.

When I told the Prince about my hope to climb a Fourteener with Weihenmayer, he coined an instant description: the Bald Leading the Blind. The truth, however, is that Weihenmayer goes uphill faster.

It's 4 a.m., and sixteen of us plod up the long approach to Wilson Peak. Many in the group grumble about the early start time. With no moon, the sky is pitch-black, which means that everyone has to wear a headlamp, or just hike like Erik.

Of course, no one hikes like Erik. He is amazing.

Much of the first stretch of the hike is on an old miners' road made of rocks the size of bowling balls. I stub my toes and trip about every sixth step in the dark. Erik does about the same. He pokes ahead with his eye-high hiking poles, using them like bug antennae to feel and sense bumpy terrain. He hunches his back to absorb uneven foot placements and high-steps his boots to shin level to clear the boulders strewn across our path. He works twice as hard as I, but I still struggle to keep up with him. Makes me wonder how I'd do hiking without a headlamp.

I ask Erik why he still climbs, even after the Seven Summits, and he goes off on a long stream-of-consciousness answer: He loves the camaraderie, the male bonding, the swearing, pissing in the woods, the work, tears, feeling of accomplishment, the feel of the wind and the sound of the rocks and the taste of his sweat when he thinks he can't go any farther but still does. Most of all, he loves when people tell him he can't do something, and then he does it anyway.

He went blind from retinoschisis at age thirteen, and took to rock climbing in a gym because he could feel his way up walls. He had a buddy in Phoenix who found that climbing helped his attention deficit disorder. So together they began taking on mountains—the guy who couldn't focus and the guy who couldn't see. They tried Mount Sherman in winter and failed. They tried Longs Peak in winter and failed again. But they learned enough on summits of other Colorado peaks to give them the confidence to try to succeed at Denali, the tallest in North America. He followed that peak with high walk-ups of Kilimanjaro and Aconcagua, the tops of Africa and South America, respectively, and then announced plans for Everest.

Much of the mountaineering world recoiled. A blind man up Everest? A circus sideshow on the world's tallest peak! Even in the narcissistic world of big-mountain climbing, Weihenmayer was denounced as an amazingly selfish man with a death wish for himself and his team members.

On May 25, 2001, he summited Mount Everest. He made the cover of *Time, Outside,* and *Climbing* magazines, and yukked it up with Jay Leno on *The Tonight Show.* He wrote an autobiography that sold more than 350,000 copies, and hit the motivational speech circuit for $40,000 a talk, as often as fifty times a year. (He waived today's fee to help raise money to buy the Wilson Peak access.)

Erik says he doesn't want to be the Blind Climber. He wants to be a good climber, a full team member who pulls his weight on a big mountain. "I am living proof of the promise of teamwork, and the need for teamwork," he says. This becomes readily apparent when he stops and asks if the setting is appropriate for him to heed nature's call. Someone says yes, so Erik does. At that very moment, the only woman on the trip hikes right by. The climber who had given Erik the all-clear signal admits his mistake. Erik just laughs it off.

We start up again, and, before we can settle back into our uphill rhythm, Erik jams his boot against a rock and lurches forward. Instinctively, I reach out and grab him by the elbow. "Thanks, but I really didn't need that," he says firmly. He's used to newcomers babying him, but clearly doesn't like it.

It's also clear he doesn't need babying. As the wide but rough jeep road turns into a narrow but rough hiking trail, Erik's hiking guide and business manager, Gavin Attwood, leads Erik by dangling a bell from his backpack. Erik follows the jingle that comes with every step.

For the next ten minutes, Erik and Gavin launch off on some opaque argument that seems to be about their schedule over the next few days. It's hard to tell if they're truly testy or just trash talking, but Gavin has finally had enough. He rips off the bell from the backpack and tells Erik, "You know what I'm going to do? Here's what I'm going to do!" And he pretends to throw the bell over a cliff into the darkness. Erik obviously has heard this threat before, and mocks Gavin with overly enthusiastic laughter. In other words, a blind guy and a buddy who have been up dozens of mountains together treat each other pretty much the same sarcastic way that two sighted guys who have been up dozens of mountains treat each other.

From the top of a false peak at 13,900 feet, we face a tricky stretch—a steep seventy-foot downclimb on loose rock over a drop-off of several hundred feet. All banter stops. Though I wish I couldn't see the consequences of a fall here, I also can't imagine trying this while blindfolded. With a few pointers from others about footholds and handholds, Erik feels his way down the rock face. I sweat more than Erik.

The downclimb is followed by an equally hairy upclimb to the summit. The instinct is to whoop with the exhilaration of a difficult climb accomplished, but the top of Wilson Peak is no place to cheer. Eleven months earlier, a private plane from Texas slammed into the mountain about two hundred feet below the summit and scattered wreckage everywhere. Four friends in their twenties were killed; the pilot's body was never recovered. On the summit is a plaque commemorating the dead, a twisted propeller, and dozens of pieces of clothes, toiletries, and other personal artifacts. When someone in our climbing group sits for a summit photo, she recoils after finding a dental retainer next to her boot. The weather is clear, but nobody wants to linger. We all clear off the summit. Life and death are not far away on any Fourteener.

After descending the hardest climbing sections, I ask Gavin if everyone views Erik with awe. He snorts. In a few weeks, he says, Erik will speak to six thousand people in Hawaii, and they'll give him a standing ovation and tell him how great he is and rush the podium to ask for his autograph on his best-selling book. And when all the crowds are gone, Gavin will tell him, "Erik, you know you're an ass and full of shit." And Erik will agree. He has a serious disability, but according to Gavin, he's still a pretty normal person with an unusually small ego, especially by world-class mountaineering standards.

On the ascent of Wilson Peak, other hikers flitted around Erik like moths to a summer porch light; celebrity seemed like something he tolerated as part of the job, but didn't particularly enjoy. On the descent, however, his handicap became more noticeable, and he moved at a slower pace than just about everyone else on the mountain. I stayed as part of a smaller group hiking down with him.

Surrounded by fewer adoring people, Erik seemed weary of his Mr. Clean image. Somebody asks if he's ever faced a climb that was too hard. In fact, he has. He was once climbing a wall with a Frenchwoman when the route turned tough enough to make Erik pause. There was a language barrier, but the woman was clearly taken aback. She hesitated, considered, stammered, and then finally blurted out with her best translation, "What's the English word for wuss?" Said Erik: "I could tell she was smiling, or I would have bitch-slapped her." Big guffaws from Erik's entourage.

Of course, at the end of a long day on the mountain, men will go to extraordinary lengths to distract fellow sufferers with a laugh. Erik tries again by asking everyone: What's the bird that symbolizes liberty? The bald eagle. What's the bird that symbolizes peace? The dove. What's the bird that symbolizes true love? The swallow.

Nobody laughs. He gets more points for effort than content.

By the time we descend to a slope of basketball-size boulders at 11,000 feet, Erik and I are so desperate to fill the time with something that we've been reduced to swapping stories about journalism.

Suddenly the slope gives way.

It's an avalanche of rock and we're both caught in it—dust billowing, a thousand rocks crashing, rolling, tumbling down the hill, a moving mountain slope forty feet long and sixty feet wide. I'm just on the back edge of it and stop after being carried down the hill four or five feet. Erik, however, is trapped in the middle of it, flailing his poles, twisting his body, pointing his hands uphill to guard against bouncing rocks. The slide carries him forty feet down the slope and buries him to his shins.

"Erik! Are you OK?" I cry out.

"I'm OK! I'm OK! Is it over?"

I try moving, but send another rock rolling down the unstable slope.

"Stay right there!" another hiker calls.

Erik faces uphill with back hunched and arms and hands crossed across his torso like a judo warrior. Rogue rocks roll past him. "Stay right there!" the hiker calls again. He scrambles gingerly over to Erik, and helps him wrest his trapped legs from the boulders. They move swiftly to the side.

From sixty feet away, I can hear Erik sigh with relief.

"Was that scary?" he asks. "I mean, I felt all the rocks and then I was going downhill and then I couldn't move my feet. That must have been a little scary. Was it scary?"

Nobody answers.

I think of the horror films I'd seen as a teenager and remember that the most terrifying scenes were always the ones I could not see, but only imagine.

Still nobody answers.

Yeah, I call to Erik. That was pretty scary.

Chapter 22

Homestretch

HANDIES PEAK 14,058'

MOUNT SNEFFELS 14,150'

SNOWMASS MOUNTAIN 14,099'

KIT CARSON PEAK 14,165'

CHALLENGER POINT 14,081'

MOUNT HARVARD 14,421'

CAPITOL PEAK 14,130'

EL DIENTE PEAK 14,159'

MOUNT WILSON 14,246'

NORTH MAROON PEAK 14,019'

CRESTONE PEAK 14,294'

It may have been out of pity, or maybe just curiosity. Either way, I wasn't complaining. My fair bride had decided to go hiking with me. I thanked her, told her how grateful I was, thanked her again, and then smothered her in a nice, long, warm hug. She looked at me a little funny.

Listen, Merrill said, you're not the only one in this house who wants you to get these peaks done. We're all ready to have you home again too. Besides, this will be fun.

No argument from me, especially after a summer of you-sleep-on-your-side-of-the-tent man-dates. I was so excited that I hosed out the back of the pickup truck, fluffed up Merrill's ages-old sleeping bag, and picked out my favorite freeze-dried camping dinner (Mountain House Mexican-Style Chicken with Rice for Two). Because Merrill is a coffee junkie, I even splurged on an espresso press for her Nalgene bottle. I was packed up and ready to backpack.

Well, no.

My wife was a trouper, but still not a saint. What this meant was no sleeping in the back of pickup trucks on vacation. A clear preference was expressed for indoor plumbing, and, if possible, food that did not have to be eaten out of a bag with a spork. Hot showers would be appreciated by her, and if nighttime company was desired, for me as well.

Adjustments were made. Grandparents were lined up to babysit. And then we were off, two people married for seventeen years together in a vehicle without a single child inside. We talked and laughed and gossiped and played the music really, really loud and then talked and laughed some more. The one thing better than the summer she was giving to me was the part of the summer I was sharing with her. The dipping sun blasted the world orange just as we crested the Continental Divide at Monarch Pass. We stopped and stared. We could have been newlyweds giddy on our honeymoon—until the motel room alarm exploded at 3:30 a.m. At this point I was grateful my wife decided to remain married to me.

We set off from the trailhead for our intended target, Handies Peak in the San Juan Mountains of southwest Colorado, and we were soon struck speechless. The peaks were jagged, with couloirs filled with snow and whole hillsides carpeted with columbines, cinquefoil, and Indian paintbrush. If I were a yodeling man, this would be the place. We were walking through Monet's garden, except at 11,000 feet. We were so giddy, we felt like skipping schoolchildren.

I had chosen to do this mountain with Merrill not only because it was gorgeous, but also because it was straightforward. In fact, about the only complicated thing about Handies Peak was the source of its name. By the time the first government surveying crews reached it in the 1870s, local miners were already calling it Handies Peak, even though nobody seemed to know anything about the identity or where-abouts of Mr. or Mrs. Handies. Better to have a mountain named after a nobody, I suppose, than an unexceptional and forgotten politician like Bross (an Illinois lieutenant governor), Evans (the second pre-statehood governor of Colorado), and Elbert (the sixth).

At about 13,000 feet, the solid and well-engineered trail on Handies took its big turn upward. Merrill, like every other runner I have hiked with this summer, could not resist. The summit was a carrot, and she was a racehorse. She galloped up the trail. I tried to keep pace until she was fifty feet, then a hundred feet, and then a hundred yards ahead of me. That's when I declared defeat, again, and settled back into my oxen pace. At some point on an overlook, she stopped and realized she was far, far ahead of me. She seemed to slow after that, but there was still no way for me to catch up. I'd been climbing peaks all summer; this was her first in fifteen years. Yet she smoked me up the hill. Thankfully, it was a perfectly balmy day on the summit, which worked out well for Merrill, because she had to wait so long for me to get there.

No way was I complaining, though. She was the one who had scored that great deal on a particularly nice hotel room that night in Telluride. I took a hot shower before our meal at a restaurant—with tablecloths!—and it felt so good that I took a shower afterward too.

Next up for us was another curiously named peak near Telluride called Mount Sneffels. According to the Hayden expedition of 1874—the same one that had survived the hair-raising electrical storm on Sunshine Peak—this towering pyramid reminded them of the Icelandic volcano Snaefele, which had contained the mysterious crater allowing passage to adventurers in the Jules Verne sci-fi thriller of the day, *Journey to the Center of the Earth*. To me the two mountains looked nothing alike. There was little doubt, though, that Mount Sneffels offered one of the most gorgeous mountain landscapes in the Rocky Mountain West. The valley below has been featured around the world in ads for Marlboro, Budweiser, Coors, and, oh yes, a guy from the Bronx named Ralph Lifshitz. Ralph loved the cowboy view so much that he bought a ranch in the valley with the best view of the peak. There was one problem: His sprawling ranch house, built anew to look weathered and old, had a front door that, when opened, did not creak like the doors in classic Western movies. So a ranch hand labored for hours to make the new door sound as if it had been slammed for decades by grizzled cowpunchers. This manufactured squeak greatly pleased the owner, who had changed his name from Ralph Lifshitz to Ralph Lauren and branded his fashionable spread the Double RL.

Our goal for the day was to gallop high above the Polo King. First, however, we had to conquer a long and steep gully that seemed to have been made of ball bearings marinated in Vaseline. Some jackasses above us kicked down a basketball-size rock from three-point range without shouting any warning. We dodged the bounce, and I instantly felt like Einstein for insisting that Merrill wear her new climbing helmet. We hiked closer together.

At the top of the steep and loose gully came a saddle, then a steep gully with snow, which made us hike even closer. Because Sneffels was such an iconic peak, dozens of people were scaling it, and some seemed to be pushing their limits. Hikers around us were slipping, and panting, and nervously eyeing the rest of the climb, which certainly ain't the boulevard trail of Handies Peak. Merrill and I bunched up a little closer. At the top of all the snow was a V-shaped notch in a high cliff wall. The notch required a full climbing move, with hands and feet, to pass through, so I scrambled to the other side and waited with camera to photograph my wife. She did not pose in the gap. She did not even smile in it. In fact, the resulting picture showed her with a look on her face that cannot be considered happy, or relieved, or thrilled. Mostly, the look says, Get me the hell out of here! Oblivious as usual, I failed to notice, or, more importantly, warn my bride that there was a drop-off of several hundred feet just to the left of the V-notch.

It was a short hike, not climb, to the summit, and it was a spectacularly calm and clear day to lollygag there. Brimming with adrenaline and testosterone, I scrambled around the airy top for the best view, but Merrill stayed planted on her rear. Finally she snapped: "Would you please sit down? You're making me nervous." Her eyes welled.

And so, after three children, seventeen years of marriage, and a million nights of talk about hopes and dreams, I suspected the love of my life had one unannounced fear: heights.

My suspicion turned to reality a few days later. On the sharp white summit ridge of Snowmass Mountain—finally, a peak with a name that made sense—she stopped, sat down, and announced she would continue no farther. We were only three hundred feet from the top. For the remaining route I saw a succession of large gray blocks chiseled with sturdy handholds; she saw hundreds of feet of air beneath them.

You go, she told me.

But what about the . . .

You go, she said. Just be careful. She thought I might be able to catch two women who had hiked part of the trail up with us.

But . . .

Go!

And so I did. I summited with the two other women, both close to my age. One was a teacher's aide at a school a few miles from our house; the other had had two boyfriends. On the return from the summit to meet Merrill on the ridge, I listened to the women talk about love triangles. I fiddled with my wedding ring.

On the long pack back to the trailhead, Merrill told me that Snowmass would be the last airy Fourteener for her. Her love of the workout and the beauty of Fourteeners was overwhelmed by her fear of falling off them. She told me how nervous she was watching me scramble down from the summit. Though it wasn't for her, she could see that the challenge was rewarding to me. She understood it. She respected it. She just didn't want to personally see me do it again.

There was less than a month left until Labor Day, and she wanted me to take my best shot at finishing by then.

I didn't know whether to be thrilled or terrified, so I just put my arm around her and kept plugging along on the twisting trail.

Just because I had her blessing didn't mean I could do it alone. I was still in the hunt for hiking partners.

A neighbor across the street, a runner, was washing his car. I offered to finish up for him if he'd climb one peak with me. No dice. I offered to wash his other car too. He just laughed.

I e-mailed old hiking partners. They were either burned out on hiking (StevieTwoShoes), preoccupied with more relaxing summer vacations (just about everyone else), or mysteriously incommunicado (Del Sur). I tried my barber, my postman, and the guy who usually checks my groceries at Safeway. Nada.

Still, if many seeds are planted, one may take root. Out of the blue I got a call from the coach of my middle son's soccer team. Alan Greenberg was a runner. He was a backpacker. As a boy, he was even an Eagle Scout. He told me he'd love to camp and climb—a hiking partner dream come true!—so I gave him a list of my remaining peaks and told him to pick any one.

The good news was that he selected two. The bad news was that he's squeamish about heights. The two mountains he selected, Kit Carson and Challenger Point, were picked mainly because they're the least airy on my list.

Still, we're both gung ho to go. He hasn't backpacked for years and he's looking forward to it. We stop at a store on the drive out to pick up sandwiches that we'll eat later at camp. He orders the same as me, except without the bacon. Alan is Jewish—he tells me he fulfilled every Jewish grandmother's dream by meeting his wife at a reception for an Israeli member of parliament—and has never eaten pork in his life.

At the trailhead I remind Alan that there is supposed to be some exposure on both peaks, but he says he's game to try. He's used to trying things outside his comfort zone. Growing up, he was always the smallest kid and the last one picked for sports in gym class. Little League coaches parked him in right field. His mother, a concert pianist, thought he might find a niche in music. He tried playing clarinet, but his fingers were too small to reach the keys. Thus was born Alan Greenberg, oboe man. Today he plays for a Yiddish salsa band that plays "Hava Nagila" but breaks into "Wipe Out." They do a lot of bar mitzvahs.

Of course, that's just for fun. A childhood in right field taught Alan the absolute advantage of tenacity. He blasted through Stanford University for economics and the University of California at Berkeley for a law degree, and now nails polluters for a living at the U.S. Justice Department. He has no body fat. He runs fast. He carries a twenty-year-old backpack that weighs as much as I do, and still beats me up the hill. He does not complain about anything.

His natural tendency to face obstacles and scrap right through them quickly becomes a great advantage about three miles into our five-mile backpack. The clouds open and we are drenched. Thunder rumbles, lightning crackles, and the sun goes vamoose. We find our intended campsite in headlamps, and proceed to erect a tent in wind, rain, dark, and utter confusion without a single cross or curse word. (In this case I imagine it's an advantage not being married to each other.) We squirm out of the rain and into our down sleeping bags to stop our shivering. It is nine o'clock at night. We are famished. Like wolves, we rip into our sandwiches.

Alan stops, awfully, in midbite. "This has bacon," he says, but I'm the one who feels like spitting up. A decent and devout man has spent a life wholly off the hog and then ends up with a mouthful only because he is doing an incredibly generous favor for me? I'm sorry, I'm sorry, I'm sorry, I tell him.

Oh, don't worry about it, he says. It's all about the intent, he says, and he didn't intend to eat bacon. He had grown up with the sound of it sizzling on dozens of Boy Scout campouts, and was used to having clothes that smelled like it.

We swap sandwiches and eat mostly in silence. He falls asleep. He snores, loudly. I blame the pig.

If Alan seemed quick yesterday with a heavy backpack, then he's a gazelle up the mountain with a light daypack today. On top of Challenger Point, which was named in 1987 after the space shuttle disaster, I am thrilled that it had taken us so little time to navigate up such a squirrely gully. Though Alan made the climb look easy, he's uneasy now.

The reason: He can see our next objective.

All the climbing books call it Kit Carson Avenue, but whoever named it has a warped sense of humor. It is no avenue. From here it appears to be barely a crack. It is a geologic freak of nature, a quarter-mile of angled shelf cut perfectly through the heart of a cliff face. Kit Carson Avenue offers climbers access to more manageable paths to the summit from the other side of the mountain.

I give Alan all the usual advice: It almost always looks worse from afar than it really is up close; all the guidebooks say it's not that bad; everybody I know who has climbed it says it's more of a hike than a climb. The look on Alan's face tells me he's not buying it. After the sandwich debacle last night in the tent, he's in no mood for new surprises.

We're about to hit the money question—go or no?—when another hiker joins us on the Challenger summit. Amazingly, it's Matt Ellis, aka Del Sur, the self-diagnosed ADD tai chi Catholic pharmacist from New Mexico who had joined me on that glissade to safety from the squabbling miners on Mount Antero. He is a calming influence.

Come on, let's just take a look at it, he tells Alan, and we all descend three hundred feet to the saddle. At the start of Kit Carson Avenue we can see it's clearly not as wide as a street, but it's no narrow curb either. It's mostly about the width of a sidewalk, albeit a sidewalk hanging about seventy stories in the sky.

Matt asks Alan, You nervous about heights? Before Alan can answer, Matt says, "Try this," and slaps his left hand against the cliff wall—away from all that air. Alan does, and then we're off, me oblivious as usual to anything more than ten feet in front of me, and Alan walking with his left shoulder rubbing against the solid side of the mountain.

When I e-mail Alan a few days later with some hero photos of him on top of Kit Carson Peak, I note, jokingly, that he appears hunched over in every shot. His response: The reason I am hunched over is to MINIMIZE EXPOSURE.

Ever since my highly charged experience with the brothers Spannring atop Mount Massive, I'd had a hankering to hike with my little brother, Todd. I still called him my little brother, even though our relationship had changed forever that day decades ago when he dunked a basketball directly over my head on our parents' driveway. Yes, he was taller than me, stronger than me, and faster than me, but he would always be little in my eyes, which, as he reminded me, were going bad much faster than his, mainly because mine were so much older. (Three years—hah.)

I thought living in Denver would give me a distinct advantage over my little brother in mountain sports. After all, he lived in Chicago. I invited him to my home turf on one of those Ride the Rockies bicycle tours. To prepare, he found the only two-hundred-foot hill in the Chicago suburbs and pedaled it twenty times a day. By the time the bike tour started in Colorado, I could not keep up with him. When he figured out I was trying to trail him, he ate chile cheese dogs for lunch.

Now, however, I didn't want another competition (even though I was pretty sure I could take him in left-handed arm wrestling). I just wanted him here, period. It was easy for some online contact or neighbor to say no to hiking with me. If my little brother turned me down, though, he'd risk the disappointment of our mother. Desperate times called for desperate measures. I made him a deal that he could not refuse, and he knew it. Unfair? Sure, but so was his elbow in my rib cage just before that driveway dunk.

Besides, there was a certain incentive. When I sent Todd my list of undone peaks, there was one name that stood out to both of us. More than a mountain, it was a symbol.

To me, it summed up everything that had gone wrong during the naming of some of the finest peaks in the world, an effete eastern moniker that had absolutely nothing to do with the muscular western landscape. I had a hard time separating the name from an acquaintance who was an alumnus of that esteemed university. He had once spent considerable time railing to me against the overall injustice of affirmative action in society while acknowledging that he was the fourth generation of his family, a legacy student, to be admitted to its hallowed halls.

Todd also took a personal interest in this mountain, but for a different reason. He had a soft spot for the little guy. In the past nineteen years, he had worked on or for eighteen different companies, most tiny, but all convinced they had the next big thing—a beer-of-the-month club, fingernail polish for inner-city women, window restoration for historic houses, janitorial services for office parks, pothole-fighting enzymes for dirt roads, and a bevy of high-tech start-ups selling software that I never fully understood. Every time he seemed on the brink of some giant breakthrough, something turned out to be not quite right. He never got set up with the right bankers, or the right investors, or the right club with the blazers and the cocktails that opened up access to the deals he really wanted to do. While he scrapped and scraped, he watched the third-basers—guys born on third base who thought they'd hit a triple—make that wide turn toward home.

And so in the heart of the Rockies, we hiked in more than seven miles, and gained 4,600 feet of elevation, and finished each other's sentences all along the way. Then we stood on the very top of Mount Harvard, and we pissed on it.

My little brother did it faster, though.

Mostly what I had left now were bad ones. These were the peaks that I had told my wife, just months ago, were probably too scary for me to ever climb. Now I wasn't so sure. I was stronger. I was more experienced. I was more confident. I was the kid who had started out watching *Frankenstein* and *Dracula* on black-and-white TV, but then had to move on up to *Psycho, The Exorcist,* and *Halloween* on the big screen for an increasingly elusive dose of fear. I did worry about what came next. My stomach was always too queasy to try *The Texas Chainsaw Massacre.*

Yet there they remained—Capitol, El Diente, Mount Wilson, and North Maroon. They were steep, rotten, confusing, and unforgiving, the Four Horsemen of My Apocalypse, the mountains that always got the blood curdling around the campfire.

As usual, though, the most frightening parts existed mainly in my imagination. Once I was upon them, touching the rock and moving from gully to wall to ridge, my worries eased. Sure, compared to other mountains, the problems on these four were larger, and the consequences of error or arrogance were greater. I also hiked each peak with people who had done the same route several times. Still, a summer of hiking had prepared me for this. I'd moved up. I was ready. There were no waiting chainsaws.

On Capitol Peak, climbers often fret over the infamous Knife Edge, a hundred-foot traverse across a balance-beam ridge with a thousand feet of air on one side and six hundred feet on the other. I climbed it mainly by keeping my hands atop the knife and my boots dug into the solid rock on the wall below. My biggest memories of that climb, though, came from Scott Scharin, an Aspen local and my guide for the day, who regaled me with tales of bombing avalanches with mortars during his winter work as a patroller of the steeps at the Aspen Highlands ski resort. If Peter Pan and his never-grow-up smile ever turned forty, he might look nearly as happy as Scott.

For El Diente Peak and Mount Wilson, there was a one-mile traverse that required work atop eight-hundred-foot cliffs. My main concern was whether I had the physical endurance to do it, because I had opted for a nontraditional route via the Kilpacker Basin that required fourteen miles of hiking and nearly 5,500 feet of elevation gain in a day. What kept me going were the stories, many true, from my guide, Drew Ludwig. Just when I thought I was getting tired, a sarcastic Drew let me in on the secrets of interior design in Telluride, where his main job was as a photographer of slopeside McMansions for real estate agents: "If you want to sell your five-thousand-square-foot mountain house," he told me, "you've got to have the elk antler chandeliers, and the elk antler candlesticks, and the elk antler silver-ware handles, and, especially, the sofa with the hairy cow skin pillows. The silver Land Rover in the garage helps, but if you're feeling really wild, you can go for the black Land Rover." The hardest part of his job was making every house look different.

On North Maroon Peak, the other half of the deadly Bells, I scrambled along crumbly ledges while trailing a half-dozen mountain goats and my hiking partner, Steve Lipsher, an old newspaper buddy on his third ascent of this peak. Steve had finished the Fourteeners years ago and went on to climb the highest mountains of four continents—Denali in North America, Aconcagua in South America, Kilimanjaro in Africa, and Elbrus of Europe, plus the world's sixth-highest peak, 26,864-foot Cho Oyu, in Asia. His favorite mountaineering moment, however, came on top of Colorado's own Mount Elbert, where Steve served as a guard warding other hikers away from the summit while his climbing partner proposed marriage to his girlfriend—and then consummated the engagement at 14,440 feet.

And no run down a Fourteeners homestretch would be complete for me without another struggle for a hiking partner. Seventeen years after we bungled our way up and down Crestone Needle, Gottlieb was planning to join me for a climb of its gnarly bookend, Crestone Peak. Then he and his wife drove cross-country to drop off their only daughter at college in Vermont. Gottlieb returned from that trip too drained, emotionally and physically, to join me for Crestone Peak.

Only because it was Labor Day weekend, when all peaks would be crowded with climbers, Merrill granted me a special exemption from the no-solo law. It turned out I didn't even need it. At the base of the stiff climb up the 1,800-foot Red Gully, I met up with a group of four that included the non-love-triangle woman from Snowmass Mountain. Instant hiking partners!

Problem was, we were having so much fun on the descent yakking—it went downhill fast when a large-chested single woman lamented the number of dates she'd had with men who could not remember the color of her eyes—that we weren't paying enough attention to the rock beneath our boots. Another woman who had already climbed more than forty Fourteeners slipped into a wet crack and slid twenty feet down the mountain. Just before an especially steep drop-off she slammed butt-first into a boulder blocking the way. She was lucky the boulder stopped her; she was unlucky to have her pelvis slammed and her wrist sprained.

Breathless, we all raced to help her. Just when we thought the worst was behind us, one of the most experienced climbers on the mountain had an unplanned date with gravity. She was OK, but we were all shaken.

We had eased up. The mountain hadn't.

Chapter 23

Return

LONGS PEAK 14,259'

The easiest thing to do was to keep taking the next step up. In hindsight, though, that was also the most dangerous thing to do.

On a group climb of the steep and glaciated Cooper Spur of Mount Hood in Oregon, Rick Goss saw many of the warning signs: leaders in his group who pressed on to the summit despite worsening weather; few people climbing with proper tension in their ropes; many people standing directly beneath others on steep and icy sections; some people too nonchalant to don helmets; no group discussion after a temporary whiteout; and, perhaps most telling of all, a group leader who slipped, fell, and slid down an unforgiving stretch of the mountain without trying to stop himself with his ice axe. Luckily, he was saved by his rope.

After gaining the summit, the assistant leader of the climb—sponsored by the renowned Oregon mountaineering club the Mazamas—proceeded to guide the group down the wrong descent path. "This isn't the way we came," Rick shouted. Others told him to pipe down. Rick was only twenty years old. The assistant trip leader was experienced and knew what he was doing, everyone said. Then came the call from the front of the line: "This is the wrong way. We need to traverse over."

They were off-route in slippery, difficult terrain. There were five rope teams—three teams of three climbers, and two teams of two. Someone finally felt uneasy enough to call for a handrail belay, which let climbers descend one at a time down a line of rope and ice axes.

Rick was the lowest man on the 50-degree slope when, from above, he heard yelling. He looked up and saw three people from his climbing group tumbling out of the clouds. They slammed into one climber above him, then another, and again and again until the tangled mass of people and rope slammed into him, too, and pitched him down the mountain.

Memories in bits and pieces: Ten people tangled and plunging. Somebody's pelvis crushing his head. Screaming. Too much speed to brake with an axe. Snow flying. Crampons slashing clothes. Crying. Legs and arms akimbo. Axes dangling. Waiting to black out. Bodies somersaulting. Silence.

They had fallen more than 1,500 vertical feet—about the height of the John Hancock Building in Chicago—and stopped in an awful heap. There was moaning and weeping and red snow all over. Rick was groggy with a severe concussion, but still managed to stand. Nobody else could. He found his knife and started cutting away the web of rope. The trip leader couldn't talk, but did follow Rick's movements with his eyes. Then his eyes went glassy, and he slumped over. It was the first time Rick had seen a dead body. As he sliced apart the tangles of rope he found three other corpses.

Of the ten who fell, four were dead. One was about to die. Four others were too hurt to move. Rick Goss hiked down to get help.

The first time I heard this story, Goss and I were good enough college buddies to be on a last-name basis. We had both just returned to school in the fall of 1981, and I had just asked him that all-purpose return-to-campus question: So what did you do on your summer vacation?

In the flat voice of an earnest engineering student, he outlined the basic details of his accident, which, to my mind, may as well have

happened on Mars. I was from Chicago, and had never hiked a mountain in my life. He was from Portland, and had summited dozens of
them. Our conversation, like most others in college, moved on to
classes, girls, and beer.

Goss's mind, however, never moved on. He had spent much of the
summer after the accident contacting and grieving with the families
of the dead. He was horrified. He was tormented. Mount Hood was
more than two thousand miles from our college in Illinois, but the
peak weighed heavily on his dreams.

The next summer, Goss returned home to Oregon and decided to
confront his doubts head-on. He signed up for another group climb
with the Mazamas, this time of North Sister, another steep and glaciated peak. He had climbed this peak the summer before the tragedy
on Mount Hood. He was determined to try North Sister with the lessons of Hood in mind.

All was fine until the group reached the final summit pitch, an airy
scramble up a rotten gully that, like a similar mess on Little Bear Peak
in Colorado, was called the Bowling Alley. At this gully, group leaders realized they had not brought enough rope to protect the ascent,
and, especially, the descent.

At this point, Goss knew he was done. The last time he had
climbed this peak he had roped up, and he did not want to attempt
such a steep and loose route without protection. There was no debate
in his mind about this decision to stop.

His issue was whether to announce it. He didn't want to unduly
rattle the confidence of other climbers preparing for an unroped
climb. To this day, however, he still regretted his failure on Mount
Hood to stridently object to unsafe climbing decisions by trip leaders.

So he just said he didn't feel comfortable going on without ropes.
He sat down.

Three others sat with him. The rest of the group continued on.
Goss and the three waited.

A few minutes later, he heard noises. He looked up—and saw the rest of the group returning. Without enough rope in iffy conditions, the whole group had decided to retreat.

After the turnaround on North Sister, Goss lost the interest and stomach for hard climbs. He worried that he was being too cautious, that his safety-first attitude was ruining others' enjoyment of the mountains. The years passed, and he spent less and less time in the high country. He became a doctor. He married, and he and his wife had two kids. He took up golf.

While pleading for climbing partners for my Fourteeners summer, I asked Goss on a lark. He didn't say no, but he didn't say yes either. I pegged him as one of those guys too polite to say outright that he really preferred to sleep past dawn on a weekend. I moved on to beg elsewhere.

And then, out of the blue, Goss called and said yes.

Actually, he said yes on one condition. Decades ago, as a teenager on family vacations, Goss had tried twice with his mother and father to summit Longs Peak in Rocky Mountain National Park. Both times they had failed. If he was going to come out of mountaineering retirement, he wanted to do it on Longs.

He would not be the first to heed the siren call of Longs Peak. The undisputed king of the northern Front Range, and the crown of Rocky Mountain National Park, Longs has hosted more triumph and heartbreak than any other Colorado mountain. In his novel *Centennial*, James Michener called it "the best mountain of them all," and few Colorado climbers will dispute him. There are more than a hundred ways up and down. Some routes call for ropes and amazing technical skill; others require only steely nerves and tough legs. No path is easy.

The first ascent of this magnificent peak remains in dispute. An elderly Arapaho claimed that his father, named Old Man Gun, had scaled the peak, dug a pit, covered himself with rocks, and hid with a dead coyote atop him until hungry eagles tried to snatch the carcass. Old Man Gun supposedly nabbed the eagles with his bare hands. The younger Arapaho, Gun Griswold, said he and five friends in 1859 repeated his father's climb, which destroyed several pairs of moccasins but yielded no eagle feathers. The only evidence of summits by Old Man Gun and the son of a gun was their word, and the word of Indians in that era was, to put it mildly, viewed by white frontiersmen with suspicion.

Numerous white men attempted the same climb for years after, but none returned with any firm proof of success. The renown of the insurmountable mountain spread so far and wide that, in 1865, the great French author Jules Verne situated a vast reflector telescope atop it to track the progress of a moon rocket launched from Florida in his sci-fi classic *From the Earth to the Moon*.

Three years later, man tried to match part of the fiction. A government expedition led by John Wesley Powell, a Civil War amputee, scratched and clawed its way to the top of Longs Peak and set the stage for a question repeated tens of thousands of times since: If a guy with one arm can do it, why can't I?

Unfortunately, many couldn't. On the list of the deadliest Fourteeners, no mountain comes close to Longs, with at least fifty recorded fatalities. Longs has claimed both the expert and novice in fair weather and foul. Few stories are as heartbreaking as the tale of hardwoman Agnes Vaille.

In the Roaring Twenties, while her peers were turning into flappers and doing the Lindy Hop at the Cotton Club, Vaille was pioneering tough routes up frightening peaks. She wasn't content to be the first woman on a treacherous climb; she wanted to be the first person up it, period.

On January 11, 1925, she and climbing partner Walter Kiener set out to record the first winter summit of the eastern face of Longs Peak. She had tried but failed three times before, but was determined to make this one count. Despite foreboding weather, and strident protests from family and friends, Vaille and Kiener set off at 9:30 a.m. and spent the next nineteen hours pushing through snowdrifts and dangling across icy ledges on a scramble considerably harder than the standard route up Longs today. At 4 a.m. the next day, they summited. It was 14 degrees below zero, and the west wind howled. Soon they were engulfed in a blizzard. While descending the north face, Vaille fell and slid 150 feet. Kiener rushed down and spent an hour comforting her, but found that twenty-five hours of subzero temperatures, combined with just an hour of sleep in the prior fifty hours, had taken its toll. Vaille was too exhausted to move. She urged Kiener to continue down by himself for help, saying she would sleep for a half-hour and then resume her descent through the less technically demanding sections of the mountain.

Several thousand feet down the mountain Kiener was met by a search party. They all raced back up the mountain to save his climbing partner. They found Vaille frozen to death a few steps from where Kiener had left her. Too weary to bring her body down the mountain, the despondent rescuers retreated. On the descent one member of the search party, Herbert Sortland, became lost and was found frozen to death six weeks later. Kiener's severe frostbite cost him all his toes, part of a foot, and several fingers. Agnes Vaille was memorialized by her family with construction at 13,200 feet of an emergency shelter stone hut.

I was hoping we wouldn't need it.

In a coincidence, another college friend of ours, Moog—his real name was Erich Meihoff, but he was the only adult I'd ever met whose nickname from first grade had stuck—planned to be in Colorado the weekend of our Longs Peak attempt. Moog wanted to climb too. After a summer of begging for hiking partners, I was now awash in them. The arrival of two friends from two decades ago meant one thing: I needed a bigger flask. This problem I was grateful to have.

Because Goss and Moog were coming from sea level—Goss from Seattle, Moog from Portland—they, and I, grew concerned about their ability to handle the big altitude change. Based on my luck with Mike Brislin at Mount Belford and Mount Oxford, and with my brother on Mount Harvard, I decided that a night at a high camp was in order. We decided to split the climb of Longs Peak into two days—the first a backpack up to a campsite at 12,500 feet, the second an attempt on the summit itself.

Our trek did not start well. At the trailhead sign-in sheet I found signatures from earlier that day from two of my earlier hiking partners, Dean Toda and David Just from Mount Lindsey, who reported that they had failed to summit. Their explanation was one word, capitalized and exclaimed: ICY!

A mile or so up the trail, we met Scott Scharin, my guide from Capitol Peak, now descending Longs with his wife and mother-in-law. They, too, had turned back from the final summit push because of ice.

Though Goss and Moog expressed amazement at the small world of Fourteeners climbers, I was more preoccupied with the nasty conditions being reported high over our heads. How much ice was above us? Would it melt out before we reached it? If not, then what?

With Goss on this hike, I knew the answer to the last question would be to turn back. This only increased my sense of desperation. It was September 7, and the high country had already been socked with two substantial snowstorms. My window for Fourteener climbing was closing.

Goss and Moog both did much to settle my nerves, mainly by not talking about hiking or climbing.

Since college, Moog had become a master of personal reinvention. After seven years of engineering window glass for factories in Wichita Falls, Texas; Perry, Georgia; Chehalis, Washington; and Mount Zion, Illinois, Moog was anxious to try living someplace with at least one other non–gun-owning Democrat. He enrolled at the University of Washington for business school, but got so bored that he spent one summer learning Japanese at Stanford University and another summer speaking it in Niigata, Japan. He left school with a freshly minted MBA diploma and no desire to ever use it. For the next year he traveled the Southern Hemisphere with hopes of figuring out what he wanted to do with his life. There was one nice detour: On a backpack of the classic sixty-kilometer Kepler Track in New Zealand, he spotted a very cute woman hiking ahead of him with a mug from Coffee People, the chain from his hometown of

Portland. Though Moog is notoriously shy, he used the mug as an excuse to talk with her. Seven thousand miles from home, he had found a woman who lived ten miles from him. They married. Moog still needed a career, though, so at the age of thirty-five he enrolled in medical school. This led to some interesting moments four years later during hospital rounds, when patients spotted his graying hair and assumed he was the senior physician on duty when in fact he was only an intern. No matter. This career was sticking. So was his college physique. Moog's shoulders were twice as wide as his backpack, and his waist had no apparent body fat. He didn't walk uphill; he charged. I tried to have him talk as much as possible, if only to slow him down to our pace.

Luckily, Goss was a yakker too. Like Moog, he was working as an internal medicine doctor, but with a heavy dose of public health administration. He had started his career ready to cure the world, but then realized, to his regret, how much of his time was eaten up by mind-numbing business—stacks of paperwork, fights with insurance companies, accounting detail, and wrestling matches to get basic health care for the working poor. He tried to change the system by working for Michael Dukakis's 1988 presidential campaign. When that didn't work, he moved on to manage health care policy for state government, the county jail in Seattle, and a hospital in Washington. He tried change; he met resistance. Specialists vs. general practitioners, physician assistants vs. physicians, providers vs. insurers, the elected vs. the unelected—name the medical conflict and Goss was there. He found it harder and harder to stay idealistic. He found too many people subscribing to a simple but infuriating philosophy: Privatize the gain, socialize the loss.

At this point on the trail, we needed more gains and less socialization. The sun was dipping below the ridge, and we still had several miles to backpack before reaching our camp. I couldn't say Goss was hurting, or even breathing heavily, but he was moving slowly. Moog and I tried to hike a little faster to avoid hiking an unfamiliar route in the dark, but Goss wasn't budging. We transferred cooking supplies and other weight from Goss's backpack to ours. Still no change. He had his pace and he was sticking with it.

We headlamped up, and arrived at our campsite a solid half-hour after all light had been extinguished from the sky. Our campsite was in a place called the Boulder Field, which we couldn't see, but could guess was named correctly because we had traversed about a billion boulders to reach the igloo-shaped rock walls of our official National Park Service campsite. The best we could tell, the nearest tree was at least a mile away on the other side of 12,000-foot Granite Pass. Unfortunately, the wind knew this too. Erecting a three-man tent in a gale at night instantly changed our names to Moe, Curly, and Larry. Somehow we survived.

And then what? It was too cold and dark to stand around outside, but too early to fall asleep. Then we remembered: The flask! Amazing how a lone palm-size device can warm the body, excavate college memories, make bad jokes good, and promote sleep in a raging wind on barren alpine tundra—all at the same time.

Though it would be macho to claim that we emptied the flask that night, the truth was not quite so manly. The flask was small; our impact on it was even smaller. The sad reality of three middle-aged married guys in a tent together for the first time since college: We were cheap dates.

The next morning—or, more accurately, the next predawn—we awoke to a wild sight: a mile-long parade of hundreds of headlamps, bobbing and weaving down the switchbacks from Granite Pass and headed our way. It was a Saturday morning with a clear weather forecast on one of the most popular alpine hikes in North America. Ah, Colorado: the one place in America where people wake up earlier on weekends than workdays. We had to get moving to beat the morning rush hour.

I stirred with worries. What if the steepest moves on this peak were still glazed with ice? What if Goss was still moving slowly?

What if we got caught behind the climbing crowds at the most precarious spots? What if I got dressed so slowly that Goss and Moog took off without me?

That last fear was about to become reality. Goss and Moog were packed, ready to go, and wondering what in the hell was taking me so long.

We stepped outside the tent and saw for the first time why our campsite was called the Boulder Field—a sloping basin, flanked by three mountains over 13,000 feet and jammed rim-to-rim with rocks the size of our backpacks and tents. To our left towered the 1,000-foot Diamond of Longs Peak. I told my buddies that I had a climbing partner earlier this summer, Walt Johnson from the Chicago Basin, who had scaled that face. Simultaneously, three jaws dropped. The rock looked smoother than the walls on my kids' bedrooms. I said out loud what Goss and Moog clearly were thinking: You've got to wonder about the judgment of a guy who could climb *that*—and then decide to go climb something with me.

At the top of the Boulder Field, next to the Agnes Vaille stone hut, rises our first goal of the day. For climbers, the Keyhole is a geological miracle—a sixty-foot oval of overhanging rock in a headwall that allows easy access to the backside of the mountain. We punch through the gap and see a transformed mountain. It's still Longs Peak, but the clear trail has been replaced by ledges, cliffs, and slabs with hundreds of feet of drop-offs.

I check the faces of Goss and Moog for signs of fear. Instead, I find jubilation.

"Damn, this looks pretty interesting," Goss says.

And then they were off. Up and down along a half-mile traverse across the Ledges; up a stiff six-hundred-foot climb of a mostly solid gully called the Trough; and a third-of-a-mile scramble across the Narrows, a two-foot ledge with hundreds of feet of air below. Two more flatlanders smoking me up the mountain—by now I was used to it, but that still didn't stop me from being surprised by it. While stopping to catch my breath at the base of the final push to the summit, I asked Goss how he had struggled with a pack yesterday while firing up the turbochargers on his boots today. "Guess I just got a little excited," he tells me. "This is fun."

Above us juts the Homestretch, the three-hundred-foot pitch up smooth, slabby rock with ice that turned back so many climbers the day before. Maybe it was evaporation from last night's winds, or maybe it was the warmth of this morning's sun. No matter: The Homestretch is in dramatically better shape for climbing today.

There's some ice, but also clear ways to scramble carefully around it. Though a slip here would result in a long slide to nowhere, we soon find ourselves safely on somewhere—the summit of Longs Peak. A few dozen people are ahead of us on the summit, and a few hundred people are behind us. Lucky for everyone, the summit is flat and the size of two football fields. The sky is blue, the sun is blasting, and the wind has returned home to Wyoming. We can see from here to forever. Goss and Moog bask in all the glory with giddy schoolboy grins.

"Wow," Goss says.

"Huh?" I ask.

"Wow," he says. "Just wow."

"Is it what you expected?"

"Even better. I'd forgotten what this was like. Wow."

Chapter 24

Summit

PIKES PEAK 14,115'

"I don't want to go!"

"Come on, let's go."

"I want to sleep!"

"You sleep every day. You can't climb a mountain every day."

"Go without me!"

"I'm not going to leave you alone out here. We're a long way from anything."

"I'm not going! Leave me alone!"

"Listen, you said you would do this. We drove an hour-and-a-half from home last night and I paid for a motel room because you said you would do this. Now we're at the trailhead and we're dressed and ready to go. Let's do this."

"I'm not doing this!"

"Come on, you promised. You'll feel better once you get going."

"I just want to stay here!"

"Please?"

"No!"

"Pretty please?"

"Leave me alone!"

So I did. I walked away from the truck in the darkness and considered my options. I had a 14,000-foot mountain to climb, and I had a teenage son. One I thought I could manage. The other I clearly could not.

For the past ten days I had only one peak left to do. I had held off on it because Cass wanted to climb it with me. The symmetry was pretty cool for both of us: Pikes Peak was where it all began for him, and where it would all end for me. He knew the route. He knew how much this climb meant to me.

He also knew how to drive me crazy.

I rolled him out of the motel room bed at 4 a.m. without much difficulty, then served up our lucky mountain breakfast of chocolate doughnuts, Gatorade, and Ho Hos on the half-hour drive to the trailhead. All seemed according to plan until I glanced over at the passenger seat and saw a half-eaten doughnut dangling from the side of his mouth. No problem, I figured. There's no reason for him to be awake until we actually start hiking.

Until he wouldn't wake up to actually start hiking.

I called his name and got a snore in response. I nudged him. Nothing. I jostled him enough to make the doughnut drop, which got his attention, because to him the only thing worse than a cell phone with no battery charge is junk food with no clear path to his gullet.

With chocolate smeared on his chin but a serious look on his face, he was adamant. No. Hiking. Today. Instead. Sleep.

I didn't want to be that jackass dad pushing his kids to do stupid things that the kids really, really didn't want to do. Still, I figured, a deal's a deal. A big snowstorm was being forecast for tomorrow. If we didn't hike this peak now with just a dusting of early fall snow, I'd be struggling with it later in knee-deep winter misery. No way I would subject my son to that.

Now or never, I figured as I approached the truck again. My adult brain struggled for some argument, any argument, that could penetrate a teenager brain two hours before dawn on a day with no school. It was hopeless. In desperation, I beat the same drum again.

"Come on, you just got another ten minutes of sleep. Let's go now."

"I told you—I'm not going!"

"There's a big storm coming in tonight. If we don't do it now, then we won't be able to do it."

"So we won't do it."

"Please?"

"Leave me alone! I want to sleep!"

"Come on, it's always hard to start. You'll be fine once we get going. You love hiking."

"I hate hiking!"

"You said you wanted to show me the place on this mountain where you got hurt."

"I hate hiking!"

"What?"

"I hate hiking!"

"What do you mean, you hate hiking? When we went up Missouri Mountain, you loved hiking. Didn't it feel good to work hard and accomplish something? You loved being on the top of that mountain? Come on, you'll love being on the top of this mountain."

"I hate hiking!"

"You always told me you liked hiking. You hate hiking?"

"Dad, you know I hate hiking. I only love summiting."

I snort Gatorade out my nose. This was about the most ridiculous thing I'd ever heard. I chortle so loud, and so hard, that I can hardly breathe.

"Hate hiking! Love summiting! BWWAAA HAAAH!"

My headlamp dances across the treetops as my face convulses with laughter. My eyes tear. I grab the side of the truck to support myself.

From the open passenger window I hear an unexpected sound: giggles. Nervous giggles maybe, but laughter nonetheless.

I shine my headlamp inside the truck. He's grinning. Better yet, his eyes are open.

"I guess that sounds pretty stupid, doesn't it?" he asks.

"I guess."

"Well, it's true."

"I'd never thought of it that way, but you do have a point."

He opens the truck door, hops out, and straps on his backpack.

"Let's go," he says.

I make sure we both start walking fast before he has a chance to reconsider.

We move through the darkness up the trail without a word. Our back-and-forth in the Crags trailhead parking lot blew a half-hour of time. If the argument was with anybody else, I would have been mad, but now I'm just grateful to be done with it.

Because we're hiking up the west side of Pikes Peak, the sun takes a long time to clear the high shoulder above us. The wait, however, is worth it: yellow light, red crags, green meadow, and golden aspen quaking in the fall breeze. The awesome sights break the silence between my son and me.

"I was a real jerk back there and I'm sorry," he tells me.

"You were just tired. No big deal."

He points to the aspens. "You were right. This is worth it."

For the next four hours, we can't shut up. We talk about school, girls, QWERTY vs. non-QWERTY cell phones for texting, cars he wants to drive someday (Audi TT), cars I might think about letting him drive someday (1984 Crown Victoria), and how Mom held up while I was gone so many days this summer. (The house stayed a lot cleaner, but the kids ate at fewer restaurants.) More lips loosened by the elixir of altitude.

The higher we hike, the more my son recognizes the route. We clear a saddle and reach a jumble of red sandstone formations. My son tells me the area just beyond this is called the Devil's Playground. I assume this is because of the weirdly shaped red rock, but he assures me it's because of the way lightning dances from pinnacle to pinnacle. I learned on our trek up Missouri Mountain to stop doubting him, and, sure enough, a sign on the trail proves him right.

A few more steps and we reach the most unpleasant part of this Fourteener, the toll road. A steady stream of cars and trucks rumbles up the road—twelve miles with 156 hairpin turns—while a work crew with backhoe and Bobcat assaults it. If any Fourteener feels conquered by man, it's Pikes Peak. The lower slopes boast a world-class collection of cheesy knickknack shops, including Santa's North Pole. There's an abandoned railroad grade that gains two thousand feet in one mile and regularly attracts gold-medal Olympians, including skater Apolo Ohno and wrestler Rulon Gardner, to run up it. A cog railroad shuttles tourists eight times daily during peak season to the summit, where a store serves up fresh doughnuts and pizza. It's the one Fourteener that smells more like aftershave and cigarettes than B.O.

Yet Pikes also inspires amazing feats. In 1893, a Massachusetts professor of English literature hired a horse wagon with some school-teacher friends and rolled and bumped their way up the mountain road. They finished their trek on mules. On the top Katharine Lee Bates felt like a typical Fourteeners climber—exhausted but inspired. From the purple mountain majesty she looked out above the fruited plain and wrote the first lines to "America the Beautiful."

Pikes inspired others in less glorious ways. In 1929, a Texan named Bill Williams spent three weeks pushing a peanut to the summit with his nose. Others have kicked a soccer ball up it, walked backward up it, and even unicycled up it. Every August there's a famous marathon up and down it, but another Texan, Alan Brock, figured that was for slackers. After his marriage busted up, and he lost his job as a minister, and he gained more than one hundred pounds, he wanted a goal to turn around his life. He trained for three years, and, starting in July 2007, ran 38 days and 918 miles from Austin, Texas, to Manitou Springs at the base of the mountain. He rested one day. On his fortieth day, he ran the Pikes Peak Marathon. He finished in 625th place.

My summer was certainly no race, but from the talus Cass and I can see my finish line. We stop just below, and he shows me the place that forced his first Fourteeners phone call, the hacksawed highway signpost that slashed open his leg. On a mountain with millions of other obstacles, we both think the same thing, but he's the one who actually says it: "How did I fall on this?"

"The important thing is," I tell him, "you survived it."

His summer camp trek up Pikes is also what got me going on my whole Fourteeners quest. I thank him for that, and we take our last steps up to the top. In the parking lot there's a giant wood-and-stone sign proclaiming the summit, and a guy who drove to the top in a Volvo takes our picture in front of it. My son gives me a hug. My first tear rolls somewhere down his back. I'm done. I'm thrilled. I'm relieved. We walk inside the Pikes Peak summit store and celebrate with two doughnuts and four slices of pepperoni pizza. Tomorrow we can both sleep in.

Bibliography

There is no such thing as climbing a Fourteener by the book, but it does help to read before venturing afield. Like mountaineering, the guidebooks have changed considerably over the years.

The first modern tome was Robert Ormes's *Guide to the Colorado Mountains*, first published in 1952. His directions were sparse—routes on complicated peaks were described in just a few sentences—but his wit was sharp. About Lizard Head, a spindly Thirteener of awful rock near Telluride, Ormes famously wrote, "Take photograph and go away." Not all did.

In 1978, Walter Borneman, a lawyer, and Lyndon Lampert, a part-time fishing guide, first released *A Climbing Guide to Colorado's Fourteeners*, which described the geology and history of the mountains, and added a few paragraphs of slightly more detailed route descriptions. It was the standard text for more than a decade of hikers.

Then came Gerry Roach, a ponytailed computer coder from Boulder. The second man on earth to have completed the Seven Summits—the highest peak on each of the seven continents—Roach was a world-class mountaineer who went nuts in his own backyard, climbing more than 1,500 Colorado peaks as well as every Fourteener via many routes. His 1992 guidebook, *Colorado's Fourteeners: From Hikes to Climbs*, became a climbing sensation. There were topographic maps, more detailed written directions than ever, and as many as twenty different hikes for a single mountain. Few serious Fourteeners climbers set out for the high country without a well-thumbed Roach at home or in the backpack.

While thousands still head for the hills today with their trusty Roaches, even more ply the trails with an avalanche of information downloaded from Web sites. The most popular is 14ers.com, which offers free downloads of extremely detailed directions, including dozens of photographs, for the most common route on every Fourteener. Owned and operated without advertisements by former software executive Bill Middlebrook, 14ers.com also stores more than three thousand trip reports written by other Fourteeners hikers. While climbing Fourteeners, I usually relied on 14ers.com downloads and topographic maps to help find my way up a mountain. Despite all the pictures and GPS waypoint downloads and written trail descriptions, I still got lost. Book knowledge is nice, but mountain judgment and experience are far more important.

Borneman, Walter R., and Lyndon J. Lampert. *A Climbing Guide to Colorado's Fourteeners*. 3rd ed. Boulder, Colorado: Pruett Publishing Co., 1994.

Bueler, William M. *Roof of the Rockies: A History of Colorado Mountaineering*. Golden, Colorado: The Colorado Mountain Club Press, 2000.

Buys, Christian J. *A Quick History of Leadville*. Montrose, Colorado: Western Reflections Publishing Co., 2004.

Chronic, Halka, and Felicie Williams. *Roadside Geology of Colorado*. Missoula, Montana: Mountain Press Publishing Co., 2002.

Cox, Steven M., and Kris Fulsaas, eds. *Mountaineering: The Freedom of the Hills*. Seattle: The Mountaineers Books, 2006.

Dawson, Louis W. II. *Dawson's Guide to Colorado's Fourteeners*. Vol. 1, *The Northern Peaks*. Colorado Springs: Blue Clover Press, 1999.

———. *Dawson's Guide to Colorado's Fourteeners*. Vol. 2, *The Southern Peaks*. Colorado Springs: Blue Clover Press, 1999.

Ellis, Amanda M. *Bonanza Towns: Leadville and Cripple Creek*. Colorado Springs: The Dentan Printing Co., 1954.

Fenwick, Robert Wesley. *Alferd Packer: The True Story of the Man-Eater*. Denver: The Denver Post, 1963.

Gantt, Paul H. *The Case of Alferd Packer, the Man-Eater*. Denver: University of Denver Press, 1952.

Griswold, Don L., and Jean Harvey. *The Carbonate Camp Called Leadville*. Denver: University of Denver Press, 1951.

Hales, Peter B. *William Henry Jackson and the Transformation of the American Landscape*. Philadelphia: Temple University Press, 1988.

Jackson, William Henry. *Time Exposure: The Autobiography of William Henry Jackson*. New York: Van Rees Press, 1940.

Jacobson, Mark I. *Antero Aquamarines*. Coeur d'Alene, Idaho: L. R. Ream Publishing. 1993.

Johnston, Dick. *The Taylor Ranch War*. Bloomington, Indiana: AuthorHouse, 2006.

Klucas, Gillian. *Leadville: The Struggle to Revive an American Town*. Washington, D.C.: Island Press, 2004.

Kushner, Ervan F. *Alferd G. Packer: Cannibal? Victim!* Frederick, Colorado: Platte 'N Press, 1980.

MacDonald, Dougald. *Longs Peak: The Story of Colorado's Favorite Fourteener*. Englewood, Colorado: Westcliffe Publishers, 2004.

Matthews, Vincent, Katie Keller-Lynn, and Betty Fox, eds. *Messages in Stone: Colorado's Colorful Geology*. Denver: Colorado Geological Survey, 2003.

Nesbit, Paul. *Longs Peak: Its Story and a Climbing Guide*. Halstead, Kansas: Mills Publishing Co., 1990.

Oldham, Ann. *Alferd G. Packer: Soldier, Prospector, and Cannibal*. Pagosa Springs, Colorado: A. Oldham, 2005.

Ormes, Robert M. *Guide to the Colorado Mountains*. 10th ed. Randy Jacobs, ed. Golden, Colorado: Colorado Mountain Club Press, 2000.

Roach, Gerry. *Colorado's Fourteeners: From Hikes to Climbs*. 2nd ed. Golden, Colorado: Fulcrum Publishing, 1999.

Waitley, Douglas. *William Henry Jackson: Framing the Frontier*. Missoula, Montana: Mountain Press Publishing Company, 1998.

Williamson, Ruby G. *Gold, God, the Devil, and Silver: Leadville, Colorado 1878–1978*. Gunnison, Colorado: B&B Printers, 1977.

Acknowledgments

Many were called, but most had the good sense to stay away. Luckily, there were a few gluttons for punishment, and I am grateful for their help and encouragement on my Fourteeners quest.

Good hiking partners are hard to find. I thankfully ended up with many: Alan Gottlieb, Shad Mika, Kirk Tubbs, Matt Ellis, Doug Spannring, Steve Spannring, Mike Brislin, Prakash Manley, Skip Perkins, David Wallace, David Just, Dean Toda, Jordan White, Walt Johnson, Alan Greenberg, and Steve Lipsher. To join me on hikes, some traveled long distances: Steve Mott from New York, Rick Goss from Washington, Erich Meihoff from Oregon, and my little brother, Todd, from Illinois. Rob Witwer and Tim Wohlgenant won me permission to climb peaks with limited access. On four of the most difficult mountains, I relied on the advice and expertise of guides Jeff Fassett and Scott Scharin of Aspen and Drew Ludwig of Telluride.

I learned much about the Fourteeners and the people who climb them from Caroline Moore, Josh Friesema, Gary Rohrer, Dave Gaffield, Greg Thomas, Cleve McCarty, Quade Smith, Tyle Smith, Adrian Crane, Ricky Denesik, Rick Trujillo, Teddy Keizer, Andrew Hamilton, Danelle Ballengee, Lou Dawson, Chris Davenport, Christina Graham, Marcia Omafray, and Debbie Welle-Powell.

Vince Matthews, director of the Colorado Geological Survey, compiled for me the latest and most accurate elevations for the summits of Fourteeners. These revised numbers, which vary from prior government maps and published field guides, result from new satellite and mapping information assembled by the National Geodetic Survey and the U.S. Geological Survey. Matthews also gave me a crash course on the birth of the Rocky Mountains. Chris Ray of the University of Colorado and Dan Blumstein of the University of California at Los Angeles taught me about animal life on those mountains.

My time in the mountains convinced me that these peaks need help. One of the best ways is to donate time or money to the trail builders of the Colorado Fourteeners Initiative: www.coloradofourteeners.org. The Trust for Public Land is still raising money for public access to Wilson Peak and other backcountry hikes: www.tpl.org.

At the Free Press of Simon & Schuster, my thanks go to Martha Levin and Dominick Anfuso, who set me loose in the high country, and to Leslie Meredith, editor extraordinaire, whose enthusiasm, wisdom, and patience helped keep me climbing and typing. My agent, Jody Rein, was, as always, a bighearted professional.

My parents, John and Alice Obmascik, started my infatuation with the Rockies during our family's annual summer camping trips in the West. (Driving two days from Chicago with three kids in the back of a station wagon with no air-conditioning—how did we all survive?) Their love, visits, and babysitting helped me reach the top of the Rockies.

The hardest part of scaling peaks was all the time away from my family. I can only hope to help our sons, Cass, Max, and Wesley, achieve their goals with as much praise and joy as they gave to mine. My wife, Merrill, gave me the encouragement to start this project, the heart to continue, and the will to finish. This book is dedicated to her.

About the Author

MARK OBMASCIK is the author of *The Big Year,* a national best seller that received five "Best of 2004" citations from major media. He was lead writer for the *Denver Post* team that won the 2000 Pulitzer Prize, and winner of the 2003 National Press Club award for environmental journalism. He lives in Denver with his wife, Merrill Schwerin, and their three sons, Cass, Max, and Wesley.